DEDICATION

To all black women that never wavered in
maintaining their true roots and that
served as an example to all those on the
path to re-awakening.

To everyone that paves the way for the
younger generation to love and accept
them self for whom they are and not what
society dictates they should be and most
importantly look like.

BEAUTY IS <u>NOT</u> ONLY SKIN DEEP

TELL PUBLICATIONS

NOW HAIR THIS!

THE DESTRUCTION OF BLACK HAIR

EMBARK ON A JOURNEY OF PERSONAL AWARENESS AND SELF ACCEPTANCE

DEBE DENE

PUBLISHED BY TELL PUBLICATIONS

NORTH HOLLYWOOD, CA

Published by Tell Publications
5062 Lankershim Blvd. Suite 1008
North Hollywood, CA 91601

Art Director: Debe Dene
Interior Layout Conversion &
Cover Illustration:
DesignsbyRachelle.com

ISBN 978-0-9801242-0-0

CONTENTS

ACKNOWLEDGEMENTS

To everyone that encouraged me,
as well as added to my life force
in a positive way.

I am especially thankful to
the Most High God for all my blessings.

Note from the Author

For generations black women whether out
of tradition, lack of knowledge, or
conformity have chosen to alter the
texture of their hair. The desire is to
blend into a society that although
emulates their music, fashion and various
physical attributes; it does not always
embrace their true culture. There have
been books written about the care of the
black woman's hair in its natural state, but
let's go a step further and discuss the

deeper issues of why black women choose to alter their hair texture. Let's start the process of self discovery and for us all to begin to think!

Introduction

Where have all the flowers gone ....
This song written by Pete Seeger in the
50's seems to come to mind, with one
exception. I find myself singing where
have all the black women gone?

I know you're saying to yourself, what
is she saying? Where have all the black
women gone? We're right here! Let me
show you what I mean. Turn on the
television to one of your favorite black
sitcoms or switch to the latest black music

video, better yet look in the mirror. What you will see is an image of another culture but your own. There are self help books and DVD's telling us - love ourselves first only then can you love someone else. This seems near impossible when we don't love ourselves enough to stop altering what we were naturally born with. We are changing the texture of our hair; the color of our eyes and in extreme cases the color of our skin to "fit in". This could be part of why most of us end up with the wrong mate. With all the other issues that come along with relationships, we begin them with a false representation of ourselves.

This book *isn't* about finding a soul mate, it is about finding ourselves and it begins with the crown that we mutilate with chemicals, straightening combs, harsh dyes and the list goes on.

Black women spend billions on products that stretch, press, iron or relax our kingly hair and have not taken the time to think why we so adamantly try to be in the image of every culture but our own.

My whole purpose for sharing this information with my Nubian sisters is just that, you are Nubian and your hair is a royal crown, **be who you were born to be.**

OCTOBER 2002

TODAY

The Author

Approximately two years after I made the choice to grow out the "unnatural" the inspiration for this book began to materialize. As I was on the journey of re-discovering who I was with my own natural textured hair I was better able to process the change that was taking place both physically and mentally. During the growing out phase I was able to capture what many of us do not talk about, the emotional aspect of the transition from unnatural to natural hair. Each period of

new hair growth taught me something new

about whom I was and sadly I initially

found myself rejecting the whole going

back to natural. During this time I felt

most vulnerable, almost naked to the

world, and as I will explain later, wore

wigs for 2 years before totally exposing

my natural locks out of fear of what I

thought everybody else would think or say.

I've learned that in relation to my hair

the only concern should have been what I

thought and not the opinion of others.

For over 25 years I "relaxed" my hair approximately every four to six weeks and before each new growth a sense of melancholy would set in. My addiction to the chemical processing of my hair made me convinced that without it I was not normal. This is a feeling many of you I'm sure can relate to.

It is extremely disheartening that we have conditioned ourselves to accept what is unnatural as natural. In fact when most black women decide to no longer straighten their hair the common phrase is

"I am going natural", when technically the saying should be "I am growing out the unnatural".

Starting at the age of seven, I've had my hair pressed, jheri curled, and relaxed or also known as "permed". What I failed to realize as this tradition continued into my adult years is the only thing I was permanently changing was my self esteem and love of self.

The growing out process did not come easy. I attempted to remove the chemicals several times, each time succumbing to applying more "relaxer" to my hair before I finally stuck to my convictions and did not reach for the "lye".

My reasons for applying the chemicals stemmed from frustration at the onset of the new growth because it was more thick than what I was accustomed to and I'm ashamed to say, I was also afraid of how people, especially my own race would look at me.

I've found that when you stop caring about something it will no longer exist. Hence when you neglect and not care for your hair in its natural state or at the very least portray a hairstyle that more closely resembles your natural hair you are in effect saying that _you_ do not exist.

Unfortunately that is the mind set of the majority of black women today who choose to depict a way of life that is not for them. Continuing to embrace an image that goes against the grain of who you really are will undeniably result in forgetting who you are.

The natural look of your hair is an extension of you, it defines you and to ignore that chips away daily at your self

esteem and self worth.

Why We Flatten, Stretch, Iron Our Hair

The reason for straightening our hair differs from person to person. It primarily boils down to texture, styling options, length, society, family, friends, boyfriends or husbands. Black women, me included have shared that initially they felt ugly with their own hair texture.

There is a great emphasis placed on length and volume even in its natural state. Somehow these attributes have been associated with having "good hair" (a topic to be discussed further), especially if the hair grows past the shoulders. On the opposite end of the spectrum mainstream society has also resorted to labeling/stereotyping black women and/or women in general with closely cropped hair as being a butch or lesbian. With this type of stereotyping it's no wonder why black woman stray even further away from removing the chemicals.

There are many styling options available with natural hair locked or loose.

The frustration sets in due to the majority of styling products that are available for hair care do not cater to our sensitive locks that require a lot of moisture.

THE CHEMICAL PROCESS REVEALED

All too often we tend to overlook the, who, where, how, what and why's of something and just follow the crowd. Choosing to apply chemicals to our hair has also become commonplace without really thinking as to *why* it's applied, it's just something that is done.

A little research can reveal the true meaning behind what in most cases appear to be harmless on the surface. In relation to chemically processing our hair this will hopefully provide a more clear understanding of the actual damage taking place. If it takes visualizing the hair dissolving and the chemicals penetrating the skin layers perhaps it will deter you from applying the chemicals in the first place.

The lack of knowledge on the composition of hair itself is perhaps one of the biggest factors in the destruction of hair. When you are unaware of what is being destroyed the tendency is to continue on the path of destruction.

Following is a simplified explanation of the
hair structure in order to get a better
understanding of its layers and make-up.
The structure of hair is composed of
protein called keratin, the same kind of
protein which makes up the nails and the
outer layer of skin. The skin on the scalp
is porous and also has layers of skin that
are made up of blood vessels, nerves,
glands, etc.

Each strand of hair (**shaft**) consists of
the **Medulla** – the inner most layer (only
present in thick hair), **Cortex** – middle

layer (attributes to strength, color and texture of hair) and **Cuticle** – outermost layer (thin and colorless and acts as a protector of the cortex).

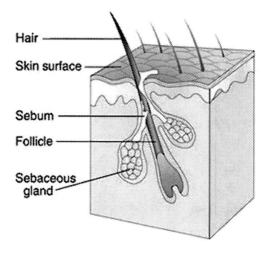

Hair

Skin surface

Sebum

Follicle

Sebaceous gland

Sodium hydroxide and ammonium thioglycolate are just two types of chemicals used in "relaxers" that are found on the market today that are to say the least, extremely toxic. The chemicals in the "relaxer" penetrate the **cortex** and **cuticle** layers and alter the hairs natural curl pattern. This process also strips the hair of its natural moisture causing the hair to lose elasticity, resulting in limp, dry, damaged locks.

Applying petroleum based products to combat the dryness only aid in the problem as it will clog the pores thus increasing dryness. The use of hot combs, flat irons and curling irons, also attribute to altering the structure of already damaged hair resulting in excess dryness and more breakage.

All products have an alkaline level that is measured by its pH (potential of hydrogen) factor which ranges from 1-14 with 7 considered as neutral. The chemicals found in hair straightening products such as Sodium hydroxide and ammonium thioglycolate have a very high pH factor of 10-14! The higher the pH factor the more corrosive the product is which is why after a "relaxer" is applied the hair is prone to consistent breakage.

In order to minimize the chemicals from continuing to be active or lessen the pH factor (strength) a neutralizing shampoo or deep conditioner is applied to the hair after the "relaxer" is rinsed out. The shine you experience after is the cuticle being coated with the neutralizing or deep conditioning ingredients. By outer appearances you may think your hair is healthy but the damage is done.

Think about this...the beauty industry makes claim to wonder creams, lotions and moisturizers that will penetrate the skin layers for softer, smoother younger looking skin. Skin is porous and most anything applied to it will be absorbed. Regardless of the outcome of these beauty aids the products are penetrating the skin layers, whether it's on the scalp or the body.

Take for instance, birth control patches that are placed on the skin and absorbed into the bloodstream in an effort to prevent unwanted pregnancies. Patches are also placed on the skin to help those that want to quit smoking.

If these external aids are absorbed by the skin it is obvious that harsh chemicals in "relaxers" are also absorbed by the layers of skin on the scalp which in turn enters the bloodstream, the brain and other internal organs.

Beauticians are also in danger as they are inhaling toxic fumes for hours on end and some go even as far as applying the chemicals without using gloves!

There are some beauticians that use a mask and wear gloves to protect their hands, so ask yourself if they are going to these lengths to protect themselves, what's being used to protect your scalp from this harmful substance that needs to stay on the hair for at least **15-20** minutes to be absorbed by the hair shaft. When the "relaxer" is burning your scalp it does not mean that it's working. It's actually burning your scalp! Your extremely sensitive scalp and scabs that appear a few days later are a painful proof of this.

If scientific research has been conducted, it has not been publicly disclosed to disprove or prove these findings, but it would be ignorant to think that internal damage does not occur over the long term use of chemical straightening agents being applied to the hair and scalp.

Black women are not regularly informed, if at all of the toll that chemicals and other hair straightening methods have on their mental and spiritual well being, why then would any time or effort be spent on the toll it has on their physical state.

Become more informed and that will allow you to make a more sound and educated approach before engaging in habits that are harmful to you.

Dark Skin Light Skin

Yes, unfortunately this is still an issue. The old mentality of light is right and dark is undesirable still thrives in mainstream society and especially amongst our own. Sadly some retailers and advertisers add to this warped way of thinking by oftentimes projecting in their marketing campaigns those with darker complexions as a fad or trend and hot only for a particular season.

Whether extremely light or dark, both sides have been taunted as a child mercilessly from family members, friends and playmates, causing them to feel that they do not belong. While there are individuals with a darker complexion that have naturally long hair the tendency is to think that someone with light skin and naturally long hair has "good hair".

This way of thinking as we all know dates back to slavery where the separation of dark skinned slaves and light skinned slaves were a common practice. It was a system set up to breed hatred amongst ourselves that lives on to this day. This dissension and division with skin complexion also plays a great role in acceptance of natural hair.

The dark skin verses light skin, good hair verses bad hair issue is so deeply rooted that some black women will only align themselves with a mate of the opposite sex that they feel would guarantee they bare children with "good hair" and "fair skin."

Some might say, sometimes you can't help who you fall in love with or love happens when you least expect it. We all have a choice in whatever we do, but, if you find yourself deliberately seeking to partner with someone that you believe is going to bare you "good haired" babies simply means you are struggling with your own perception of what you define is beautiful and in your eyes it is not being black.

Bringing this particular topic to light is so those with this point of view can take an honest look at themselves and perhaps embark on re-evaluating their thought process about their heritage and culture and begin the process of healing and self love.

The pre-conception is if you're a lighter complexion you automatically have "good hair" and if you're of a darker complexion you have "bad hair", "coarse hair", "nappy". This should not come as a surprise, but there is no such thing as "good hair" or "bad hair" furthermore, black women should be happy to be nappy! By continuing to allow society to define what is beautiful will only allow this ignorance to continue. We have to embrace and accept that we all have

different textured hair and love what we

are born with.

How Society Describes our Mane

"Unruly", "unmanageable", "dreadful",

no, I'm not talking about an undisciplined

animal. These words are just a brief list of

what we have conditioned ourselves to

accept as fact about our hair and in turn

ourselves. In fact most of the top hair

product manufacturers go so far as using

slogans with these very words to market

their products that you essentially end up

buying.

Why such venom for something given

to us by our Creator? Do you think our

creator made a mistake when he made his

children in his own image? Do you believe

that our creator wanted his children to go

through life feeling ugly, devalued,

worthless, or inferior? Wake Up!

Curiosity from different cultures is

always welcomed but at times can

borderline on being insulting. Often times

I get looks and stares from someone that

is of a different nationality and once these

individuals feel comfortable enough to

engage in conversation, shortly thereafter,

I get the "questions". I believe the

questions are not directed in a malicious

way or meant in any way to embarrass me,

but at the end of the day it is a little

unnerving to be asked in public when I

choose to wear braids, "how do I wash my

hair and how often" or if I should wear my

hair loose "how does your hair do that"? I can't help but think that I'm being viewed as an alien, although it's not too difficult to understand why anyone with natural hair would be viewed that way due to the fact that so few black women choose to wear natural hair and in the eyes of another culture, those that do are a rarity, a sight to be seen somewhat. I understand that my kingly hair is intriguing so I often answer the questions politely all the while educating them about the differences between our hair textures.

How Black Women Define Themselves

Black women for decades have come to define each other using terms and or phrases that are demeaning and degrading not realizing that the continuous use of negative connotations when describing our tresses are cutting away at the core of their self esteem and well being. Sadly this hate of self is passed on to our children. When will this vicious cycle end?

We march, protest and even ban certain retailers the very moment we feel a negative or racial connotation has been expressed in any form. We rally for certain doors to be broken down in tinsel town, demanding for equal roles etc., yet we don't project who we really are to the world. Why should anyone show us respect or accept us if we don't even respect or accept ourselves!

Church goers are claiming to be in the image of God, but go to worship with an altered image of what God gave them. In actuality these women are saying, we don't like how you made us, why did you give us this hair, these lips, my eyes are too dark and the darker sisters ask why their skin is so black. The complaints go on and on, yet the realization of what incredible gifts we have been given goes unnoticed.

Besides hair trends, other nationalities are paying top dollar for lip injections, butt implants and darkening agents to name a few of the many procedures performed to achieve what Nubians are born with.

Some more food for thought...do you realize that no other race on this planet can inherit the very hair that we seek to destroy; not by mixing races or concocting a mixture in a laboratory, can anyone reproduce, unless by birth a Nubians natural hair.

The misconception that has been perpetuated is that our hair texture and its various styles are worn only at 70's theme parties or costume events that are allocated to certain calendar days throughout the year. Our hair and the styles we wear it in are not a trend or a fad. That's equivalent to saying _you_ are a trend or a fad...in today out tomorrow, hot this season not the next. Know the power of your natural hair and origin and you can go on to become all that you were meant to be.

How much more empowered you will be once you've embraced the true essence of you. No more hiding behind a chemical process that leaves your hair dead and limp which in effect is leaving you spiritually dead adding to that a scalp that is on the verge of being severely

damaged and/or permanently destroyed.

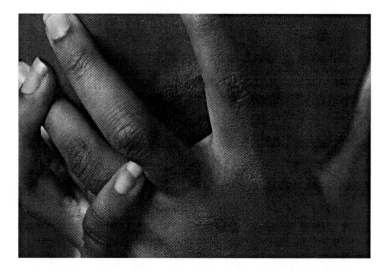

Have Patience in the Growing Out Process

Knowledge coupled with patience is

the key to the re-awakening of ultimately

what is your soul. If you're in your 30's

chances are you have been straightening

your hair for more than half of your life.

Taking that first step and not applying any straightening agents to your hair be it a "relaxer" or straightening comb, etc., will seem like a major deal. It can at times feel like your going through withdrawal and you may even change your mind after a few weeks, maybe even a few days.   So, you do what you've always been accustomed to doing and you plunge right back into that "lye" or you flaunt that hair piece or weave that has no resemblance to your natural hair texture. I know...I've been there.

I truly understand what years of telling yourself that you are not beautiful unless your hair is lying flat on your head will do to your self- esteem. Through personal experience, once you miss that first touch up you are well on your way.

Making the transition from unnatural to natural hair begins really with some quiet time, soul searching and strengthening of the mind. Ask yourself some questions to the nature of *why* am I straightening my hair, *who* am I really without chemicals in my hair (see section -

Questions to ask yourself)...

Preparation is the key to any new venture and growing the chemicals out of your hair once and for all is no different (see chapter on Maintaining and Making the Transition to Natural Locks).

Refrain from the temptations of the airbrushed over glamorized images on magazine covers, television, billboards, etc. 95% of the images we see in society do not resemble Nubians. A daily bombardment of images that do not resemble you will inevitably persuade you to conform to what is seen as the majority, and completely forgetting about yourself.

Nubians eventually will and in most cases have already adapted and embraced these idealisms of what society constitutes as being beautiful, acceptable or the norm.

What Are We Teaching Our Children?

Love of self leads to self discovery which encourages one to seek knowledge that leads to self empowerment. These steps will enable you to live the life that you were meant to live and to never ever feel inferior to anyone. This will enable you to teach your children the skills they need to become confident productive individuals and later on successful well adjusted adults.

You're probably wondering, how can the removal of straightening chemicals from my hair or using other straightening

methods to change my hair texture and

image, lead to all of that. A love of one's

self goes a long way. When you love and

accept yourself, your confidence levels

increase substantially and you will also

emanate a positive energy, that in turn

allow you to go after and seek

opportunities that you otherwise would

not think of pursuing.

This confidence comes from deep

within and you begin to give and share

that light with others, essentially passing it

on to those that will come after you and those that are currently in your life.

Little black girls grow up loving dolls that in most cases do not look like them. Mommies hair does not look like theirs, and in some cases, their playmates do not look like them. How do you think they will eventually feel about themselves?

Little black boys are also getting their first impression of what is beautiful and at an impressionable age form in their mind that straight hair looks better. Already the tone of who they will find attractive when they get older is being ingrained in their minds. We wonder why today most black men prefer straight hair over kinky hair and it starts from what they were exposed to on a daily basis growing up.

Nubians are congested with images that do not resemble them on a regular basis forcing them to think they need to change what they are made to believe needs to be **"fixed"**, when everything is right in the first place. Usually something is "fixed" when it is broken or not working and is in need of repair. There is absolutely nothing wrong with wearing your natural hair and literally speaking the only time your natural hair is "broken or prone to breaking" is when it has been chemically processed.

Getting Support
(What to Expect from your co-workers, friends and family)

One of many concerns when thinking about removing the unnatural hair is not being taken seriously in the corporate world (if that is where you currently earn a living). Have you asked yourself, why? One good guess is self awareness, which is a powerful tool to utilize because being aware of self leads to a deeper connection of who you really are, your true roots. Not everyone around you will be quick to

support this new frame of mind.
Remember, your talents and skills have not
changed only your hair texture and style.

Surprisingly support for taking the
step to wearing your hair in its natural
texture will not come from those closest to
you, at least not everyone. You might
even hear "you look ugly with your hair
like that" or "you need to invest in some
tcb" or some may remark, "the hot comb
was invented, use it." It's disappointing to
know that these kinds of comments are
coming from other Nubians.

Both black women and men are guilty of displaying this type of ignorance. In most cases you may receive compliments from other races before a Nubian brother or sister says something positive or encouraging. The silence or negative comments stem from the realization of knowing deep down they too have the same hair texture and fear embracing their true roots.

I always encourage the women that approach me and compliment my hair them that they too can achieve the same.

The most common response is "no I can't wear my natural hair, I've tried and it just doesn't look right, or it doesn't work for me." I know firsthand why they've come to this conclusion. The number one reason would be the use of the wrong products in their hair. You can not continue using the same products in relaxed hair on natural kinky hair, doing this will not get the desired results.

Natural hair thrives on moisture and most of the products for relaxed hair or on the market period are detergent based which simply means when you apply

theses same products to natural textured

hair you are stripping your already

sensitive hair of much needed moisture.

The outcome is crispy, dry hair that is

prone to extreme breakage not to mention

hair that is difficult to style.

Seek out other black women who have

made the transition. When you see

another black woman on the street, at your

grocery store, workout class, etc. ask their

advice on what they did to remove the

chemicals and what they do to maintain

their natural hair. If you want to go a step further start your own natural hair group, small or large.

Accepting the "lye's" for so long has the majority of Nubian women going to any lengths to wipe out their true identity. Stop annihilating what our creator has given us. It is detrimental to your mental and physical well being.

Must Be The Money

Most black hair salons unfortunately cater to the flat and bone straight hair image. Black owned distributors and manufactures that are fortunate enough to have any foot hold in the beauty manufacturing industry share in the billions that are generated from the production of chemical based products and other straightening agents. The dollars that are generated supersede what is healthier for natural hair textures and will only continue to push the notion of chemically processed or the pursuit of straight hair.

The black community and even more so the non-black communities have profited greatly, selling the latest "relaxer", European wig, European weave, flat iron, etc., when the focus should be on products that are suitable for and that resemble our natural hair type.

Uplifting your self-esteem and empowering yourself is not anyone else's concern, *you* are responsible for your own mental and physical well being. It is not the responsibility of society to change our minds about how we view ourselves; it is solely up to us.

New businesses have been popping up to cater to the extremely small population of women who already got rid of the "lye" but we also have to be careful of the ingredients used in this new wave of "all natural" and "botanical" or "herbal" hair solutions. Some have chemicals in it that are still extremely harsh and drying to already sensitive hair that will leave you even more frustrated when trying to maintain your natural locks.

Contrary to what a lot of people say, your natural hair is not difficult to manage. The difficulty is finding quality products that are compatible with our natural hair texture.

I've listed several of many ingredients that are harmful to your hair and skin which are commonly found in shampoos, conditioners, hair pomade and other hair and skin care items that are used on a regular basis. When you purchase hair maintenance products and don't understand what some of the ingredients are then conduct your own research to find out what you are applying to your hair/scalp and skin.

Taking a few minutes to read the ingredients on the products you purchase you will find that they may not differ from some of your daily household cleaning solutions.   If you're cleaning the house it's beneficial but using these agents in areas that are inches away from your eyes, ears, mouth and penetrating the layers of skin on your head and body are a whole different matter.

SODIUM HYDROXIDE (LYE-BASED) GUANIDINE HYDROXIDE (NO-LYE) - Severe irritant. Corrosive! Swallowing may cause severe burns of mouth, throat, and stomach. Severe scarring of tissue and death may result. Symptoms may include bleeding, vomiting, diarrhea, fall in blood pressure. Damage may appear days after exposure. Contact with skin can cause irritation or severe burns and scarring with greater exposures. Causes irritation of eyes, and with greater exposures it can cause burns that may result in permanent impairment of vision, even blindness. Chronic Exposure: Prolonged contact with dilute solutions or dust has a destructive effect upon tissue. [JT Baker - Material Safety Data Sheet]

CALCIUM HYDROXIDE: Used as a Lye substitute in no lye hair relaxers. A common ingredient in plaster, poison, can destroy the hair, skin, nerves, blood and glands causes an increase in the blood pH which is damaging to internal organs. [Wikipedia]

ISOPROVYL ALCOHOL: Isopropyl alcohol is also commonly used as a cleaner and solvent in industry. It is also a very good cleaning agent and often used for cleaning electronic devices. It is most often found in lotions, color rinses, cosmetics, etc. It is also used as a gasoline additive for dissolving water or ice in fuel lines Isopropyl alcohol is oxidized by the liver into acetone. Symptoms of isopropyl alcohol poisoning include flushing, headache, dizziness, CNS depression, nausea, vomiting, anesthesia, and coma. Use in well-ventilated areas and use protective gloves while using. Poisoning can occur from ingestion, inhalation, or absorption. [Wikipedia]

SODIUM LAURYL SUFATE (SLS) & SODIUM LAURETH SULFATE (SLES): SLES, is a detergent and surfactant found in many personal care products soaps, shampoos, toothpaste etc. Products containing these substances can affect those prone to eczema and other irritants. These substances provide a foaming quality to the product, allowing for better distribution of the product while washing hair or skin and while brushing teeth. When rinsed off, the product will have cleaned the area but will have taken moisture from the top layers of skin. In people with sensitive skin (prone to dermatitis, acne, eczema, psoriasis and chemical sensitivity), the drying property of these type of detergents can cause flare-ups of skin conditions or may worsen existing conditions. The large majority of toothpastes sold in the U.S. contain Sodium laureth sulfate (SLS), which is known to cause aphthous ulcers in certain individuals. **Both SLS and SLES can enter the blood stream.** [Wikipedia]

MINERAL OIL/ PETROLATUM: Mineral oil or liquid petrolatum is a by-product in the distillation of petroleum to produce gasoline. Mineral oil with added fragrance is marketed as baby oil in the US, UK and Canada.   Used as an ingredient in baby lotions, cold creams, ointments and other pharmaceuticals and low-grade cosmetics. Alternative – Raw Almond Oil or Raw Shea Butter. [Wikipedia]

DIETHANOLAMINE (DEA): DEA and its variants are suspected of increasing the risk of cancer. Studies also show that DEA directly inhibits fetal brain development in mice by blocking the absorption of choline, a nutrient required for brain development and maintenance. DEA is also associated with miscarriages in laboratory studies. [Wikipedia]

DMDM HYDANTOIN: - releases a powerful acid and neuro toxin formaldehyde which causes joint pain, skin reactions, allergies, depression, headaches, chest pains, ear infections, chronic fatigue, dizziness, and loss of sleep. Exposure also irritates the respiratory system, triggers heart palpitations or asthma, and aggravates coughs. Other side effects are a weakened immune system and cancer. [Organic & Natural Skin Care by Monica Olsen]

HYDROQUINONE: - This ingredient is commonly used in skin whitening products. It is also commonly used in plastics manufacturing and is a highly toxic chemical. This ingredient should not be used on humans or animals. Hydroquinone is a well known carcinogen and is known as a liver, blood, lung and respiratory, reproductive organ and skin toxicant. [Organic & Natural Skin Care by Monica Olsen]

SYNTHETIC FRAGRANCES: - The synthetic fragrances used in cosmetics can have as many as 200 ingredients. There is no way to know what the chemicals are, since on the label it will simply say "Fragrance". Some of the problems caused by these chemicals are headaches, dizziness, rash, hyper-pigmentation, violent coughing, vomiting, skin irritation, and the list goes on. Advice: Don't buy a cosmetic that has the word "Fragrance" on the ingredients label. [Organic & Natural Skin Care by Monica Olsen]

In the transition phase of going from straight to curly, wavy or kinky hair, you might say to yourself this is too much for me to handle or I don't have time to tend to/manage my hair.

It will take re-learning your hairs texture and what products work best for it and so on before it becomes second nature to maintain. Be prepared to take at least 6 months to truly get used to your natural hair and playing with different styling options until you get comfortable with your natural hair once again.

Experiment with different products and styling options to determine what works best for you. It may actually get challenging but during that time (which does not last for long), you will really feel free and unlimited for the first time in your life.

Be True to Yourself

Going natural does not mean having your chemical free tresses hidden under a European style wig or European style weave, something I did initially because the "relaxer" had badly eaten away at my hair that I was nearly bald on certain sections of my scalp. Wearing these wigs created a new addiction, which I kept up for two years. I once again conditioned myself to feel more comfortable with straight haired wigs instead of using alternative styling options that resembled my natural hair.

Take into consideration that even though you have your hair natural and choose to press or flat iron it, the end result is the same, you are still opting for "straight is great" instead of opting for something more along the lines of what is naturally kinky, curly or wavy hair, the true texture of your hair.

You might think well it's all about style and I just want to change my look, just like I change my outfits or accessories.

Opting to change the very texture of your hair goes far beyond making a fashion statement. It is a mental statement and how you truly feel about yourself and heritage.

Most likely, after many years of living with what society deems as "beautiful" chances are you are still not accepting your true self and feel it necessary to make your hair straight to feel better about yourself or accepted.

Start discovering the many styling options that you can do with your own hair texture without feeling the need to alter the hair to achieve a so called fashionable look.

The most common complaint amongst black women is that their natural hair is too hard to comb or maintain on a daily basis, but sadly will go to great lengths caring for hair that is chemically processed by spending countless dollars on expensive shampoos, conditioners, oil sheens, etc.

The amount of effort given to maintaining straight hair should also be put into practice towards, natural hair care and finding products that work with natural hair textures. The effort is not given because the truth is, it's not difficult to care for natural hair, the desire and acceptance of natural kinky hair is what is difficult for most to embrace.

You'll soon discover that you won't need as many products and styling tools to maintain your natural hair as you did when your hair was relaxed or pressed, etc. Avoiding activities you enjoy such as exercising or something as simple as taking a steamy hot shower to name just a few things avoided because of the likely

hood of sweating out the "perm" or "press"

will be a thing of the past.

   With that revelation most would think

that black women would be excited to

grow out the chemicals, throw out the

pressing combs and return to natural hair

with the realization that they no longer

have to spend what amounts to a work

day time wise at the beauty salon for their

weekly visits not to mention the dollars

spent on additional styling tools and hair

maintenance products. Money will also be

spent maintaining your natural hair, but in comparison it will not amount to what is spent sporting a European hair style.

Your natural hair is fighting to make a breakthrough by the onset of new growth and each time you fight back by beating it up with harsh chemicals, ironing combs, etc. Your natural hair loves you...you need to love it back. Nurture it, love it, take care of it and it will take care of you.

Recently at a recording studio a female musician who was admiring my hair, shared that she just recently "relaxed" her hair again because she is going to perform oversees and that the older audiences would not accept her natural hair because it is not sophisticated.

It is unsettling to think that you can tell someone their hair is not sophisticated, when that is how it naturally grows! Must hair be bone straight in order to have class? This singer went on to say that she could where braids on the stage just as long as they were micro braids and looked like "real hair". In other words society feels nappy hair is not real hair.

A friend was overwhelmed with moving into her new home and desperately needed to have both of her sons' corn rowed hair re-done. I mentioned that she should just have them where it loose. She responded that they would end up in detention or get suspended for wearing their hair out because the school looks at it as being unruly. That would be equivalent to telling a Caucasian child that his blue eyes need to be covered up with dark sunglasses or he/she could be expelled.

I mention these incidents to demonstrate how we accepted to not embrace ourselves the way we were created and allowed others in society to dictate and put rules in place as to what is acceptable.

Many times I have conversed with friends and they still make reference to "good hair" verses "bad hair" with comments such as my other siblings have that half black half Indian (or some other nationality) mix in their hair and with disdain state that they don't know why they ended up with their nappy hair.

We have allowed society to dictate what is sophisticated and acceptable and leaving our image and culture totally out of the equation. A multitude of damage is being inflicted on a child when you enforce a rule that tells them they can not get an education if they chose to wear their hair the way it naturally grows.

The end result is seen in my encounter with the singer, who as an adult agrees instantly to straighten her hair to look "presentable", this would not have been her mindset if as a child it was instilled that there is nothing wrong with her

natural hair.

Physical Damage Caused By Straightening Agents

The signs of damaged hair are obvious. What's even more alarming are black women who continue to add more stress to their scalp that is already showing signs of balding, especially around the hair line.

Over processed hair tends to break off at weak points all over the scalp. The hair will most often look frail and thinned out. Extreme breakage usually occurs near the hairline and in the middle, as most black women are prone to wearing their hair in a ponytail. Regardless of the obvious signs of permanent damage, all common sense is thrown out the window because of the overwhelming desire to straighten the hair. Women will have hairlines that start as far back as the tip of the upper ear and still pull the hair back in a ponytail. What's worse is this look is usually accompanied by a ponytail that is too heavy for the overall hair density on the scalp adding more strain to the already thinning, damaged hair line and mid section.

A hairline in this condition normally indicates that the damage is irreversible. It is however not too late to save what hair remains, by not exposing it to more chemicals or straightening methods.

The key component here is to catch the signs of balding and thinning especially around the hairlines in the early stages. Even if you find your hair is thinning one month and then looks full or more dense a couple of months later as you may have waited a few extra weeks to do a touch up does not mean the hair will continue to get thick and that it's okay to continue applying the chemicals, as it won't be long before permanent damage is the end result.

Look Great With Your Hair In Its Natural State

You've made the choice to wear your hair in its natural state or you've chosen a more natural hair style alternative. Whether you choose to lock, twist, free-style or cornrow your textured tresses, the old adage that our hair is hard to style is far from the truth. Following are several styles that are easy to achieve and maintain either on your own or with the assistance of a professional stylist.

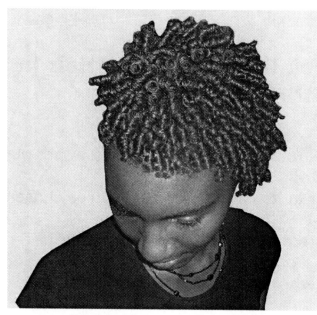

Mohawk with Cornrows and a rod set

Mohawk with Cornrows and a rod set
(see Step by Step -How to Create look)

Straight Two Strand Twist

Two Strand Twist
(see Step by Step - How to Create look)

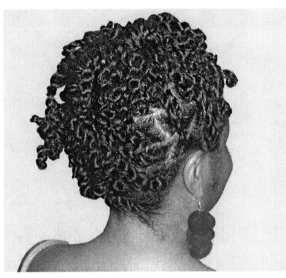

Two Strand Twist w/ Flat Twists and Pin Up

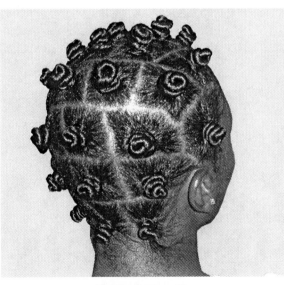

Nubian Knots with
(see Step by Step – How to Create look)

Kinky Twist

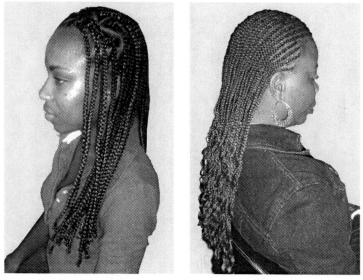

Geo Braid Extensions   Layered Cornrow Ext.

(see Step by Step – How to Create look)

Lock Maintenance & Bun   Pin Up Locks w/ Rod Set

Locks and Rod Set
(see Step by Step How to Create look)

Nutrition and Exercise and The Effects on the Hair and Skin

Living in a society that is fast paced, can make it extremely difficult to maintain a healthy way of living. Most often many opt to stop off at a fast food restaurant and pick up dinner after a long day at work out of ease and convenience. Trying to fit in an exercise routine at least 3 times a week and eating nutritious healthy meals throughout the day sounds like you would need to hire a personal trainer and cook. Incorporating moderate exercise and healthy eating does not have to empty your wallets or exhaust you mentally from trying to schedule it in your daily lives.

You've probably heard it a million times, but eliminating fried and processed foods from your daily food intake and increasing/adding nuts, whole grains, fruits and vegetables will make a difference in your weight and overall health overtime.

Weight loss is different for everyone but following the basic guidelines of eating healthier foods and exercising, whether it is a brisk walk, swimming, biking, or a session at the gym will increase your odds of maintaining healthier skin and hair and an overall healthier you.

Most people complain that eating healthy is not fun - life is too short. Exactly! Life is too short to live it without quality health. The average person takes better care of their car then they do their body. When you consistently put poor gas in your vehicle or don't maintain the vehicle on a regular basis eventually major problems will occur with the performance of the vehicle. Think of your body in the same context.

When the body has tried all possible ways to eliminate toxins found in the junk foods without success one of the tell tale signs is not only your mental condition, but the condition of your skin and hair.

Outbreaks, in the forms of acne, rashes, boils, lesions, etc is the skins way of telling us we need to make a drastic change not only in our lifestyle, but nutritionally. Thin, constant shedding and dull hair is also an indication of poor nutrition. Nourishing your body correctly amongst the obvious benefits it provides, it greatly benefits your hair.

Health Tips

Drink at least 6 – 8 oz glasses of water daily (water aids in flushing out toxins from your system and overall healthy function of internal organs)

Make sure at least 3 of your meals have at least 8-10 grams of fiber which aids in the digestive process

Eliminate or cut back on caffeine products (soda, coffee, etc.) which contributes to dehydration

Stay away from man made juices and other sugar filled beverages.

(invest in a juicer and purchase fruits and vegetables to make fresh and healthy drinks – look for a low rpms on your new juicer purchase to ensure you are not killing enzymes which provides needed nutrients in the product)

Incorporate more fruits, nuts, grains and vegetables in your meals

Eliminate or cut back on fried foods and fast foods

Eliminate or cut back on sweets or other high sugar content foods (sweet tooth alternatives – fruits, natural granola bar, etc.)

Exercise at least 3 times a week (attain maximum heart rate level to burn sufficient calories)

Try to go for a walk after a meal

Don't eat at least 2 – 3 hours before going to sleep

Eat smaller meals throughout the day (approx. 5 meals with snacks included) this will keep your metabolism at a healthy calorie burning rate

Eating well balanced meals of fruits and vegetables and drinking plenty of water will enrich your blood with the right nutrients that go to the root of your hair, strengthening the hair and promoting growth. Hair grows 1/2 an inch every month. That's 6 inches per year! Sadly the new growth is not visible because of the harmful products used in the hair that attribute to breakage.

To the Brothers

I implore our brothers to also wake up and to love yourself enough to appreciate your true Nubian queens and not continue to be seduced by "straight is great".

The perception that our black men have towards black women that choose to wear their hair natural range from such comments as they're lazy, not clean and are poor. It is shocking and disturbing that black men would view black women in such a demeaning and negative light. As well, comments like those mentioned prompt black women to state, that if they do remove the "unnatural" that they will only do it after they are married. This invokes the notion that states if black women with natural are currently single will remain single unless her hair is altered and resembling that of a Caucasians hair.

There are black men that embrace black women that choose to not alter their natural hair, but those men are far and few between.

Our black sisters need, love encouragement and acceptance from our black men which will undoubtedly lead to the strengthening of our black families.

Maintaining and Making the Transition to Natural Locks

- Make the commitment <u>today</u> to not put any straightening agents in your hair ("relaxers", hot comb, etc.)

- If you are used to a lengthy hair style, opt for braids until your natural hair grows to a desired length. Keep in mind that the braids, your hair and especially the scalp must be well maintained while using this method to eliminate the chemicals from your hair. Do not braid the hair too tight! Do not keep the braids in too long to avoid a fusion of your hair and the extensions.

- During the growing out phase opt for styles or other hair style alternatives that are closely related to you culturally. This will increase your self-esteem and self awareness.

- Use a detangling shampoo or just conditioner to cleanse your natural textured hair. This will allow your hair to retain moisture. Avoid shampoos that may have some of the

ingredients I listed (Must be the

Money) as the top ingredients (or at

all) as they only dry out the hair or

cause more damage. A great hair

rinse is Apple Cider Vinegar or

Lemon Juice.

- Use oils that are not petroleum

  based which will clog the pores and

  produce product buildup.
  (recommended oils: Raw Shea Butter, Almond
  Oil, Primrose Oil, Rosemary Oil, Jojoba Oil,
  Avocado Oil – to name a few)

- With each new growth trim off the chemically damaged hair on the ends (unless you of course decided to cut all the "relaxed" hair off from the very beginning).

- Protect the hair when sleeping by covering it with a silk head wrap as most pillow cases can cause the hair to pull and break when snagged by the materials that the pillow case is composed of.

- Ignore the negative comments. Keep in mind that when another black woman may not take kindly to you wearing your hair natural, most likely they to minus the European weaves, wigs, etc have hair that looks exactly like what you are trying to achieve and maintain.

- Educate yourself by reading magazines that cater to natural texture hair and discover new styles and practice new ways to wear your chemical free hair.

The long term benefits of going chemical free

- Healthy hair and scalp

- Healthier attitude about yourself and self-image

- Positive outlook on life

- Setting an example for the younger generation that will inevitably instill within themselves more confidence

- Saving money by cutting down on purchasing "relaxer kits" or other straightening agents which can amount to thousands each year

- Never worrying about your hair being exposed to the elements, such as rain, snow, or the sun.

- Discovering who you are really meant to be.

- Positive energy

- Going after things in life with confidence and surety

A New You

If you've been inspired after reading this book and decided to make the transition, we applaud you. This book is meant to encourage, educate, and provoke thought and insight. Tell your sister (s), girlfriends, mother, aunt (s), what you've learned and how they too can make the transition, and if they are not at that point in their lives let them know that you need to be encouraged through your transitional phase that those who do not agree or are

A NEW YOU

not on board should keep the negative comments to themselves.

Once I made the choice to remove all straightening agents from my hair and letting my hair just be, I am discovering how truly beautiful I am inside and out which in turn is realigning my soul, spirit and body. I am no longer tempted to alter my hair in an effort to achieve a look or image that was not meant for me. Wake up! **Black women discover who you are...you won't be disappointed!**

128

Questions to ask Yourself

In order to get a better understanding of how we as black women view ourselves especially when it comes to our hair I have put together some questions to probe deeper about your thoughts on your natural hair and self image.

HOW LONG HAVE YOU STRAIGHTENED YOUR HAIR AND BY WHAT PROCESS/METHOD DO YOU STRAIGHTEN YOUR HAIR (PERM, PRESS, TEXTURIZER, ETC)

GROWING UP DID YOU THINK THAT YOUR HAIR WAS SUPPOSED TO BE STRAIGHT? WHY?

WHO DO YOU LOOK TO FOR YOUR HAIRSTYLE IDEAS (TELEVISION, VIDEOS, MAGAZINES)

QUESTIONS TO ASK YOURSELF

DO YOU THINK ANY OF THE ABOVE MEDIA OUTLETS
INFLUENCE YOUR HAIRSTYLE IDEAS AND YOUR PERSONAL
IMAGE

WOULD YOU FEEL, EMBARRASSED OR UGLY TO WEAR YOUR
HAIR NATURAL? IF YES EXPLAIN WHY.

DO YOU FEEL THE THAT THE MAN THAT YOU ARE CURRENTLY
DATING WILL REACT NEGATIVELY TO YOU IF YOU DECIDED TO
GO NATURAL? WHY?

IF YOU ARE SINGLE, ARE YOU WAITING TO GET MARRIED FIRST
BEFORE GOING NATURAL? WHY?

HAVE YOU ATTEMPTED TO GROW OUT THE CHEMICALS ONLY
TO GIVE UP AND APPLY MORE CHEMICALS? IF YES WHAT WERE
THE REASONS FOR YOU GIVING IN.

IF YOU SUCCEEDED IN THE GROWING OUT PROCESS ONLY TO
GO BACK TO STRAIGHTENING YOUR HAIR HOW DID YOU FEEL
FOR THAT MOMENT WEARING YOUR HAIR NATURAL?

HOW DID SOCIETY MAKE YOU FEEL WHEN YOU WORE YOUR
HAIR NATURAL (STARES, COMMENTS, ETC)

WHO DID THE REMARKS COME FROM (MEN, WOMEN, BLACK, WHITE)

WHAT KIND OF COMMENTS WERE MADE. (GOOD OR BAD)
DO YOU THINK BLACK WOMAN LOOK BETTER WITH EUROPEAN TEXTURE HAIR, IF YES EXPLAIN WHY

WOULD YOU FEEL UNCOMFORTABLE WEARING YOUR HAIR NATURAL AT YOUR PLACE OF WORK? IF YES, EXPLAIN WHY

DO YOU STRAIGHTEN YOUR DAUGHTERS HAIR? IF YES, WHY?

IF YOU WERE TO ASK YOUR DAUGHTER/SON WHICH HAIR LOOKED BETTER STRAIGHT OR NAPPY WHAT WOULD SHE/HE SAY

IF YOUR DAUGHTER/SON ANSWERED STRAIGHT HAIR TO THE ABOVE QUESTION, ASK SHE/HE WHY?

WOULD YOU LIKE TO SEE MORE IMAGES OF BLACK WOMAN WITH NATURAL HAIR IN THE MEDIA

DO YOU THINK BY SEEING MORE WOMAN THAT RESEMBLE THE REAL YOU WILL ENCOURAGE YOU TO MAKE THE TRANSITION TO NATURAL HAIR

QUESTIONS TO ASK YOURSELF

IF YOU ARE A HAIRSTYLIST DO YOU THINK YOUR BUSINESS WOULD SUFFER FINANCIALLY IF MORE BLACK WOMEN WORE NATURAL HAIR OR WOULD YOU RE-VAMP YOUR BUSINESS TO CATER TO NATURAL

STEP BY STEP – How to Create Look

Mohawk with cornrows and a rod set

1. Part the hair in small sections, separate with long duck bill clips, cornrow your design. Start from the nape of the neck and work your way up the head. Do one side at a time making sure to leave a section of hair out in the middle for your Mohawk. Be sure to oil the scalp with an all natural hair butter like Warm Spirit's Anahita Hair Butter.

2. For the hair left out for the Mohawk, separate into small sections and wet set on rods, use a styling foam that has no alcohol in it like Fantasia's styling foam. Be sure that the hair is taut, start twisting it around the curl rod at the bottom of the rod and work your way up.

3. Place the client under the hair dryer for 30-60 minutes. Then spray the hair with hair oil such as Warm Spirit's Anahita Hair Conditioning Oil and using your fingers, pluck the rods out to make them fuller. Use a moisturizing hair butter like

Warm Spirit's Anahita Hair Butter to separate the rods and as you pluck, be sure to go in the same directions as the curls are going. Spray with an oil free moisturizer like Fantasia's Hair Polisher for high shine.

Straight Two Strand Twists

1. Blow dry hair with a comb attachment to slightly straighten the hair, but be sure to leave the ends slightly natural. Part the hair in small sections, separate with long duck bill clips. Separate the section of hair into 2 equal parts and twist in a clock wise motion. Twist to the bottom of the hair and repeat on the next section. Be sure to oil the scalp with an all natural hair butter like Warm Spirit's Anahita Hair Butter.

2. For the flat twists in the front, part into the desired design and flat twist the hair along the scalp. Then twist the hair out to the ends.

3. Spray with an oil free moisturizer like Fantasia's Hair Polisher for high shine.

Two Strand Twist w/ Flat Twists and Pin Up

1. Part the hair in small sections, separate with long duck bill clips. Separate the section of hair into 2 equal parts and twist in a clock wise motion. Twist to the bottom of the hair and repeat on the next section. Be sure to oil the scalp with an all natural hair butter like Warm Spirit's Anahita Hair Butter. For added curl, you can dampen the hair with water and use a clear gel with no alcohol in it like Fantasia's Aloe Vera Styling Gel.

2. For the flat twists, part into the desired design and flat twist the hair along the scalp. If hair was dampened place client under the dryer for 20 minutes.

3. For Pin Up, pin hair starting from the back working your way to the front in the desired style and secure with hair pins. Spray with an oil free moisturizer like Fantasia's Hair Polisher for high shine.

Nubian Knots with Cornrows

1. Blow dry hair with a comb attachment to slightly straighten the hair, but be sure to leave the ends slightly natural. Part the hair in medium sections, separate with long duck bill clips. You may apply a small amount of styling foam like Fantasia's styling foam to help the hair shine. Twist the entire section of hair in a clock wise motion until it twists around itself, twists in a coil and tuck. Secure it with a small rubber band making sure to hide it under the knot. Be sure to oil the scalp with an all natural hair butter like Warm Spirit's Anahita Hair Butter.

2. For the cornrows on the side, part into the desired design and cornrow the hair along the scalp. Then twist the hair into the nubian knots.

3. Spray with an oil free moisturizer like Fantasia's Hair Polisher for high shine. Hint: when you remove the knots, the hair will have a natural curl. Separate the large coil curls by plucking them out with hair butter and leave the cornrows in for a funky curly afro look.

Kinky Twist (and Kinky Twist with Rod Set)

1. Part the hair in small sections, separate with short clips. Add kinky twist hair with a short cornrow stitch and begin twisting two strands of hair in a clock wise motion. Twist to the bottom of the hair and repeat on the next section. Be sure to oil the scalp with an all natural hair butter like Warm Spirit's Anahita Hair Butter.

2. For the rod set ends, put 2 to 3 twists on a rod curler. Be sure that the hair is taut, start twisting it around the curl rod at the bottom of the rod and work your way up. Twist about 2 to 3 inches of the kinky twist on the rod curler. Dip the curlers in hot water that has been brought to a boil. Let the rod curlers sit in the hot water a few moments, remove, dry with a towel and after 10 minutes, remove all of the rod curlers.

3. Spray with an oil free moisturizer like Fantasia's Hair Polisher for high shine.

Geo Braid Extensions

1. Part hair into geometric shapes and use long duck bill clips to separate the hair.

2. Add kanekalon braid extension hair and cornrow down a short stitch and then begin braiding down to the bottom of the braid extension hair. Be sure to oil the scalp with an all natural hair butter like Warm Spirit's Anahita Hair Butter.

3. Secure the ends by folding the end of the braid on to itself, attaching a small rubber band and clipping off the excess hair. Use scissors to clip stray hairs in the braids. Spray with an oil free moisturizer like Fantasia's Hair Polisher for high shine.

Layered Cornrow Extensions

1. Part hair across from ear to ear horizontally and separate using long duck bill clips. Add kanekalon braid extension hair and cornrow down and then begin braiding down the hair to the bottom of the braid extension hair. Be sure to oil the scalp with anall natural hair butter like Warm Spirit's Anahita Hair Butter.

2. Repeat in the front making sure to part the hair in the desired design.

3. Style the ends into waves by gathering all the braids together, braiding them into 3 big braids, and dipping the ends (about 5-6 inches) in hot water that has been brought to a boil. Hold the ends in the boiling water for several moments, remove and dry with a towel. After a few minutes, unbraid the 3 big braids. Trim the length as desired. Use scissors to clip stray hairs in the braids. Spray with an oil free moisturizer like Fantasia's Hair Polisher for high shine.

<u>Lock Maintenance and Bun</u>

1. Wash locks with a nature based product such as Warm Spirit Essential Spa Shampoo, and moisturize with essential oils such as Warm Spirit Anahita Conditioning Hair Oil.

2. While locks are damp, palm roll and clip down each individual lock until the entire set of locks have been palm rolled and secured with short clips. Locks should be palm rolled with a healthy and natural mixture of alcohol free aloe vera gel

such as Fantasia's Styling Gel with Aloe, mixed with a natural based hair butter such as Warm Spirit Anahita Hair Butter.

3. Sit client under the dryer for 45-60 minutes. For bun styling, start gathering locks from the back first, twist them up together in 3 separate rows, gather all the locks together then wrap them around and tuck. Spray with oil free moisturizer from Fantasia for high shine.

<u>Pin Up Locks w/ Rod Set</u>

1. Wash locks with a nature based product such as Warm Spirit Essential Spa Shampoo, and moisturize with essential oils such as Warm Spirit Anahita Conditioning Hair Oil.

2. While locks are damp, palm roll and clip down each individual lock until the entire set of locks have been palm rolled and secured with short clips. Locks should be palm rolled with a healthy and natural mixture of alcohol free aloe vera gel such as Fantasia's Styling Gel with Aloe, mixed with a nature based hair butter such as Warm Spirit Anahita Hair Butter. Sit client under the dryer for 45-60 minutes.

3. For rod set, remove clips and set two locks on a rod curler using Fantasia's styling foam. Be sure that the locks are taut before you roll them on the curler. Once all locks are secured on rod curlers, set client under the dryer for 60-90 minutes. Remove rods, and separate each curly lock for fullness. Pin up into desired style and secure with hair pins. Spray with oil free moisturizer from Fantasia for high shine.

Locks on Rod Set (2)

1. Wash locks with a nature based product such as Warm Spirit Essential Spa Shampoo, and moisturize with essential oils such as Warm Spirit Anahita Conditioning Hair Oil.

2. While locks are damp, palm roll and clip down each individual lock until the entire set of locks have been palm rolled and secured with short clips. Locks should be palm rolled with a healthy and natural mixture of alcohol free aloe vera gel such as Fantasia's Styling Gel with Aloe, mixed with a natural based hair butter such as Warm Spirit Anahita Hair Butter. Sit client under the dryer for 45-60 minutes.

3. For rod set, remove clips and set two locks on a rod curler using Fantasia's styling foam. Be sure that the locks are taut before you roll them on the curler. Once all locks are secured on rod curlers, set client under the dryer for 60-90 minutes. Remove rods, and separate each curly lock for fullness. Spray with oil free moisturizer from Fantasia for high shine.

1. Wash locks with a nature based product such as Warm Spirit Essential Spa Shampoo, and moisturize with essential oils such as Warm Spirit Anahita Conditioning Hair Oil.

2. While locks are damp, palm roll and clip down each individual lock until the entire set of locks have been palm rolled and secured with short clips. Locks should be palm rolled with a healthy and natural mixture of alcohol free aloe vera gel such as Fantasia's Styling Gel with Aloe, mixed with a nature based hair butter such as Warm Spirit Anahita Hair Butter. Sit client under the dryer for 45-60 minutes.

3. For rod set, remove clips and set two locks on a rod curler using Fantasia's styling foam. Be sure

that the locks are taut before you roll them on the curler. Once all locks are secured on rod curlers, set client under the dryer for 60-90 minutes. Remove rods, and separate each curly lock for fullness. Pin up into desired style and secure with hair pins. Spray with oil free moisturizer from Fantasia for high shine.

ALL HAIR STYLES AND PHOTOS IN THE CHAPTER **LOOK GREAT WITH YOUR HAIR IN ITS NATURAL STATE** ARE PROVIDED BY:

Danisha Nicole, Washington DC Metropolitan Area
Natural Hair Care Specialist
www.myspace.com/danishanicole
Warm Spirit Business Owner
www.warmspirit.org/danishanicole

FOR ADDITIONAL COPIES OF

NOW HAIR THIS!
THE DESTRUCTION OF BLACK HAIR

PLEASE SEND $12.95 U.S
CURRENCY PER COPY VIA
MONEY ORDER OR CERTIFIED
CHECK TO:

TELL PUBLICATIONS
5062 LANKERSHIM BLVD
SUITE 1008
NORTH HOLLYWOOD, CA 91601
(PLEASE ALLOW 7 TO 10 DAYS FOR DELIVERY)

OR
VISIT WWW.DEBEDENE.COM
EMAIL: debe@debedene.com

DEBE DENE

NOW HAIR THIS!

LaVergne, TN USA
09 March 2011
219466LV00001B/169/A

PENGUIN BUSINESS LIBRARY
MANAGEMENT CLASSICS
SERIES EDITOR: GEORGE

SELF-HELP

Samuel Smiles (1812–1904) was a biographer, writer and popular moralist. He was born near Edinburgh, and educated at Haddington High School and Edinburgh University, where he studied medicine. After practising in Scotland, he took up journalism, and later business as secretary to several of the fast-developing railway companies. In the midst of these various occupations, and drawing material from them, he produced biographies of successful industrialists such as Josiah Wedgwood and George Stephenson. He used these works to put forward his ideas of political and social reform, as well as his economic and ethical doctrine, largely derived from the 'Manchester School'. *Self-Help* (1859) is his most famous work.

The Rt. Hon. Sir Keith Joseph, M.P., was educated at Harrow and at Magdalen College, Oxford, and was a Captain in the Royal Artillery, 1939–46. He is a Fellow of All Souls College. He first took his seat as Conservative M.P. for Leeds North-East in 1956, and has had a distinguished political career ever since. He has been Secretary of State for Education and Science since 1981, and is a member of the Cabinet.

George Bull is Consultant Editor to the Penguin Business Library. He has translated five volumes for the Penguin Classics and has worked for the *Financial Times*, for McGraw-Hill *World News* and for *The Director* magazine, of which he was Editor-in-Chief until 1984.

SELF-HELP

with illustrations of
Conduct and Perseverance *by*
SAMUEL SMILES

Abridged by GEORGE BULL

WITH AN INTRODUCTION BY
SIR KEITH JOSEPH, Bt, M.P.

PENGUIN BOOKS

Penguin Books Ltd, Harmondsworth, Middlesex, England
Viking Penguin Inc., 40 West 23rd Street, New York, New York 10010, U.S.A.
Penguin Books Australia Ltd, Ringwood, Victoria, Australia
Penguin Books Canada Ltd, 2801 John Street, Markham, Ontario, Canada L3R 1B4
Penguin Books (N.Z.) Ltd, 182–190 Wairau Road, Auckland 10, New Zealand

First published 1859
Published in Penguin Books 1986

Introduction copyright © Sir Keith Joseph, 1986
All rights reserved

Made and printed in Great Britain by
Richard Clay (The Chaucer Press) Ltd, Bungay, Suffolk
Filmset in 10/12½ pt Monophoto Ehrhardt by
Northumberland Press Ltd, Gateshead, Tyne and Wear

Contents

Introduction
by Sir Keith Joseph, Bt, M.P.

Smiles' *Self-Help* was published in 1859 – the same year as
Darwin's *Origin of the Species* and Mills' *Essay on Liberty*. A quarter of
a million copies were sold in his life time and the book has been through
many editions. It has been translated into scores of languages, including
Japanese, Hindi and Albanian. Quotations hung from the Khedive's
wall.

One of the great merits of the work [wrote the reviewer in *Fraser's Magazine*]
is the proof with which it overflows that the most important results achieved
in life are generally obtained through imperfect means – the exercise of ordinary
qualities such as courage, patience, perseverance, integrity, self-culture, self-
discipline, self-respect, above all strict conscientiousness in the performance,
thorough and prompt, of whatever duty may be nearest in the course of life of
everyday.

'Energy,' wrote Smiles, 'accomplishes more than genius.'
Smiles built the book – the most successful of many improving books
of the Victorian era – on a series of talks he had given to about 100
young artisans who had formed in Leeds an evening school for mutual
improvement. Such schools were not unusual in the largely peaceful,
prosperous years of the second half of the nineteenth century. It was a
time when little was expected of government but much was expected
of individuals; the cults of self-help and self-improvement were strong
and widespread – representing the value of achievement over that of
birth. There were in 1860 over 200,000 members of Mechanics Institutes. There were mutual improvement societies, lyceums and
libraries – and adult education took place at most of them. There were
three million members of Friendly and Provident societies and three
million members of Temperance societies.
Smiles filled his book with an endless and fascinating tapestry of
precept and anecdote. His writing was muscular and succinct, often in
the form of aphorisms such as 'The Nation comes from the Nursery'.
His descriptions of achievements and inventions were clear. He was by

7

any yardstick an outstandingly successful writer, exercising an almost universal appeal. Asa Briggs wrote of his 'remarkable ability to say something of interest and importance to generations of ordinary men and women. He proves his precepts by illustration upon illustration, heaping example upon example, drawn as much from the lives of men of humble as of exalted birth and all of them interesting and relevant.'

He was not, strictly speaking, original: he expressed ideas already widely current in the mid-Victorian period. But he was not banal. Although he reflected the ideas of his time, he conveyed the commonplace in terms so vigorous and vivid as to persuade generations of readers, both his contemporaries and their descendants. In short, he managed to catch what Lionel Trilling has called 'a culture's hum and buzz of implications'.

Because of his emphasis upon progress – particularly in his three separate volumes on engineers – his work not only appealed to the new urban middle class and all those seeking to join it but also promulgated an appropriate ethic for people in those rural areas of Victorian Britain where rapid industrialization and the new technology followed the extension of the railways. Indeed, the book broadcast the achievement ethic far more widely than in Britain, influencing directly or indirectly American businessmen and Chinese revolutionaries, and Smiles himself was honoured in Serbia and in Italy.

What Smiles hymned was not so much success itself as the moral character that lies behind it; in tune with the religious professions of the age, he celebrated patience, courage, endeavour, and the perseverance with which worthy objectives were pursued. He lauded individualism not as a means to worldly gain but as the path to independence and to self-fulfilment. 'It is not ease but difficulty – not facility – that makes men,' he wrote.

Smiles cannot be dismissed as a humbug or as a smug moralist: of radical inclination, sensitive and compassionate, he believed in the work of ordinary man and in his capacity to realize himself. He judged not in terms of money or social status but of the fullest use by each individual of every quality, skill and talent he possessed. The joy of success was in the effort not the achievement. 'It is doubtful,' he wrote, 'whether any heavier evil could be imposed on man than the complete gratification of all his hopes without effort on his part.'

8

True, he had his sharp limitations: he was no abstract thinker, and he was naïve about art, believing that effort and will alone could make an artist. But he did not judge by financial results or ignore men who left no impress on society. He criticized false gentility, praised manual skills and labour, urged working-class progress. He condemned fraud, bad work, drunkenness, pilfering. Energy and determination he picked out to admire – but only for worthy aims. 'Failure,' he wrote, 'in any good cause is honourable while success in a bad cause is mostly infamous.'

He condemned money-making or career-making without self-cultivation. He saw the love of money, not money itself, as the root of evil – 'a love which contracts the soul and closes it against generous life and action'.

He had no time for snobbery or social climbing, always taking the side of the moral against the narrowly 'social' values. For Smiles, to get knowledge merely to get on in life was a 'low idea'. Self-culture and potential, or at least duty fulfilled, were their own reward. He gave the 'crown and glory of life' to character – the idea of the gentleman – attainable by all regardless of birth or means; to independence, integrity and dignity. Smiles' emphasis, of course, was on individual not collective or government help. He wrote that 'your own exertions are the key to life ... Anything else – government policy, state intervention, group support – is incidental to the all-important effort made by each individual on his own behalf.' For these reasons, Smiles was definitely in favour of economic laissez-faire. But from his early days he also wanted social reform. He was sympathetic to Chartism (though not to physical force); he was against the Corn Laws and in favour of extending the suffrage. He supported cooperation, producer cooperatives, mutual benefit, though he was not sympathetic to trade unions – in his view an imperfect form of cooperation – nor to strikes. He resented the charge that he preached a gospel of material success; he was disappointed that his biographies of Robert Dick, the Thurso baker, a financial failure in his trade but eminent in geology and botany, and of Thomas Edward, the Scots cobbler and natural historian, sold much less well than that of George Moore – whose biography he needed much persuasion by Mrs Moore to write – a man who rose from Cumberland poverty to City wealth and large-scale philanthropy by his own efforts. 'What I

9

wanted to do,' he wrote, 'was to show that courage and perseverance would lead to success of the best sort.'

In a powerful passage in a later book, Smiles exclaimed:

When typhus or cholera breaks out, they tell us that Nobody is to blame. That terrible Nobody! How much he has to answer for. More mischief is done by Nobody than by all the world besides. Nobody adulterates our food. Nobody poisons us with bad drink ... Nobody leaves towns undrained. Nobody fills jails, penitentiaries, and convict stations. Nobody makes poachers, thieves, and drunkards. Nobody has a theory too – a dreadful theory. It is embodied in two words: laissez-faire – let alone. When people are poisoned with plaster of Paris mixed with flour, 'let alone' is the remedy ... Let those who can, find out when they are cheated: caveat emptor. When people live in foul dwellings, let them alone, let wretchedness do its work; do not interfere with death.*

As this passage shows, Smiles saw that much was beyond individual cure. True, he did not recognize the need for collective action other than the few safety nets that existed: the workhouse for the destitute and islands of help from churches, voluntary bodies and charity. But it would be anachronistic to blame him for this; and it would be to miss the importance of what he *did* see – that 'help from without is often enfeebling in its effect but help from within invariably invigorating'. The pendulum of welfare – however benignly intended – has swung counter-productively; and the further it swings the more relevant the philosophy of self-help becomes. The welfare state can only sensibly aspire to provide a base on which the individual can build. It was not intended to create dependency. Private savings and private provision are crucial still, morally and socially. Smiles shows how they were possible albeit difficult – even in infinitely poorer times.

The combined effects of the cost of the welfare state and the particular tax system which we have over recent decades constructed to pay for it – by bringing for many net-of-tax earning levels so close to benefit levels and by adding insurance contributions to wages – has inadvertently blunted the will both to work and to employ. Moreover, the advances of collectivism have meant the contraction for many of the area of personal decision and responsibility. If the need for decision is constantly eroded, and if rights are over-emphasized in relation to

* Quoted by Asa Briggs in his *Victorian People* (1965).

duties, the power of decision may well dwindle too. In our times there is a perceptible depressing limpness in individual attitudes, a limpness that might be corrected by a dose of Smiles.

One of the greatest contrasts between Smiles' time and ours is that in his time we in England were, for all our poverty compared with today, the most productive and prosperous society in the world. Now we are at the bottom of the league of developed nations: our standard of living and the quality and extent of our public and social services are below those of many others. The cause is part of the contrast. Productivity in Britain is lower – much lower in many cases – than it is in other developed societies: that is to say that the average output per man and woman in Britain today is less, often much less, than the average output per man and woman in many other societies. As a result, people in other countries can be and are better paid: and their higher pay yields more to support both public social services and private beneficence. We enjoy neither the success nor the scope for generosity for which Smiles hoped.

Moreover, our low average productivity is one of the realities behind our high contemporary unemployment. Now, as in Smiles' time, the disaster of unemployment is all too frequently blamed on the mythical 'Nobody'. And a new 'Nobody' has been invented: the 'public purse' – a mythical entity that can supposedly create work without cost and wealth without effort. We all know – we need only a little of Smiles' honesty to admit – that the blame should not fall on 'Nobody' but on many politicians, many managements, many trade unions, many academics and many commentators, on our own failure to exhibit those qualities of effective industriousness, perseverance and self-discipline that Smiles celebrated. Only when we match the qualities – the moral qualities – of our more productive competitors abroad can we hope to employ all those here who seek work. It is true, of course, that as we acquire these qualities, as productivity rises, fewer people are needed to make the same quantity of goods and services; but the lower prices achieved by greater productivity extend the market, making new ventures profitable that would not otherwise have been so, thus increasing the number of jobs.

Smiles would have rejoiced that the drudgery of his time has been relieved. He would have rejoiced the more that, as productivity rose, the working week and the working year could become shorter and shorter, leaving time for the self-culture that he so much desired. But he would also have warned us against the illusion that 'help from without' – this time in the form of collective redistribution – could replace individual energy, efficiency and productiveness at work as a means of widening and deepening prosperity. He would have seen clearly – what has taken us many years to see – that such 'help', if offered as an alternative to effective and cooperative work, destroys wealth, destroys jobs, and ultimately destroys the nation's moral life.

But there is another lesson that Smiles and his great gallery of enterprisers has for us today. His books assume an agreed answer to a question which concerns us closely, but which, in the stream of talk about unemployment, is all too often left unasked: the question, where do jobs come from?

And an agreed answer there is. When the government recently emphasized that jobs come, directly or indirectly, from consumers and from nowhere else, there was no disagreement. The criticism was, rather, that the government was saying nothing new. Nor is it surprising that jobs should come from consumers, because we are all – everyone in the world to a greater or lesser extent – consumers. And most people – that is, all except children, the retired and the permanently ill or handicapped – are also workers, producers of goods and services in one form or another. The problem in any society is to reconcile the interests of people as workers with the interests of the same people and their dependants as consumers.

The least ineffective way yet discovered to achieve this balance is by decentralized ownership and decision-making within the rule of law and subject to competition. We call this, for short, free enterprise or capitalism. You can (perhaps with less than ideal results) abstract any service you wish – such as health or education – and finance it in such a way that it is free at point of use. But the more that trade and manufacture are handled by free enterprise, the more likely it is both that prosperity, employment, social services and philanthropy will flourish and that political freedom will remain.

For free enterprise or capitalism – that is, decentralized ownership and decision-making subject to competition and within the rule of law –

is the necessary (though not the sufficient) condition for political freedom. You can have free enterprise of a sort without having political freedom but you cannot have true political freedom without free enterprise because a state that takes complete economic power thereby exercises totalitarian social power.

It is also common ground politically that the central figure in free enterprise is the middle-man, the entrepreneur. (The word was invented by Jean Baptiste Say to mean somebody who puts existing resources to more productive uses whether inside an existing organization or by setting up a new one.) The entrepreneur is the person who seeks to identify what consumers, at home or abroad or both, want and would be willing to buy at a profitable price. These entrepreneurs are the job-creators because it is they who gather the men and women, the material, the machinery and the money to turn the vision of a market into a reality. It is they who, in the hope of profit but under the risk of bankruptcy, within the law – and subject, of course, to competition from every similar product or service and from every other use to which consumers can put their money – create the jobs. They need drive as well as vision; they need energy and will and courage.

Entrepreneurs are economic prime movers; they come in every degree of size and vitality, ambition and skill. They can be merchants, manufacturers, farmers, providers of services, importers, retailers, wholesalers and much else; many seek independence – to be their own boss; some want power; some want to found an expanding enterprise; some have large financial ambitions. We should not underrate the risks that even the less ambitious take: most have worries; some have great worries; some go bankrupt.

Entrepreneurs in one form or another are the subject of many of Smiles' anecdotes, bringing new or improved products or services to market, pioneering new methods of production: opening up new means of linking producers and consumers or new sources of supply. His entrepreneurs can be owners risking their own money in the venture, or managers. Their main motives may be the fulfilment of a dream, the making of a fortune, the desire to succeed, the joy of creating – sometimes a mixture.

Smiles made heroes of men with these qualities. We need not make heroes of them. But we do need to realize that their pioneering and risk-

13

taking, however self-interested it may be, is necessary to bring into existence the jobs we seek.

Any government that wants to preside over low unemployment will need to copy Smiles' enthusiasm for entrepreneurship. And this cannot be achieved by collectivization. It can be brought about only by increasing the incentive and the freedom of action that entrepreneurs enjoy; by creating a fiercely competitive climate in business with real prospects for making capital as well as losing it, with substantial possibilities for earning and saving and with not too many regulations and restrictions. Whether a government relies almost entirely upon the existing network of capital provision or seeks to supplement it by becoming itself an even larger lending agency, it will depend upon entrepreneurs to identify, define and lead new projects. The purposes of entrepreneurs are harnessed to the interests of the public by the law and by competition. It is competition in addition to the law that compels businessmen, be they manufacturers or traders, to serve the interests of consumers; if they fail to satisfy, they go bankrupt. It is the entrepreneur who adjusts business to markets, filling a gap here, making improvements there; it is the entrepreneur who makes markets and destroys them, rendering obsolete or outflanking whole industries and sub-industries. If competition is to fulfil its function of enlarging choice, increasing jobs and prosperity and social services while simultaneously reducing the working week and the working year, then it must indeed be, as Schumpeter described it, a 'perennial gale of creative destruction'.

But, alas, governments have long neglected and hampered Smiles' entrepreneur. Indeed, through nationalization, municipalization, excessive taxation and over-regulation, they have positively prevented entrepreneurs from following their endless, self-interested quest to serve customers and provide employment.

How can it be that the entrepreneur, so fully recognized and respected by Smiles and his age, has now been so neglected? The failure is partly, at least, among the very people who should have kept the activity of the entrepreneur firmly in the centre of debate, but who have virtually ignored it.

Opening his lecture at a colloquium on entrepreneurship in 1983, the economist Professor Henderson said:

I think I should begin with a confession, a confession of failure or at least of oversight. In University College London, where I now work, I give a course of lectures which is concerned particularly with government policies in Britain towards industries and enterprises, mainly those which are in the public sector but with some consideration also of the private sector. In these lectures I have never made any reference to the problem of entrepreneurship or the role of the entrepreneur; and in making no such reference I did not take a conscious decision to exclude the subject – it simply never crossed my mind to refer to it. Moreover, I suspect that if I had sent my lecture notes for comment to a representative group of fellow-economists who were likewise interested in this range of topics, while I would have received a wide variety of criticisms and suggestions for improvement, probably no one would have remarked: 'There's one rather important omission: you've said nothing about entrepreneurship.' Until recently, I had never heard of Professor Kirzner's *Competition and Entrepreneurship* and I learned of its existence only by accident, not from a fellow-economist but from a reference in Robert Nozick's book, *Anarchy, State and Utopia*. Without consciously reflecting on the matter, I had fallen into thinking that the subject of entrepreneurship had disappeared from economics with Joseph Schumpeter's doctrine of 'the obsolescence of the entrepreneurial function', which was set out in his great book, *Capitalism, Socialism and Democracy*, in the early 1940s.*

Professor Tom Wilson of Glasgow said at the same conference: 'Professor Henderson said that it had not occurred to him very much to talk about entrepreneurship in his lectures on public policy. This is characteristic of nearly all of us in academic life. And it is not only a matter of academic interest.'

Why have economists as a group neglected the entrepreneurial function? They appear to have misled themselves by their own highly abstract model of perfect competition – which exists nowhere – and have assumed away the risk and the uncertainty to which all business decision-making is in fact inevitably subject. The result has been that they have tended to obscure rather than to clarify understanding about unemployment; they have not drawn sufficient attention to low productivity, to uncompetitive unit labour costs nor to the discouragement of and indifference to entrepreneurship. They have mostly clamoured for more public spending, either ignoring the experiences

* 'The Prime Mover', Institute of Economic Affairs (1983).

15

of the past when most of it seeped into prices or dreaming of pay controls to prevent the same happening again. Economists have tended to treat choice as concerned only with the means of implementing an already-made decision as to aim. They have tended to ignore the decision as to aim. Yet it is the choice of aim that is even more crucial – whether to seek to serve an as yet unexplored and unexploited potential market sector, or whether to compete in a part, and if so, which part of an existing market – while all the time the market itself and those who strive to serve its innumerable sectors and sub-sectors are all subject to huge, unpredictable, continuous and kaleidoscopic changes.

Different in emphasis has been and are some, though some only, of the brethren of the economists – the economic historians. They have tended to identify entrepreneurs, their number and vigour as crucial factors in the vitality and prosperity of different economies at different times. It is a salutary and eye-opening exercise to look for the references to 'risk' and 'entrepreneurs' in the indices of most economic and many economic history textbooks.

But, of all the economic histories ever written, it is Smiles' *Self-Help* that most explicitly and vividly portrays, celebrates – above all, *understands* – the entrepreneur and the virtues that make him what he is. For that reason, if for no other, this book, so deeply expressive of the spirit of its own times, is also a book for *our* times: the purveyor of a message that we, government and governed, employer and employee, in work and out of work, need to take to heart and keep in mind.

Preface by the author
to the edition of 1886

This is a revised edition of a book which has already been received with considerable favour at home and abroad. It has been reprinted in various forms in America; translations have appeared in Dutch and French, and others are about to appear in German and Danish. The book has, doubtless, proved attractive to readers in different countries by reason of the variety of anecdotal illustrations of life and character which it contains, and the interest which all more or less feel in the labours, the trials, the struggles, and the achievements of others. No one can be better aware than the author of its fragmentary character, arising from the manner in which it was for the most part originally composed – having been put together principally from jottings made during many years – intended as readings for young men, and without any view to publication. The appearance of this edition has furnished an opportunity for pruning the volume of some superfluous matter, and introducing various new illustrations, which will probably be found of general interest.

In one respect the title of the book, which it is now too late to alter, has proved unfortunate, as it has led some, who have judged it merely by the title, to suppose that it consists of a eulogy of selfishness: the very opposite of what it really is – or at least of what the author intended it to be. Although its chief object unquestionably is to stimulate youths to apply themselves diligently to right pursuits – sparing neither labour, pains, nor self-denial in prosecuting them – and to rely upon their own efforts in life, rather than depend upon the help or patronage of others, it will also be found, from the examples given of literary and scientific men, artists, inventors, educators, philanthropists, missionaries, and martyrs, that the duty of helping one's self in the highest sense involves the helping of one's neighbours.

It has also been objected to the book that too much notice is taken in it of men who have succeeded in life by helping themselves, and too little of the multitude of men who have failed. 'Why should not Failure,' it has been asked, 'have its Plutarch as well as Success?' There is, indeed, no reason why Failure should not have its Plutarch, except that a record of mere failure would probably be found excessively depressing as well as uninstructive reading. It is, however, shown in the following pages that Failure is the best discipline of the true worker, by stimulating him to renewed efforts, evoking his best powers, and carrying him onward in self-culture, self-control, and growth in knowledge and wisdom. Viewed in this light, Failure, conquered by Perseverance, is always full of interest and instruction, and this we have endeavoured to illustrate by many examples.

As for Failure *per se*, although it may be well to find consolations for it at the close of life, there is reason to doubt whether it is an object that ought to be set before youth at the beginning of it. Indeed, 'how *not* to do it' is of all things the easiest learnt: it needs neither teaching, effort, self-denial, industry, patience, perseverance nor judgement. Besides, readers do not care to know about the general who lost his battles, the engineer whose engines blew up, the architect who designed only deformities, the painter who never got beyond daubs, the schemer who did not invent his machine, the merchant who could not keep out of the Gazette. It is true, the best of men may fail, in the best of causes. But even these best of men did not try to fail, or regard their failure as meritorious; on the contrary, they tried to succeed, and looked upon failure as misfortune. Failure in any good cause is, however, honourable, whilst success in any bad cause is merely infamous. At the same time success in the good cause is unquestionably better than failure. But it is not the result in any case that is to be regarded so much as the aim and the effort, the patience, the courage, and the endeavour with which desirable and worthy objects are pursued:

> *'Tis not in mortals to command success;*
> *We will do more – deserve it.*

London
May, 1866

1. Self-Help: National and Individual

'Heaven helps those who help themselves' is a well-tried maxim, embodying in a small compass the results of vast human experience. The spirit of self-help is the root of all genuine growth in the individual; and, exhibited in the lives of many, it constitutes the true source of national vigour and strength. Help from without is often enfeebling in its effect, but help from within invariably invigorates. Whatever is done *for* men or classes, to a certain extent takes away the stimulus and necessity of doing for themselves; and where men are subjected to over-guidance and over-government, the inevitable tendency is to render them comparatively helpless.

Even the best institutions can give a man no active help. Perhaps the most they can do is to leave him free to develop himself and improve his individual condition. But in all times men have been prone to believe that their happiness and well-being were to be secured by means of institutions rather than by their own conduct. Hence the value of legislation as an agent in human advancement has usually been much overestimated. To constitute the millionth part of a Legislature, by voting for one or two men once in three or five years, however conscientiously this duty may be performed, can exercise but little active influence upon any man's life and character. Moreover, it is every day becoming more clearly understood, that the function of Government is negative and restrictive, rather than positive and active; being resolvable principally into protection – protection of life, liberty and property. Laws, wisely administered, will secure men in the enjoyment of the fruits of their labour, whether of mind or body, at a comparatively small personal sacrifice; but no laws, however stringent, can make the idle industrious, the thriftless provident, or the drunken sober. Such reforms can only be effected by means of individual action, economy, and self-denial, by better habits, rather than by greater rights.

The Government of a nation itself is usually found to be but the reflex of the individuals composing it. The Government that is ahead of the people will inevitably be dragged down to their level, as the

Government that is behind them will in the long run be dragged up. In the order of nature, the collective character of a nation will as surely find its befitting results in its law and government, as water finds its own level. The noble people will be nobly ruled, and the ignorant and corrupt ignobly. Indeed, all experience serves to prove that the worth and strength of a State depend far less upon the form of its institutions than upon the character of its men. For the nation is only an aggregate of individual conditions, and civilization itself is but a question of the personal improvement of the men, women, and children of whom society is composed.

National progress is the sum of individual industry, energy, and uprightness, as national decay is of individual idleness, selfishness and vice. What we are accustomed to decry as great social evils, will, for the most part, be found to be but the outgrowth of man's own perverted life; and though we may endeavour to cut them down and extirpate them by means of Law, they will only spring up again with fresh luxuriance in some other form, unless the conditions of personal life and character are radically improved. If this view be correct, then it follows that the highest patriotism and philanthropy consist, not so much in altering laws and modifying institutions, as in helping and stimulating men to elevate and improve themselves by their own free and independent individual action.

It may be of comparatively little consequence how a man is governed from without, whilst everything depends upon how he governs himself from within. The greatest slave is not he who is ruled by a despot, great though that evil be, but he who is the thrall of his own moral ignorance, selfishness, and vice. Nations who are thus enslaved at heart cannot be freed by any mere changes of masters or of institutions; and so long as the fatal delusion prevails, that liberty solely depends upon and consists in government, so long will such changes, no matter at what cost they may be effected, have as little practical and lasting result as the shifting of the figures in a phantasmagoria. The solid foundations of liberty must rest upon individual character; which is also the only sure guarantee for social security and national progress. John Stuart Mill truly observes that 'even despotism does not produce its worst effects so long as individuality exists under it; and whatever crushes individuality *is* despotism, by whatever name it be called'.

Old fallacies as to human progress are constantly turning up. Some call for Caesars, others for Nationalities, and others for Acts of Parliament. We are to wait for Caesars, and when they are found, 'happy the people who recognize and follow them'. This doctrine shortly means, everything *for* the people, nothing *by* them – a doctrine which, if taken as a guide, must, by destroying the free conscience of a community, speedily prepare the way for any form of despotism. Caesarism is human idolatry in its worst form – a worship of mere power, as degrading in its effects as the worship of mere wealth would be. A far healthier doctrine to inculcate among the nations would be that of Self-Help; and so soon as it is thoroughly understood and carried into action, Caesarism will be no more. The two principles are directly antagonistic; and what Victor Hugo said of the Pen and the Sword alike applies to them. 'Ceci tuera cela.' [*This will kill that.*]

The power of Nationalities and Acts of Parliament is also a prevalent superstition. What William Dargan, one of Ireland's truest patriots, said at the closing of the first Dublin Industrial Exhibition, may well be quoted now. 'To tell the truth,' he said, 'I never heard the word independence mentioned that my own country and my own fellow townsmen did not occur to my mind. I have heard a great deal about the independence that we were to get from this, that, and the other place, and of the great expectations we were to have from persons from other countries coming amongst us. Whilst I value as much as any man the great advantages that must result to us from that intercourse, I have always been deeply impressed with the feeling that our industrial independence is dependent upon ourselves. I believe that with simple industry and careful exactness in the utilization of our energies, we never had a fairer chance nor a brighter prospect than the present. We have made a step, but perseverance is the great agent of success; and if we but go on zealously, I believe in my conscience that in a short period we shall arrive at a position of equal comfort, of equal happiness, and of equal independence, with that of any other people.'

All nations have been made what they are by the thinking and the working of many generations of men. Patient and persevering labourers in all ranks and conditions of life, cultivators of the soil and explorers of the mine, inventors and discoverers, manufacturers, mechanics and artisans, poets, philosophers, and politicians, all have contributed towards the grand result, one generation building upon another's labours, and carrying them forward to still higher stages. This constant succession of noble workers – the artisans of civilization – has served to create order out of chaos in industry, science, and art; and the living race has thus, in the course of nature, become the inheritor of the rich estate provided by the skill and industry of our forefathers, which is placed in our hands to cultivate, and to hand down, not only unimpaired but improved, to our successors.

The spirit of self-help, as exhibited in the energetic action of individuals, has in all times been a marked feature in the English character, and furnishes the true measure of our power as a nation. Rising above the heads of the mass there were always to be found a series of individuals distinguished beyond others, who commanded the public homage. But our progress has also been owing to multitudes of smaller and less-known men. Though only the generals' names may be remembered in the history of any great campaign, it has been in a great measure through the individual valour and heroism of the privates that victories have been won. And life, too, is 'a soldiers' battle' – men in the ranks having in all times been amongst the greatest of workers. Many are the lives of men unwritten, which have nevertheless as powerfully influenced civilization and progress as the more fortunate Great whose names are recorded in biography. Even the humblest person, who sets before his fellows an example of industry, sobriety, and upright honesty of purpose in life, has a present as well as a future influence upon the well-being of his country; for his life and character pass unconsciously into the lives of others, and propagate good example for all time to come.

Daily experience shows that it is energetic individualism which produces the most powerful effects upon the life and action of others, and really constitutes the best practical education. Schools, academies, and colleges, give but the merest beginnings of culture in comparison with it. Far more influential is the life-education daily given in our homes, in the streets, behind counters, in workshops, at the loom and the plough, in counting-houses and manufactories, and in the busy haunts of men. This is that finishing instruction as members of society, which Schiller designated 'the education of the human race', consisting in action, conduct, self-culture, self-control – all that tends to discipline a man truly, and fit him for the proper performance of the duties and business of life – a kind of education not to be learnt from books, or acquired by any amount of mere literary training. With his usual weight of words Bacon observes that 'Studies teach not their own use; but there is a wisdom without them, and above them, won by observation'; a remark that holds true of actual life, as well as of the cultivation of the intellect itself. For all experience serves to illustrate and enforce the lesson, that a man perfects himself by work more than by reading – that it is life rather than literature, action rather than study, and character rather than biography, which tends perpetually to renovate mankind.

Biographies of great, but especially of good men, are nevertheless most instructive and useful, as helps, guides, and incentives to others. Some of the best are almost equivalent to gospels – teaching high living, high thinking, and energetic action for their own and the world's good. The valuable examples which they furnish of the power of self-help, of patient purpose, resolute working, and steadfast integrity, issuing in the formation of truly noble and manly character, exhibit, in language not to be misunderstood, what it is in the power of each to accomplish for himself; and eloquently illustrate the efficacy of self-respect and self-reliance in enabling men of even the humblest rank to work out for themselves an honourable competency and a solid reputation.

Great men of science, literature, and art – apostles of great thoughts and lords of the great heart – have belonged to no exclusive class nor rank in life. They have come alike from colleges, workshops, and farmhouses – from the huts of poor men and the mansions of the rich. Some of God's greatest apostles have come from 'the ranks'. The poorest have sometimes taken the highest places; nor have difficulties apparently the most insuperable proved obstacles in their way. Those very difficulties, in many instances, would ever seem to have been their best helpers, by evoking their powers of labour and endurance, and stimulating into life faculties which might otherwise have lain dormant. The instances of obstacles thus surmounted, and of triumphs thus achieved, are indeed so numerous as almost to justify the proverb that 'with Will one can do anything'. Take, for instance, the remarkable fact that from the barber's shop came Jeremy Taylor, the most poetical of

23

divines; Sir Richard Arkwright, the inventor of the spinning jenny and founder of the cotton manufacture; Lord Tenterden, one of the most distinguished of Lord Chief Justices; and Turner, the greatest among landscape painters.

No one knows to a certainty what Shakespeare was; but it is unquestionable that he sprang from a humble rank. His father was a butcher and grazier; and Shakespeare himself is supposed to have been in early life a woolcomber; whilst others aver that he was an usher in a school and afterwards a scrivener's clerk. He truly seems to have been 'not one, but all mankind's epitome'. For such is the accuracy of his sea phrases that a naval writer alleges that he must have been a sailor; whilst a clergyman infers, from internal evidence in his writings, that he was probably a parson's clerk; and a distinguished judge of horseflesh insists that he must have been a horse-dealer. Shakespeare was certainly an actor, and in the course of his life 'played many parts', gathering his wonderful stores of knowledge from a wide field of experience and observation. In any event, he must have been a close student and a hard worker; and to this day his writings continue to exercise a powerful influence on the formation of English character.

The common class of day labourers has given us Brindley the engineer, Cook the navigator, and Burns the poet. Masons and brick-layers can boast of Ben Jonson, who worked at the building of Lincoln's Inn, with a trowel in his hand and a book in his pocket, Edwards and Telford the engineers, Hugh Miller the geologist, and Allan Cunningham the writer and sculptor; whilst among distinguished carpenters we find the names of Inigo Jones the architect, Harrison the chronometer-maker, John Hunter the physiologist, Romney and Opie the painters, Professor Lee the orientalist, and John Gibson the sculptor.

From the weaver class have sprung Simson the mathematician, Bacon the sculptor, the two Milners, Adam Walker, John Foster, Wilson the ornithologist, Dr Livingstone the missionary traveller, and Tannahill the poet. Shoemakers have given us Sir Clowdesley Shovel the great admiral, Sturgeon the electrician, Samuel Drew the essayist, Gifford the editor of the *Quarterly Review*, Bloomfield the poet, and William Carey the missionary; whilst Morrison, another laborious missionary, was a maker of shoe-lasts. Within the last few years, a profound naturalist has been discovered in the person of a shoemaker at Banff, named Thomas Edwards, who, while maintaining himself by his trade, has devoted his leisure to the study of natural science in all its branches, his researches in connection with the smaller crustaceae having been rewarded by the discovery of a new species, to which the name of 'Praniza Edwardsii' has been given by naturalists.

Nor have tailors been undistinguished. John Stow, the historian, worked at the trade during some part of his life. Jackson, the painter, made clothes until he reached manhood. The brave Sir John Hawkwood, who so greatly distinguished himself at Poitiers and was knighted by Edward III for his valour, was in early life apprenticed to a London tailor. Admiral Hobson, who broke the boom at Vigo in 1702, belonged to the same calling. He was working as a tailor's apprentice near Bonchurch, in the Isle of Wight, when the news flew through the village that a squadron of men-of-war was sailing off the island. He sprang from the shopboard, and ran down with his comrades to the beach, to gaze upon the glorious sight. The boy was suddenly inflamed with the ambition to be a sailor; and springing into a boat, he rowed off to the squadron, gained the admiral's ship, and was accepted as a volunteer. Years after, he returned to his native village full of honours, and dined off bacon and eggs in the cottage where he had worked as an apprentice. But the greatest tailor of all is unquestionably Andrew Johnson, the present President of the United States – a man of extraordinary force of character and vigour of intellect. In his great speech at Washington, when describing himself as having begun his political career as an alderman, and run through all the branches of the legislature, a voice in the crowd cried, 'From a tailor up'. It was characteristic of Johnson to take the intended sarcasm in good part, and even to turn it to account. 'Some gentleman says I have been a tailor. That does not disconcert me in the least; for when I was a tailor I had the reputation of being a good one, and making close fits; I was always punctual with my customers, and always did good work.'

Cardinal Wolsey, De Foe, Akenside, and Kirke White were the sons of butchers; Bunyan was a tinker, and Joseph Lancaster a basket-maker. Among the great names identified with the invention of the steam-engine are those of Newcomen, Watt, and Stephenson; the first a blacksmith, the second a maker of mathematical instruments, and the third an engine-fireman. Huntingdon the preacher was originally a coalheaver, and Bewick, the father of wood-engraving, a coalminer. Dodsley was a footman, and Holcroft a groom. Baffin the navigator began his seafaring career as a man before the mast, and Sir Clowdesley Shovel as a cabin-boy. Herschel played the oboe in a military band. Chantrey was a journeyman carver, Etty a journeyman printer, and Sir Thomas Lawrence the son of a tavern-keeper. Michael Faraday, the son of a blacksmith, was in early life apprenticed to a bookbinder, and worked at that trade until he reached his twenty-second year; he now occupies the very first rank as a philosopher, excelling even his master, Sir Humphry Davy, in the art of lucidly expounding the most difficult and abstruse points in natural science.

Among those who have given the greatest impulse to the sublime science of astronomy, we find Copernicus, the son of a Polish baker; Kelper, the son of a German public-house keeper, and himself the *garçon de cabaret*; d'Alembert, a foundling picked up one winter's night on the steps of the church of St Jean le Rond at Paris, and brought up by the wife of a glazier; and Newton and Laplace, the one the son of a small freeholder near Grantham, the other the son of a poor peasant of Beaumont-en-Auge, near Honfleur. Notwithstanding their comparatively adverse circumstances in early life, these distinguished men achieved a solid and enduring reputation by the exercise of their genius, which all the wealth in the world could not have purchased. The very possession of wealth might indeed have proved an obstacle greater even than the humble means to which they were born. The father of Lagrange, the astronomer and mathematician, held the office of Treasurer of War at Turin; but having ruined himself by speculations, his family were reduced to comparative poverty. To this circumstance Lagrange was in after life accustomed partly to attribute his own fame and happiness. 'Had I been rich,' said he, 'I should probably not have become a mathematician.'

The sons of clergymen and ministers of religion generally have particularly distinguished themselves in our country's history. Amongst them we find the names of Drake and Nelson, celebrated in naval heroism; of Wollaston, Young, Playfair, and Bell, in science; of Wren, Reynolds, Wilson, and Wilkie, in art; of Thurlow and Campbell, in law; and of Addison, Thomson, Goldsmith, Coleridge, and Tennyson, in literature. Lord Hardinge, Colonel Edwardes, and Major Hodson, so honourably known in Indian warfare, were also the sons of clergymen. Indeed, the empire of England in India was won and held chiefly by men of the middle class – such as Clive, Warren Hastings, and their successors – men for the most part bred in factories and trained to habits of business.

Among the sons of attorneys we find Edmund Burke, Smeaton the engineer, Scott and Wordsworth, and Lords Somers, Hardwick, and Dunning. Sir William Blackstone was the posthumous son of a silk-mercer. Lord Gifford's father was a grocer at Dover; Lord Denman's a physician; Judge Talfourd's a country brewer; and Lord Chief Baron Pollock's a celebrated saddler at Charing Cross. Layard, the discoverer of the monuments of Nineveh, was an articled clerk in a London solicitor's office; and Sir William Armstrong, the inventor of hydraulic machinery and of the Armstrong ordnance, was also trained to the law and practised for some time as an attorney. Milton was the son of a London scrivener, and Pope and Southey were the sons of linendrapers. Professor Wilson was the son of a Paisley manufacturer, and Lord Macaulay of an African merchant. Keats was a druggist, and Sir Humphry Davy a country apothecary's apprentice. Speaking of himself, Davy once said, 'What I am I have made myself: I say this without vanity, and in pure simplicity of heart.' Richard Owen, the Newton of Natural History, began life as a midshipman, and did not enter upon the line of scientific research, in which he has since become so distinguished, until comparatively late in life. He laid the foundations of his great knowledge while occupied in cataloguing the magnificent museum accumulated by the industry of John Hunter, a work which occupied him at the College of Surgeons during a period of about ten years.

Foreign not less than English biography abounds in illustrations of men who have glorified the lot of poverty by their labours and their genius. In art we find Claude, the son of a pastrycook; Geefs, of a baker; Leopold Robert, of a watchmaker; and Haydn, of a wheelwright; whilst Daguerre was a scene-painter at the Opera. The father of Gregory VII was a carpenter; of Sextus V, a shepherd; and of Adrian VI, a poor bargeman. When a boy, Adrian, unable to pay for a light by which to study, was accustomed to prepare his lessons by the light of the lamps in the streets and the church porches, exhibiting a degree of patience and industry which were the certain forerunners of his future distinction.

Of like humble origin were Hauy, the mineralogist, who was the son of a weaver of Saint-Just; Hautefeuille, the mechanician, of a baker at Orleans; Joseph Fourier, the mathematician, of a tailor at Auxerre; Durand, the architect, of a Paris shoemaker; and Gesner, the naturalist, of a skinner or worker in hides, at Zurich. This last began his career under all the disadvantages attendant on poverty, sickness, and domestic calamity; none of which, however, were sufficient to damp his courage or hinder his progress. His life was indeed an eminent illustration of the truth of the saying, that those who have most to do and are willing to work, will find the most time. Pierre Ramus was another man of like character. He was the son of poor parents in Picardy, and when a boy was employed to tend sheep. But not liking the occupation he ran away to Paris. After encountering much misery, he succeeded in entering the College of Navarre as a servant. The situation, however, opened for him the road to learning, and he shortly became one of the most distinguished men of his time.

The chemist Vauquelin was the son of a peasant of Saint-André-d'Herbetot, in the Calvados. When a boy at school, though poorly clad, he was full of bright intelligence; and the master, who taught him to read and write, when praising him for his diligence, used to say, 'Go on, my boy; work, study, Colin, and one day you will go as well dressed as the parish churchwarden!' A country apothecary who visited the school admired the robust boy's arms, and offered to take him into his laboratory to pound his drugs, to which Vauquelin assented, in the hope of being able to continue his lessons. But the apothecary would not permit him to spend any part of his time in learning; and on ascertaining this, the youth immediately determined to quit his service. He therefore left Saint-André and took the road for Paris with his haversack on his back. Arrived there, he searched for a place as apothecary's boy, but could not find one. Worn out by fatigue and destitution, Vauquelin fell ill, and in that state was taken to the hospital, where he thought he should die. But better things were in store for the poor boy. He recovered, and again proceeded in search of employment, which he at length found with an apothecary. Shortly after, he became known to Fourcroy the eminent chemist, who was so pleased with the youth that he made him his private secretary; and many years after, on the death of that great philosopher, Vauquelin succeeded him as Professor of Chemistry. Finally, in 1829, the electors of the district of Calvados appointed him their representative in the Chamber of Deputies, and he re-entered in triumph the village which he had left so many years before, so poor and so obscure.

England has no parallel instances to show, of promotions from the ranks of the army to the highest military offices, which have been so common in France since the first Revolution. *La carrière ouverte aux talents* has there received many striking illustrations, which would doubtless be matched among ourselves were the road to promotion as open. Hoche, Humbert, and Pichegru began their respective careers as private soldiers. Hoche, while in the King's army, was accustomed to embroider waistcoats to enable him to earn money wherewith to purchase books on military science. Humbert was a scapegrace when a youth; at sixteen he ran away from home, and was by turns servant to a tradesman at Nancy, a workman at Lyons, and a hawker of rabbit skins. In 1792 he enlisted as a volunteer; and in a year he was general of brigade. Kleber, Lefèvre, Suchet, Victor, Lannes, Soult, Massena, St Cyr, D'Erlon, Murat, Augereau, Bessières, and Ney, all rose from the ranks. In some cases promotion was rapid, in others it was slow. St Cyr, the son of a tanner of Toul, began life as an actor, after which he enlisted in the Chasseurs, and was promoted to a captaincy within a year. Victor, Duc de Belluno, enlisted in the Artillery in 1781: during the events preceding the Revolution he was discharged; but immediately on the outbreak of war he re-enlisted, and in the course of a few months his intrepidity and ability secured his promotion as Adjutant-Major and chief of battalion. Murat, *le beau sabreur*, was the son of a village inn-keeper in Perigord, where he looked after the horses. He first enlisted in a regiment of Chasseurs, from which he was dismissed for insubordination: but again enlisting, he shortly rose to the rank of Colonel. Ney enlisted at eighteen in a Hussar regiment, and gradually advanced step by step; Kleber soon discovered his merits, surnaming him 'The Indefatigable', and promoted him to be Adjutant-General when only twenty-five. On the other hand, Soult was six years from the date of his enlistment before he reached the rank of sergeant. But Soult's advancement was rapid compared with that of Massena, who served for fourteen years before he was made sergeant; and though he after-wards rose successively, step by step, to the grades of Colonel, General of Division, and Marshal, he declared that the post of sergeant was the step which of all others had cost him the most labour to win. Similar promotions from the ranks, in the French army, have continued down to our own day. Changarnier entered the King's bodyguard as a private in 1815. Marshal Bugeaud served four years in the ranks, after which he was made an officer. Marshal Randon, who became French Minister of War, began his military career as a drummer boy; and in the portrait of him in the gallery at Versailles, his hand rests upon a drumhead, the picture being thus painted at his own request. Instances such as these inspire French soldiers with enthusiasm for their service, as each private feels that he may possibly carry the baton of a marshal in his knapsack.

The instances of men, in this and other countries, who, by dint of persevering application and energy, have raised themselves from the humblest ranks of industry to eminent positions of usefulness and influence in society, are indeed so numerous that they have long ceased to be regarded as exceptional. Looking at some of the more remarkable, it might almost be said that early encounter with difficulty and adverse circumstances was the necessary and indispensable condition of success. The British House of Commons has always contained a number of such self-raised men – fitting representatives of the industrial character of the people; and it is to the credit of our Legislature that they have been welcomed and honoured there. When Joseph Brotherton, member for Salford, in the course of the discussion on the Ten Hours Bill, detailed with true pathos the hardships and fatigues to which he had been subjected when working as a factory boy in a cotton mill, and described the resolution which he had then formed, that if ever it was in his power he would endeavour to ameliorate the condition of that class, Sir James Graham rose immediately after him, and declared, amidst the cheers of the House, that he did not before know that Mr Brotherton's origin had been so humble, but that it rendered him more proud than he had ever before been of the House of Commons, to think that a person risen from that condition should be able to sit side by side, on equal terms, with the hereditary gentry of the land.

One member of the House, named Fox, was accustomed to introduce his recollections of past times with the words, 'When I was working as a weaver boy at Norwich'; and there are other members of Parliament, still living, whose origin has been equally humble. Mr Lindsay, the well-known ship-owner, and at one time member for Sunderland, once told the simple story of his life to the electors of Weymouth, in answer to an attack made upon him by his political opponents. He had been left an orphan at fourteen, and when he left Glasgow for Liverpool to push his way in the world, not being able to pay the usual fare, the captain of the steamer agreed to take his labour in exchange, and the boy worked his passage by trimming the coals in the coal hole. At Liverpool he remained for seven weeks before he could obtain employment, during which time he lived in sheds and fared hardly; until at last he found shelter on board a West Indiaman. He entered as a boy, and before he was nineteen, by steady good conduct he had risen to the command of a ship. At twenty-three he retired from the sea, and settled on shore, after which his progress was rapid. 'He had prospered,' he said, 'by steady industry, by constant work, and by ever keeping in view the great principle of doing to others as you would be done by.'

The career of Mr William Jackson, of Birkenhead, who represented North Derbyshire, bears considerable resemblance to that of Mr Lindsay. His father, a surgeon at Lancaster, died, leaving a family of eleven children, of whom William Jackson was the seventh son. The elder boys had been well educated while the father lived, but at his death the younger members had to shift for themselves. William, when under twelve years old, was taken from school, and put to hard work at a ship's side from six in the morning till nine at night. His master falling ill, the boy was taken into the counting-house, where he had more leisure. This gave him an opportunity of reading, and having obtained access to a set of the *Encyclopaedia Britannica*, he read the volumes through from A to Z, partly by day, but chiefly at night. He afterwards put himself to a trade, was diligent, and succeeded in it. Now he has ships sailing on almost every sea, and holds commercial relations with nearly every country on the globe.

Among like men of the same class may be ranked Richard Cobden, whose start in life was equally humble. The son of a small farmer at Midhurst in Sussex, he was sent at an early age to London and employed as a boy in a warehouse in the City. He was diligent, well conducted, and eager for information. His master, a man of the old school, warned

31

him against too much reading; but the boy went on in his own course, storing his mind with the wealth found in books. He was promoted from one position of trust to another – became a traveller for his house – secured a large connection, and eventually started in business as a calico printer at Manchester. Taking an interest in public questions, more especially in popular education, his attention was gradually drawn to the subject of the Corn Laws, to the repeal of which he may be said to have devoted his fortune and his life. It may be mentioned as a curious fact that the first speech he delivered in public was a total failure. But he had great perseverance, application, and energy; and with persistency and practice, he became at length one of the most persuasive and effective of public speakers, extorting the disinterested eulogy of even Sir Robert Peel himself. M. Drouyn de Lhuys, the French ambassador, has eloquently said of Mr Cobden that he was 'a living proof of what merit, perseverance, and labour can accomplish; one of the most complete examples of those men who, sprung from the humblest ranks of society, raise themselves to the highest rank in public estimation by the effect of their own worth and of their personal services; finally one of the rarest examples of the solid qualities inherent in the English character'.

In all these cases, strenuous individual application was the price paid for distinction; excellence of any sort being invariably placed beyond the reach of indolence. It is the diligent hand and head alone that maketh rich – in self-culture, growth in wisdom, and in business. Even when men are born to wealth and high social position, any solid reputation which they may individually achieve can only be attained by energetic application; for though an inheritance of acres may be bequeathed, an inheritance of knowledge and wisdom cannot. The wealthy man may pay others for doing his work for him, but it is impossible to get his thinking done for him by another, or to purchase any kind of self-culture. Indeed, the doctrine that excellence in any pursuit is only to be achieved by laborious application, holds as true in the case of the man of wealth as in that of Drew and Gifford, whose only school was a cobbler's stall, or Hugh Miller, whose only college was a Cromarty stone quarry.

Riches and ease, it is perfectly clear, are not necessary for man's highest culture, else had not the world been so largely indebted in all times to those who have sprung from the humbler ranks. An easy and luxurious existence does not train men to effort or encounter with difficulty; nor does it awaken that consciousness of power which is so necessary for energetic and effective action in life. Indeed, so far from poverty being a misfortune, it may, by vigorous self-help, be converted even into a blessing; rousing a man to that struggle with the world in which, though some may purchase ease by degradation, the right-minded and true-hearted find strength, confidence, and triumph. Bacon says, 'Men seem neither to understand their riches nor their strength: of the former they believe greater things than they should; of the latter much less. Self-reliance and self-denial will teach a man to drink out of his own cistern, and eat his own sweet bread, and to learn and labour truly to get his living, and carefully to expend the good things committed to his trust.'

Riches are so great a temptation to ease and self-indulgence, to which men are by nature prone, that the glory is all the greater of those who, born to ample fortunes, nevertheless take an active part in the work of their generation – who 'scorn delights and live laborious days'. It is to the honour of the wealthier ranks in this country that they are not idlers; for they do their fair share of the work of the state, and usually take more than their fair share of its dangers. It was a fine thing said of a subaltern officer in the Peninsular campaigns, observed trudging along through mud and mire by the side of his regiment, 'There goes £15,000 a year!' and in our own day, the bleak slopes of Sebastopol and the burning soil of India have borne witness to the like noble self-denial and devotion on the part of our gentler classes; many a gallant and noble fellow, of rank and estate, having risked his life, or lost it, in one or other of those fields of action, in the service of his country.

Nor have the wealthier classes been undistinguished in the more peaceful pursuits of philosophy and science. Take, for instance, the great name of Bacon, the father of modern philosophy, and of Worcester, Boyle, Cavendish, Talbot and Rosse, in science. The last named may be regarded as the great mechanic of the peerage; a man who, if he had not been born a peer, would probably have taken the highest rank as an inventor. So thorough is his knowledge of smith-work that he is said to have been pressed on one occasion to accept the foremanship of a large workshop, by a manufacturer to whom his rank was unknown. The great Rosse telescope, of his own fabrication, is certainly the most extraordinary instrument of the kind that has yet been constructed.

But it is principally in the departments of politics and literature that we find the most energetic labourers amongst our higher classes. Success in these lines of action, as in all others, can only be achieved through industry, practice, and study; and the great Minister, or parliamentary leader, must necessarily be amongst the very hardest of workers. Such was Palmerston; and such were Derby and Russell, Disraeli and Gladstone. These men have had the benefit of no Ten Hours Bill, but have often, during the busy season of Parliament, worked 'double shift', almost day and night. One of the most illustrious of such workers in modern times was unquestionably Sir Robert Peel. He possessed in an extraordinary degree the power of continuous intellectual labour, nor did he spare himself. His career, indeed, presented a remarkable example of how much a man of comparatively moderate powers can accomplish by means of assiduous application and indefatigable industry. During the forty years that he held a seat in Parliament, his labours were prodigious. He was a most conscientious man, and whatever he undertook to do, he did thoroughly. All his speeches bear evidence of his careful study of everything that had been spoken or written on the subject under consideration. He was elaborate almost to excess; and spared no pains to adapt himself to the various capacities of his audience. Withal, he possessed much practical sagacity, great strength of purpose, and power to direct the issues of action with steady hand and eye. In one respect he surpassed most men: his principles broadened and enlarged with time; and age, instead of contracting, only served to mellow and ripen his nature. To the last he continued open to the reception of new views, and, though many thought him cautious to excess, he did not allow himself to fall into that indiscriminating admiration of the past, which is the palsy of many minds similarly educated, and renders the old age of many nothing but a pity.

The indefatigable industry of Lord Brougham has become almost proverbial. His public labours extended over a period of upwards of sixty years, during which he has ranged over many fields – of law, literature, politics, and science – and achieved distinction in them all. How he contrived it, has been to many a mystery. Once, when Sir Samuel Romilly was requested to undertake some new work, he excused himself by saying that he had no time; 'but,' he added, 'go with it to that fellow Brougham, he seems to have time for everything'. The secret of it was, that he never left a minute unemployed; withal he possessed a constitution of iron. When arrived at an age at which most men would have retired from the world to enjoy their hard-earned leisure, perhaps to doze away their time in an easy chair, Lord Brougham commenced and prosecuted a series of elaborate investigations as to the laws of Light, and he submitted the results to the most scientific audiences that Paris and London could muster. About the same time, he was passing through the press his admirable sketches of the 'Men of Science and Literature of the Reign of George III', and taking his full share of the law business and the political discussions in the House of Lords. Sydney Smith once recommended him to confine himself to only the transaction of so much business as three strong men could get through. But such was Brougham's love of work – long become a habit – that no amount of application seems to have been too great for him; and such was his love of excellence, that it has been said of him that if his station in life had been only that of a shoe-black, he would never have rested satisfied until he had become the best shoe-black in England.

Another hard-working man of the same class was Sir E. Bulwer Lytton. Few writers have done more, or achieved higher distinction in various walks – as a novelist, poet, dramatist, historian, essayist, orator, and politician. He has worked his way step by step, disdainful of ease, and animated throughout by the ardent desire to excel. On the score of mere industry, there are few living English writers who have written so much, and none that has produced so much of high quality. The industry of Bulwer is entitled to all the greater praise that it has been entirely self-imposed. To hunt, and shoot, and live at ease – to frequent the clubs and enjoy the opera, with the variety of London visiting and sight-seeing during the 'season', and then off to the country mansion, with its well-stocked preserves, and its thousand delightful out-door pleasures, to travel abroad, to Paris, Vienna, or Rome – all this is excessively attractive to a lover of pleasure and a man of fortune, and by no means calculated to make him voluntarily undertake continuous labour of any kind. Yet these pleasures, all within his reach, Bulwer must, as compared with men born to similar estate, have denied himself in assuming the position and pursuing the career of a literary man. Like

Byron, his first effort was poetical (*Weeds and Wild Flowers*), and a failure. His second was a novel (*Falkland*), and it proved a failure too. A man of weaker nerve would have dropped authorship; but Bulwer had pluck and perseverance; and he worked on, determined to succeed. He was incessantly industrious, read extensively, and from failure went courageously onwards to success. *Pelham* followed *Falkland* within a year, and the remainder of Bulwer's literary life, now extending over a period of thirty years, has been a succession of triumphs.

Mr Disraeli affords a similar instance of the power of industry and application in working out an eminent public career. His first achievements were, like Bulwer's, in literature; and he reached success only through a succession of failures. His *Wondrous Tale of Alroy* and *Revolutionary Epic* were laughed at, and regarded as indications of literary lunacy. But he worked on in other directions, and his *Coningsby*, *Sybil*, and *Tancred*, proved the sterling stuff of which he was made. As an orator too, his first appearance in the House of Commons was a failure. It was spoken of as 'more screaming than an Adelphi farce'. Though composed in a grand and ambitious strain, every sentence was hailed with 'loud laughter'. *Hamlet* played as a comedy were nothing to it. But he concluded with a sentence which embodied a prophecy. Writhing under the laughter with which his studied eloquence had been received, he exclaimed, 'I have begun several times many things, and have succeeded in them at last. I shall sit down now, but the time will come when you will hear me.' The time did come; and how Disraeli succeeded in at length commanding the attention of the first assembly of gentlemen in the world, affords a striking illustration of what energy and determination will do; for Disraeli earned his position by dint of patient industry. He did not, as many young men do, having once failed, retire dejected, to mope and whine in a corner, but diligently set himself to work. He carefully unlearnt his faults, studied the character of his audience, practised sedulously the art of speech, and industriously filled his mind with the elements of parliamentary knowledge. He worked patiently for success; and it came, but slowly: then the House laughed with him, instead of at him. The recollection of his early failure was effaced, and by general consent he was at length admitted to be one of the most finished and effective of parliamentary speakers.

Although much may be accomplished by means of individual industry and energy, as these and other instances set forth in the following pages serve to illustrate, it must at the same time be acknowledged that the help which we derive from others in the journey of life is of very great importance. The poet Wordsworth has well said that 'these two things, contradictory though they may seem, must go together – manly dependence and manly independence, manly reliance and manly self-reliance'. From infancy to old age, all are more or less indebted to others for nurture and culture; and the best and strongest are usually found the readiest to acknowledge such help. Take, for example, the career of the late Alexis de Tocqueville, a man doubly well-born, for his father was a distinguished peer of France, and his mother a granddaughter of Malesherbes. Through powerful family influence, he was appointed Judge Auditor at Versailles when only twenty-one; but probably feeling that he had not fairly won the position by merit, he determined to give it up and owe his future advancement in life to himself alone. 'A foolish resolution', some will say; but de Tocqueville bravely acted it out. He resigned his appointment, and made arrangements to leave France for the purpose of travelling through the United States, the results of which were published in his great book on *Democracy in America*. His friend and travelling companion, Gustave de Beaumont, has described his indefatigable industry during this journey. 'His nature,' he says, 'was wholly averse to idleness, and whether he was travelling or resting, his mind was always at work ... With Alexis, the most agreeable conversation was that which was the most useful. The worst day was the lost day, or the day ill spent; the least loss of time annoyed him.' Tocqueville himself wrote to a friend: 'There is no time of life at which one can wholly cease from action; for effort without one's self, and still more effort within, is equally necessary, if not more so, when we grow old, as it is in youth. I compare man in this world to a traveller journeying without ceasing towards a colder and colder region; the higher he goes, the faster he ought to walk. The great malady of the soul is cold. And in resisting this formidable evil, one needs not only to be sustained by the action of a mind employed, but also by contact with one's fellows in the business of life.'

Notwithstanding de Tocqueville's decided views as to the necessity of exercising individual energy and self-dependence, no one could be more ready than he was to recognize the value of that help and support

37

for which all men are indebted to others in a greater or less degree. Thus, he often acknowledged, with gratitude, his obligations to his friends, de Kergorlay and Stofells – to the former for intellectual assistance, and to the latter for moral support and sympathy. To de Kergorlay he wrote: 'Thine is the only soul in which I have confidence, and whose influence exercises a genuine effect upon my own. Many others have influence upon the details of my actions, but no one has so much influence as thou on the origination of fundamental ideas, and of those principles which are the rules of conduct.' De Tocqueville was not less ready to confess the great obligations which he owed to his wife, Marie, for the preservation of that temper and frame of mind which enabled him to prosecute his studies with success. He believed that a noble-minded woman insensibly elevated the character of her husband, while one of a grovelling nature has certainly tended to degrade it.

In fine, human character is moulded by a thousand subtle influences; by example and precept; by life and literature; by friends and neighbours; by the world we live in as well as by the spirits of our forefathers, whose legacy of good words and deeds we inherit. But great, unquestionably, though these influences are acknowledged to be, it is nevertheless equally clear that men must necessarily be the active agents of their own well-being and well-doing; and that, however much the wise and the good may owe to others, they themselves must in the very nature of things be their own best helpers.

2. Leaders of Industry:
Inventors and Producers

One of the most strongly-marked features of the English people is their spirit of industry, standing out prominent and distinct in their past history, and as strikingly characteristic of them now as at any former period. It is this spirit, displayed by the commons of England, which has laid the foundations and built up the industrial greatness of the empire. This vigorous growth of the nation has been mainly the result of the free energy of individuals, and it has been contingent upon the number of hands and minds from time to time actively employed within it, whether as cultivators of the soil, producers of articles of utility, contrivers of tools and machines, writers of books, or creators of works of art. And while this spirit of active industry has been the vital principle of the nation, it has also been its saving and remedial one, counteracting from time to time the effects of errors in our laws and imperfections in our constitution.

The career of industry which the nation has pursued, has also proved its best education. As steady application to work is the healthiest training for every individual, so is it the best discipline of a state. Honourable industry travels the same road with duty; and Providence has closely linked both with happiness. The gods, says the poet, have placed labour and toil on the way leading to the Elysian fields. Certain it is that no bread eaten by man is so sweet as that earned by his own labour, whether bodily or mental. By labour the earth has been subdued, and man redeemed from barbarism; nor has a single step in civilization been made without it. Labour is not only a necessity and a duty, but a blessing: only the idler feels it to be a curse. The duty of work is written on the thews and muscles of the limbs, the mechanism of the hand, the nerves and lobes of the brain – the sum of whose healthy action is satisfaction and enjoyment. In the school of labour is taught the best practical wisdom; nor is a life of manual employment, as we shall hereafter find, incompatible with high mental culture.

Hugh Miller, than whom none knew better the strength and the weakness belonging to the lot of labour, stated the result of his experience

39

to be, that Work, even the hardest, is full of pleasure and materials for self-improvement. He held honest labour to be the best of teachers, and that the school of toil is the noblest of schools – save only the Christian one – that it is a school in which the ability of being useful is imparted, the spirit of independence learnt, and the habit of persevering effort acquired. He was even of opinion that the training of the mechanic – by the exercise which it gives to his observant faculties, from his daily dealing with things actual and practical, and the close experience of life which he acquires – better fits him for picking his way along the journey of life, and is more favourable to his growth as a Man, emphatically speaking, than the training afforded by any other condition.

The array of great names which we have already cursorily cited, of men springing from the ranks of the industrial classes, who have achieved distinction in various walks of life – in science, commerce, literature, and art – shows that at all events the difficulties interposed by poverty and labour are not insurmountable.

Inventors have set in motion some of the greatest industries of the world. To them society owes many of its chief necessaries, comforts, and luxuries; and by their genius and labour daily life has been rendered in all respects more easy as well as enjoyable. Our food, our clothing, the furniture of our homes, the glass which admits the light to our dwellings at the same time that it excludes the cold, the gas which illuminates our streets, our means of locomotion by land and sea, the tools by which our various articles of necessity and luxury are fabricated, have been the result of the labour and ingenuity of many men and many minds. Mankind at large are all the happier for such inventions, and are every day reaping the benefit of them in an increase of individual well-being as well as of public enjoyment.

Though the invention of the working steam-engine – the king of machines – belongs, comparatively speaking, to our own epoch, the idea of it was born many centuries ago. Like other contrivances and discoveries, it was effected step by step – one man transmitting the results of his labours, at the time apparently useless, to his successors, who took it up and carried it forward another stage – the prosecution of the inquiry extending over many generations. The steam-engine was nothing, however, until it emerged from the state of theory, and was taken in hand by practical mechanics; and what a noble story of patient, laborious investigation, of difficulties encountered and overcome by heroic industry, does not that marvellous machine tell! It is indeed, in itself, a monument of the power of self-help in man. Grouped around it we find Savery, the military engineer; Newcomen, the Dartmouth blacksmith; Cawley, the glazier; Potter, the engine-boy; Smeaton, the civil engineer; and, towering above all, the laborious, patient, never-tiring James Watt, the mathematical-instrument maker.

Watt was one of the most industrious of men; and the story of his life proves, what all experience confirms, that it is not the man of the greatest natural vigour and capacity who achieves the highest results, but he who employs his powers with the greatest industry and the most carefully disciplined skill – the skill that comes by labour, application, and experience. Many men in his time knew far more than Watt, but none laboured so assiduously as he did to turn all that he did know to useful practical purposes. He was, above all things, most persevering in the pursuit of facts. He cultivated carefully that habit of active attention on which all the higher working qualities of the mind mainly depend. Indeed, Mr Edgeworth entertained the opinion, that the difference of intellect in men depends more upon the early cultivation of this *habit of attention*, than upon any great disparity between the powers of one individual and another.

Even when a boy, Watt found science in his toys. The quadrants lying about his father's carpenter's shop led him to the study of optics and astronomy; his ill-health induced him to pry into the secrets of physiology; and his solitary walks through the country attracted him to the study of botany and history. While carrying on the business of a mathematical-instrument maker, he received an order to build an organ; and, though without an ear for music, he undertook the study of harmonics, and successfully constructed the instrument. And, in like manner, when the little model of Newcomen's steam-engine, belonging to the University of Glasgow, was placed in his hands to repair, he forthwith set himself to learn all that was then known about heat, evaporation, and condensation – at the same time plodding his way in mechanics and the science of construction – the results of which he at length embodied in his condensing steam-engine.

For ten years he went on contriving and inventing – with little hope to cheer him, and with few friends to encourage him. At length, Watt found a fit partner in another eminent leader of industry – Matthew Boulton, of Birmingham; a skilful, energetic, and far-seeing man, who vigorously undertook the enterprise of introducing the condensing-engine into general use as a working power; and the success of both is now matter of history.

Many skilful inventors have from time to time added new power to the steam-engine; and, by numerous modifications, rendered it capable of being applied to nearly all the purposes of manufacture – driving machinery, impelling ships, grinding corn, printing books, stamping money, hammering, planing, and turning iron; in short, of performing every description of mechanical labour where power is required. One of the most useful modifications in the engine was that devised by Trevithick, and eventually perfected by George Stephenson and his son, in the form of the railway locomotive, by which social changes of immense importance have been brought about, of even greater consequence, considered in their results on human progress and civilization, than the condensing-engine of Watt.

One of the first grand results of Watt's invention – which placed an almost unlimited power at the command of the producing classes – was the establishing of the cotton-manufacture. The person most closely identified with the foundation of this great branch of industry was unquestionably Sir Richard Arkwright, whose practical energy and sagacity were perhaps even more remarkable than his mechanical inventiveness. His originality as an inventor has indeed been called in question, like that of Watt and Stephenson. Arkwright probably stood in the same relation to the spinning-machine that Watt did to the steam-engine and Stephenson to the locomotive. He gathered together the scattered threads of ingenuity which already existed, and wove them, after his own design, into a new and original fabric. Though Lewis Paul, of Birmingham, patented the invention of spinning by rollers thirty years before Arkwright, the machines constructed by him were so imperfect in their details, that they could not be profitably worked, and the invention was practically a failure. Another obscure mechanic, a reed-maker of Leigh, named Thomas Highs, is also said to have invented the water-frame and spinning-jenny; but they, too, proved unsuccessful.

When the demands of industry are found to press upon the resources of inventors, the same idea is usually found floating about in many minds; such has been the case with the steam-engine, the safety-lamp, the electric telegraph, and other inventions. Many ingenious minds are found labouring in the throes of invention, until at length the master mind, the strong practical man, steps forward, and straightaway delivers them of their idea, applies the principle successfully, and the thing is done. Then there is a loud outcry among all the smaller contrivers, who see themselves distanced in the race; and hence men such as Watt, Stephenson, and Arkwright, have usually to defend their reputation and their rights as practical and successful inventors.

Richard Arkwright, like most of our great mechanicians, sprang from the ranks. He was born in Preston in 1732. His parents were very poor, and he was the youngest of thirteen children. He was never at school: the only education he received he gave to himself; and to the last he was only able to write with difficulty. When a boy, he was apprenticed to a barber, and after learning the business, he set up for himself in Bolton, where he occupied an underground cellar, over which he put up the sign, 'Come to the subterraneous barber – he shaves for a penny.' The other barbers found their customers leaving them, and reduced their prices to his standard, when Arkwright, determined to push his trade, announced his determination to give 'a clean shave for a halfpenny'. After a few years he quitted his cellar, and became an itinerant dealer in hair. At that time wigs were worn, and wig-making formed an important branch of the the barbering business. Arkwright went about buying hair for the wigs. He was accustomed to attend the hiring fairs throughout Lancashire resorted to by young women, for the purpose of securing their long tresses; and it is said that in negotiations of this sort he was very successful. He also dealt in a chemical hair dye, which he used adroitly, and thereby secured a considerable trade. But he does not seem, notwithstanding his pushing character, to have done more than earn a bare living.

In travelling about the country, Arkwright had become acquainted with a person named Kay, a clockmaker at Warrington, who assisted him in constructing some of the parts of his perpetual-motion machinery. It is supposed that he was informed by Kay of the principle of spinning by rollers; but it is also said that the idea was at first suggested to him by accidentally observing a red-hot piece of iron become elongated by passing between iron rollers. However this may be, the idea at once took firm possession of his mind, and he proceeded to devise the process by which it was to be accomplished, Kay being able to tell him nothing on this point. Arkwright now abandoned his business of hair collecting, and devoted himself to the perfecting of this machine, a model of which, constructed by Kay under his directions, he set up in the parlour of the Free Grammar School at Preston. The exhibition of his machine in a town where so many workpeople lived by the exercise of manual labour proved a dangerous experiment; ominous growlings were heard outside the schoolroom from time to time, and Arkwright – remembering the fate of Kay, who was mobbed and compelled to fly from Lancashire because of his invention of the fly-shuttle, and of poor Hargreaves, whose spinning-jenny had been pulled to pieces only a short time before by a Blackburn mob – wisely determined on packing up his model and removing to a less dangerous locality. He went accordingly to Nottingham, where he applied to some of the local bankers for pecuniary assistance; and the Messrs Wright consented to advance him a sum of money on condition of sharing in the profits of the invention. The machine, however, not being perfected so soon as they had anticipated, the bankers recommended Arkwright to apply to Messrs Strutt & Need, the former of whom was the ingenious inventor and patentee of the stocking-frame. Mr Strutt at once appreciated the merits of the invention, and a partnership was entered into with Arkwright, whose road to fortune was now clear. The patent was secured in the name of 'Richard Arkwright, of Nottingham, clockmaker', and it is a circumstance worthy of note, that it was taken out in 1769, the same year in which Watt secured the patent for his steam-engine. A cotton-mill was first erected at Nottingham, driven by horses; and another was shortly after built, on a much larger scale, at Cromford, in Derbyshire, turned by a water-wheel, from which circumstance the spinning-machine came to be called the water-frame.

Arkwright's labours, however, were, comparatively speaking, only begun. He had still to perfect all the working details of his machine. It was in his hands the subject of constant modification and improvement, until eventually it was rendered practicable and profitable in an eminent degree. But success was only secured by long and patient labour: for some years, indeed, the speculation was disheartening and unprofitable, swallowing up a very large amount of capital without any result. When success began to appear more certain, then the Lancashire manufacturers fell upon Arkwright's patent to pull it in pieces, as the Cornish miners fell upon Boulton and Watt to rob them of the profits of their steam-engine. Arkwright was even denounced as the enemy of the working people; and a mill which he built near Chorley was destroyed by a mob in the presence of a strong force of police and military. The Lancashire men refused to buy his materials, though they were confessedly the best in the market. Then they refused to pay patent-right for the use of his machines, and combined to crush him in the courts of law. To the disgust of right-minded people, Arkwright's patent was upset. After the trial, when passing the hotel at which his opponents were staying, one of them said, loud enough to be heard by him, 'Well, we've done the old shaver at last'; to which he coolly replied, 'Never mind, I've a razor left that will shave you all.' He established new mills in Lancashire, Derbyshire and at New Lanark, in Scotland. The mills at Cromford also came into his hands at the expiry of his partnership with Strutt, and the amount and the excellence of his products were such, that in a short time he obtained so complete a control of the trade, that the prices were fixed by him, and he governed the main operations of the other cotton-spinners.

Arkwright was a man of great force of character, indomitable courage, much worldly shrewdness, with a business faculty almost amounting to genius. At one period his time was engrossed by severe and continuous labour, occasioned by the organizing and conducting of his numerous manufactories, sometimes from four in the morning till nine at night. Be it for good or for evil, Arkwright was the founder in England of the modern factory system, a branch of industry which has unquestionably proved a source of immense wealth to individuals and to the nation.

All the other great branches of industry in Britain furnish like examples of energetic men of business, the source of much benefit to the neighbourhoods in which they have laboured, and of increased power and wealth to the community at large. Among such might be cited the Strutts of Belper; the Tennants of Glasgow; the Marshalls and Gotts of Leeds; the Peels, Ashworths, Birleys, Fieldens, Ashtons, Heywoods, and Ainsworths of South Lancashire, some of whose descendants have since become distinguished in connection with the

45

political history of England. Such pre-eminently were the Peels of South Lancashire.

The founder of the Peel family, about the middle of last century, was a small yeoman, occupying the Hole House Farm, near Blackburn, from which he afterwards removed to a house situated in Fish Lane in that town. Robert Peel, as he advanced in life, saw a large family of sons and daughters growing up about him; but the land about Blackburn being somewhat barren, it did not appear to him that agricultural pursuits offered a very encouraging prospect for their industry. The place had, however, long been the seat of a domestic manufacture – the fabric called 'Blackburn greys', consisting of linen weft and cotton warp, being chiefly made in that town and its neighbourhood. It was then customary – previous to the introduction of the factory system – for industrious yeomen with families to employ the time not occupied in the fields in weaving at home; and Robert Peel accordingly began the domestic trade of calico-making. He was honest, and made an honest article; thrifty and hard-working, and his trade prospered. He was also enterprising, and was one of the first to adopt the carding cylinder, then recently invented.

But Robert Peel's attention was principally directed to the *printing* of calico – then a comparatively unknown art – and for some time he carried on a series of experiments with the object of printing by machinery. The experiments were secretly conducted in his own house, the cloth being ironed for the purpose by one of the women of the family. It was then customary, in such houses as the Peels', to use pewter plates for dinner. Having sketched a figure or pattern on one of the plates, the thought struck him that an impression might be got from it in reverse, and printed on calico with colour. In a cottage at the end of the farmhouse lived a woman who kept a calendering machine, and going into her cottage, he put the plate with colour rubbed into the figured part and some calico over it, through the machine, when it was found to leave a satisfactory impression. Such is said to have been the origin of roller-printing on calico. Robert Peel shortly perfected his process, and the first pattern he brought out was a parsley leaf; hence he is spoken of in the neighbourhood of Blackburn to this day as 'Parsley Peel'. The process of calico-printing by what is called the mule machine – that is, by means of a wooden cylinder in relief, with an engraved copper cylinder – was afterwards brought to perfection by one of his sons, the head of the firm of Messrs Peel & Co., of Church.

From what can now be learnt of the character of the original and untitled Robert Peel, he must have been a remarkable man – shrewd, sagacious, and far-seeing. His son, Sir Robert, thus modestly spoke of him: 'My father may be truly said to have been the founder of our family; and he so accurately appreciated the importance of commercial wealth in a national point of view, that he was often heard to say that the gains to individuals were small compared with the national gains arising from trade.'

Sir Robert Peel, the first baronet and the second manufacturer of the name, inherited all his father's enterprise, ability, and industry. His position, at starting in life, was little above that of an ordinary working man; for his father, though laying the foundations of future prosperity, was still struggling with the difficulties arising from insufficient capital. When Robert was only twenty years of age, he determined to begin the business of cotton-printing, which he had by this time learnt from his father, on his own account. His uncle, James Haworth, and William Yates of Blackburn, joined him in his enterprise; the whole capital which they could raise amongst them amounting to only about £500, the principal part of which was supplied by William Yates. The father of the latter was a householder in Blackburn, where he was well known and much respected; and having saved money by his business, he was willing to advance sufficient to give his son a start in the lucrative trade of cotton-printing, then in its infancy. Robert Peel, though comparatively a mere youth, supplied the practical knowledge of the business; but it was said of him, and proved true, that he 'carried an old head on young shoulders'. A ruined corn-mill with its adjoining fields was purchased for a comparatively small sum, near the then insignificant town of Bury, where the works long after continued to be known as 'The Ground'; and a few wooden sheds having been run up, the firm commenced their cotton-printing business in a very humble way in the year 1770, adding to it that of cotton-spinning a few years later.

The career of Yates, Peel & Co. was throughout one of great and uninterrupted prosperity. Sir Robert Peel himself was the soul of the firm; to great energy and application uniting much practical sagacity,

47

and first-rate mercantile abilities – qualities in which many of the early cotton-spinners were exceedingly deficient. He was a man of iron mind and frame, and toiled unceasingly. In short, he was to cotton-printing what Arkwright was to cotton-spinning, and his success was equally great. The excellence of the articles produced by the firm secured the command of the market, and the character of the firm stood pre-eminent in Lancashire.

Sir Robert Peel readily appreciated the value of all new processes and inventions; in illustration of which we may allude to his adoption of the process for producing what is called *resist work* in calico-printing. This is accomplished by the use of a paste, or resist, on such parts of the cloth as where intended to remain white. The person who discovered the paste was a traveller for a London house, who sold it to Mr Peel for an inconsiderable sum. It required the experience of a year or two to perfect the system and make it practically useful; but the beauty of its effect, and the extreme precision of outline in the pattern produced, at once placed the Bury establishment at the head of all the factories for calico-printing in the country.

Among other distinguished founders of industry, the Rev. William Lee, inventor of the stocking-frame, and John Heathcoat, inventor of the bobbin-net machine, are worthy of notice, as men of great mechanical skill and perseverance, through whose labours a vast amount of remunerative employment has been provided for the labouring population of Nottingham and the adjacent districts. The accounts which have been preserved of the circumstances connected with the invention of the stocking-frame are very confused, and in many respects contradictory, though there is no doubt as to the name of the inventor. This was William Lee, born at Woodborough, a village some seven miles from Nottingham, about the year 1563. According to some accounts, he was the heir to a small freehold, while according to others he was a poor scholar, and had to struggle with poverty from his earliest years. He entered as a sizar at Christ College, Cambridge, in May, 1579, and subsequently removed to St John's, taking his degree of B.A. in 1582–3.

At the time when Lee invented the stocking-frame he was officiating as curate of Calverton, near Nottingham; and it is alleged by some writers that the invention had its origin in disappointed affection. The curate is said to have fallen deeply in love with a young lady of the village, who failed to reciprocate his affection; and when he visited her, she was accustomed to pay much more attention to the process of knitting stockings and instructing her pupils in the art, than to the addresses of her admirer.

Whatever may have been the actual facts as to the origin of the invention of the stocking-loom, there can be no doubt as to the extraordinary mechanial genius displayed by its inventor. That a clergyman living in a remote village, whose life had for the most part been spent with books, should contrive a machine of such delicate and complicated movements, and at once advance the art of knitting from the tedious process of linking threads in a chain of loops by three skewers in the fingers of a woman, to the beautiful and rapid process of weaving by the stocking-frame, was indeed an astonishing achievement, which may be pronounced almost unequalled in the history of mechanical invention. Lee's merit was all the greater, as the handicraft arts were then in their infancy, and little attention had as yet been given to the contrivance of machinery for the purposes of manufacture. According to tradition, the first frame he made was a twelve gauge, without leadsinkers, and it was almost wholly of wood; the needles being also stuck in bits of wood. One of Lee's principal difficulties consisted in the formation of the stitch, for want of needle eyes; but this he eventually overcame by forming eyes to the needles with a three-square file. At length, one difficulty after another was successfully overcome, and after three years' labour the machine was sufficiently complete to be fit for use. The quondam curate, full of enthusiasm for his art, now began stocking-weaving in the village of Calverton, and he continued to work there for several years, instructing his brother James and several of his relations in the practice of the art.

Having brought his frame to a considerable degree of perfection, and being desirous of securing the patronage of Queen Elizabeth, whose partiality for knitted silk stockings was well known, Lee proceeded to London to exhibit the loom before Her Majesty. He first showed it to several members of the Court, among others to Sir William (afterwards Lord) Hunsdon, whom he taught to work it with success; and Lee was, through their instrumentality, at length admitted to an interview with the Queen, and worked the machine in her presence. Elizabeth, however, did not give him the encouragement that he had expected; and she is said to have opposed the invention on the ground that it was calculated to deprive a large number of poor people of their employment of hand knitting. Lee was no more successful in finding other patrons, and considering himself and his invention treated with contempt, he embraced the offer made to him by Sully, the sagacious minister of Henry IV, to proceed to Rouen and instruct the operatives of that town – then one of the most important manufacturing centres of France – in the construction and use of the stocking-frame. Lee accordingly transferred himself and his machines to France, in 1605, taking with him his brother and seven workmen. He met with a cordial reception at Rouen, and was proceeding with the manufacture of stockings on a large scale – having nine of his frames in full work – when unhappily ill fortune again overtook him. Henry IV, his protector, on whom he had relied for the rewards, honours, and promised grant of privileges, which had induced Lee to settle in France, was murdered by the fanatic Ravaillac; and the encouragement and protection which had heretofore been extended to him were at once withdrawn.

Lee's brother, with seven of the workmen, succeeded in escaping from France with their frames, leaving two behind. On James Lee's return to Nottinghamshire, he was joined by one Ashton, a miller of Thoroton, who had been instructed in the art of framework knitting by the inventor himself before he left England. These two, with the workmen and their frames, began the stocking-manufacture at Thoroton, and carried it on with considerable success. The place was favourably situated for the purpose, as the sheep pastured in the neighbouring district of Sherwood yielded a kind of wool of the longest staple. Ashton is said to have introduced the method of making the frames with lead sinkers, which was a great improvement. The number of looms employed in different parts of England gradually increased; and the machine manufacture of stockings eventually became an important branch of the national industry.

One of the most important modifications in the stocking-frame was that which enabled it to be applied to the manufacture of lace on a large scale. In 1777, two workmen, Frost and Holmes, were both engaged in making point-net by means of the modifications they had introduced in the stocking-frame; and in the course of about thirty years, so rapid was the growth of this branch of production that 1,500 point-net frames were at work, giving employment to upwards of 15,000 people. Owing, however, to the war, to change of fashion, and to other circumstances, the Nottingham lace-manufacture rapidly fell off; and it continued in a decaying state until the invention of the bobbin-net machine by John Heathcoat, late M.P. for Tiverton, which had the effect of at once re-establishing the manufacture on solid foundations.

John Heathcoat was the youngest son of a respectable small farmer at Duffield, Derbyshire, where he was born in 1783. When at school he made steady and rapid progress, but was early removed from it to be apprenticed to a frame-smith near Loughborough. The boy soon learnt to handle tools with dexterity, and he acquired a minute knowledge of the parts of which the stocking-frame was composed, as well as of the more intricate warp-machine. At his leisure he studied how to introduce improvements in them, and his friend, Mr Bazley, M.P., states that as early as the age of sixteen, he conceived the idea of inventing a machine by which lace might be made similar to Buckingham or French lace, then all made by hand. The first practical improvement he succeeded in introducing was in the warp-frame, when, by means of an ingenious apparatus, he succeeded in producing 'mitts' of a lacy appearance, and it was this success which determined him to pursue the study of mechanical lace-making.

When a little over twenty-one years of age, Heathcoat went to Nottingham, where he readily found employment, for which he soon received the highest remuneration, as a setter-up of hosiery and warp-frames, and was much respected for his talent for invention, general intelligence, and the sound and sober principles that governed his conduct. He also continued to pursue the subject on which his mind had before been occupied, and laboured to compass the contrivance of a twist traverse-net machine. He first studied the art of making the Buckingham or pillow-lace by hand, with the object of effecting the same motions by mechanical means. It was a long and laborious task, requiring the exercise of a great perseverance and ingenuity.

It is difficult to describe in words an invention so complicated as the bobbin-net machine. It was, indeed, a mechanical pillow for making lace, imitating in an ingenious manner the motions of the lace-maker's fingers in intersecting or tying the meshes of the lace upon her pillow.

51

On analysing the component parts of a piece of hand-made lace, Heathcoat was enabled to classify the threads into longitudinal and diagonal. He began his experiments by fixing common pack-threads lengthwise on a sort of frame for the warp, and then passing the weft threads between them by common plyers, delivering them to other plyers on the opposite side; then, after giving them a sideways motion and twist, the threads were repassed back between the next adjoining cords, the meshes being thus tied in the same way as upon pillows by hand. He had then to contrive a mechanism that should accomplish all these nice and delicate movements, and to do this cost him no small amount of mental toil. Long after he said, 'The single difficulty of getting the diagonal threads to twist in the allotted space was so great that if it had now to be done, I should probably not attempt its accomplishment.' His next step was to provide thin metallic discs, to be used as bobbins for conducting the threads backwards and forwards through the warp. These discs, being arranged in carrier-frames placed on each side of the warp, were moved by suitable machinery so as to conduct the threads from side to side in forming the lace. He eventually succeeded in working out his principle with extraordinary skill and success; and, at the age of twenty-four, he was enabled to secure his invention by a patent.

As in the case of nearly all inventions which have proved productive, Heathcoat's rights as a patentee were disputed, and his claims as an inventor called in question. On the supposed invalidity of the patent, the lace-makers boldly adopted the bobbin-net machine, and set the inventor at defiance. But other patents were taken out for alleged improvements and adaptations; and it was only when these new paten-tees fell out and went to law with each other that Heathcoat's rights became established. One lace manufacturer having brought an action against another for an alleged infringement of his patent, the jury brought in a verdict for the defendant, in which the judge concurred, on the ground that *both* the machines in question were infringements of Heathcoat's patent. It was on the occasion of this trial, 'Boville *v.* Moore', that Sir John Copley (afterwards Lord Lyndhurst), who was retained for the defence in the interest of Mr Heathcoat, learnt to work the bobbin-net machine in order that he might master the details of the invention. On reading over his brief, he confessed that he did not quite understand the merits of the case; but as it seemed to him to be one of great importance, he offered to go down into the country forthwith and study the machine until he understood it; 'and then,' said he, 'I will defend you to the best of my ability.' He accordingly put himself into that night's mail, and went down to Nottingham to get up his case as perhaps counsel never got it up before. Next morning the learned sergeant placed himself in a lace-loom, and he did not leave it until he could deftly make a piece of bobbin-net with his own hands, and thoroughly understood the principle as well as the details of the machine. When the case came on for trial, the learned sergeant was enabled to work the model on the table with such ease and skill, and to explain the precise nature of the invention with such felicitous clearness, as to astonish alike judge, jury, and spectators; and the thorough conscientiousness and mastery with which he handled the case had no doubt its influence upon the decision of the court.

After the trial was over, Mr Heathcoat, on inquiry, found about six hundred machines at work after his patent, and he proceeded to levy royalty upon the owners of them, which amounted to a large sum. But the profits realized by the manufacturers of lace were very great, and the use of the machines rapidly extended; while the price of the article was reduced from five pounds the square yard to about five pence in the course of twenty-five years. During the same period the average annual returns of the lace-trade have been at least four millions sterling, and it gives remunerative employment to about 150,000 workpeople.

To return to the personal history of Mr Heathcoat. In 1809 we find him established as a lace-manufacturer at Loughborough, in Leicestershire. Notwithstanding the great increase in the number of hands employed in lace-making through the introduction of the new machines, it began to be whispered about among the workpeople that they were superseding labour, and an extensive conspiracy was formed for the purpose of destroying them wherever found. As early as the year 1811 disputes arose between the masters and men engaged in the stocking- and lace-trades in the south-western parts of Nottinghamshire and the adjacent parts of Derbyshire and Leicestershire, the result of which was the assembly of a mob at Sutton-in-Ashfield, who proceeded in open day to break the stocking- and lace-frames of the manufacturers. Some of the ringleaders having been seized and punished, the disaffected learned caution; but the destruction of the machines was nevertheless carried on secretly wherever a safe opportunity presented itself. In the neighbourhood of Nottingham, which was the focus of turbulence, the machine-breakers organized themselves in regular bodies, and held nocturnal meetings at which their plans were arranged. Probably with the view of inspiring confidence, they gave out that they were under the command of a leader named Ned Ludd, or General Ludd, and hence their designation of Luddites. Under this organization machine-breaking was carried on with great vigour during the winter of 1811, occasioning great distress, and throwing large numbers of workpeople out of employment. Meanwhile, the owners of the frames proceeded to remove them from the villages and lone dwellings in the country, and brought them into warehouses in the towns for their better protection.

The Luddites seem to have been encouraged by the lenity of the sentences pronounced on such of their confederates as had been apprehended and tried; and shortly after, the mania broke out afresh, and rapidly extended over the northern and midland manufacturing districts. The organization became more secret; an oath was administered to the members binding them to obedience to the orders issued by the heads of the confederacy; and the betrayal of their designs was decreed to be death. All machines were doomed by them to destruction, whether employed in the manufacture of cloths, calico, or lace; and a reign of terror began which lasted for years. In Yorkshire and Lancashire mills were bodily attacked by armed rioters, and in many cases they were wrecked or burnt; so that it became necessary to guard them by soldiers and yeomanry. The masters themselves were doomed to death; many of them were assaulted, and some were murdered. At length the law was vigorously set in motion; numbers of the misguided Luddites were apprehended; some were executed; and after several years' violent commotion from this cause, the machine-breaking riots were at length quelled.

In 1831 the electors of Tiverton, of which town Mr Heathcoat had proved himself so genuine a benefactor, returned him to represent them in Parliament, and he continued their member for nearly thirty years. On retiring from the representation in 1859, owing to advancing age and increasing infirmities, thirteen hundred of his workmen presented him with a silver inkstand and gold pen, in token of their esteem. He enjoyed his leisure for only two more years, dying in January 1861 at the age of seventy-seven, and leaving behind him a character for probity, virtue, manliness, and mechanical genius, of which his descendants may well be proud.

We next turn to a career of a very different kind, that of the illustrious but unfortunate Jacquard, whose life also illustrates in a remarkable manner the influence which ingenious men, even of the humblest rank, may exercise upon the industry of a nation. Jacquard was the son of a hardworking couple of Lyons, his father being a weaver, and his mother a pattern reader. They were too poor to give him any but the most meagre education. When he was of age to learn a trade, his father placed him with a bookbinder. An old clerk, who made up the master's accounts, gave Jacquard some lessons in mathematics. He very shortly began to display a remarkable turn for mechanics, and some of his contrivances quite astonished the old clerk, who advised Jacquard's father to put him to some other trade, in which his peculiar abilities might have better scope than in bookbinding.

His parents dying, Jacquard found himself in a measure compelled to take his father's two looms, and carry on the trade of a weaver. He immediately proceeded to improve the looms, and became so engrossed with his inventions that he forgot his work, and very soon found himself at the end of his means. He then sold the looms to pay his debts, at the same time that he took upon himself the burden of supporting a wife. He became still poorer, and to satisfy his creditors, he next sold his cottage. He tried to find employment, but in vain, people believing him to be an idler, occupied with mere dreams about his inventions. At length he obtained employment with a linen-maker of Bresse, whither he went, his wife remaining at Lyons, earning a precarious living by making straw bonnets.

We hear nothing further of Jacquard for some years, but in the interval he seems to have prosecuted his improvement in the draw-loom for the better manufacture of figured fabrics; for, in 1790, he brought out his contrivance for selecting the warp threads, which, when added to the loom, superseded the services of a drawboy. The adoption of this machine was slow but steady, and in ten years after its introduction, 4,000 of them were found at work in Lyons. Jacquard's pursuits were rudely interrupted by the Revolution, and, in 1792, we find him fighting in the ranks of the Lyonnaise Volunteers against the Army of the Convention under the command of Dubois Crancé. The city was taken; Jacquard fled and joined the Army of the Rhine, where he rose to the rank of sergeant. He might have remained a soldier, but that, his only son having been shot dead at his side, he deserted and returned to Lyons to recover his wife. He found her in a garret, still employed at her old trade of straw-bonnet making. While living in concealment with her, his mind reverted to the inventions over which he had so long brooded in former years; but he had no means wherewith to prosecute them. Jacquard found it necessary, however, to emerge from his hiding-place and try to find some employment. He succeeded in obtaining it with an intelligent manufacturer, and while working by day he went on inventing by night.

In three months Jacquard had invented a loom to substitute mechanical action for the irksome and toilsome labour of the workman. The loom was exhibited at the Exposition of National Industry at Paris in 1801, and obtained a bronze medal. Jacquard was further honoured by a visit at Lyons from the Minister Carnot, who desired to congratulate him in person on the success of his invention. In the following year the Society of Arts in London offered a prize for the invention of a machine for manufacturing fishing-nets and boarding-netting for ships. Jacquard heard of this, and while walking one day in the fields according to his custom, he turned the subject over in his mind, and contrived the plan of a machine for the purpose. His friend, the manufacturer, again furnished him with the means of carrying out his idea, and in three weeks Jacquard had completed his invention.

Jacquard's achievement having come to the knowledge of the Prefect of the Department, he was summoned before that functionary, and, on his explanation of the working of the machine, a report on the subject was forwarded to the Emperor. The inventor was forthwith summoned to Paris with his machine, and brought into the presence of the Emperor, who received him with the consideration due to his genius. The interview lasted two hours, during which Jacquard, placed at his ease by the Emperor's affability, explained to him the improvements which he proposed to make in the looms for weaving figured goods. The result was, that he was provided with apartments in the Conservatoire des

Arts et Métiers, where he had the use of the workshop during his stay, and was provided with a suitable allowance for his maintenance.

Installed in the Conservatoire, Jacquard proceeded to complete the details of his improved loom. He had the advantage of minutely inspecting the various exquisite pieces of mechanism contained in that great treasury of human ingenuity. Among the machines which more particularly attracted his attention, and eventually set him upon the track of his discovery, was a loom for weaving flowered silk, made by Vaucanson the celebrated automaton-maker.

Vaucanson was a man of the highest order of constructive genius. The inventive faculty was so strong in him that it may almost be said to have amounted to a passion, and could not be restrained. While a mere boy attending Sunday conversations with his mother, he amused himself by watching, through the chinks of a partition wall, part of the movements of a clock in the adjoining apartment. He endeavoured to understand them, and by brooding over the subject, after several months he discovered the principle of the escapement.

From that time the subject of mechanical invention took complete possession of him. With some rude tools which he contrived, he made a wooden clock that marked the hours with remarkable exactness; while he made for a miniature chapel the figures of some angels which waved their wings, and some priests that made several ecclesiastical movements.

Vaucanson, however, did not confine himself merely to the making of automata. By reason of his ingenuity, Cardinal de Fleury appointed him inspector of the silk manufactories of France; and he was no sooner in office, than with his usual irrepressible instinct to invent, he proceeded to introduce improvements in silk machinery. One of these was his mill for thrown silk, which so excited the anger of the Lyons operatives, who feared the loss of employment through its means, that they pelted him with stones and had nearly killed him. He nevertheless went on inventing, and next produced a machine for weaving flowered silks, with a contrivance for giving a dressing to the thread, so as to render that of each bobbin or skein of an equal thickness.

One of the chief features of Vaucanson's machine was a pierced cylinder which, according to the holes it presented when revolved, regulated the movement of certain needles, and caused the threads of the warp to deviate in such a manner as to produce a given design, though only of a simple character. Jacquard seized upon the suggestion with avidity, and, with the genius of the true inventor, at once proceeded to improve upon it. At the end of a month his weaving-machine was completed. To the cylinder of Vaucanson, he added an endless piece of pasteboard pierced with a number of holes, through which the threads of the warp were presented to the weaver; while another piece of mechanism indicated to the workman the colour of the shuttle which he ought to throw. Thus the drawboy and the reader of designs were both at once suspended. The first use Jacquard made of his new loom was to weave with it several yards of rich stuff which he presented to the Empress Josephine. Napoleon was highly gratified with the result of the inventor's labours, and ordered a number of the looms to be constructed by the best workmen, after Jacquard's model, and presented to him; after which he returned to Lyons.

There he experienced the frequent fate of inventors. He was regarded by his townsmen as an enemy, and treated by them as Kay, Hargreaves, and Arkwright had been in Lancashire. The workmen looked upon the new loom as fatal to their trade, and feared lest it should at once take the bread from their mouths. A tumultuous meeting was held on the Place des Terreaux, when it was determined to destroy the machines. This was however prevented by the military. But Jacquard was denounced and hanged in effigy. The *Conseil des prud'hommes* in vain endeavoured to allay the excitement, and they were themselves denounced. At length, carried away by the popular impulse, the *prud'hommes*, most of whom had been workmen and sympathized with the class, had one of Jacquard's looms carried off and publicly broken in pieces. Riots followed, in one of which Jacquard was dragged along the quay by an infuriated mob intending to drown him, but he was rescued.

The great value of the Jacquard loom, however, could not be denied, and its success was only a question of time. Jacquard was urged by some English silk manufacturers to pass over into England and settle there. But notwithstanding the harsh and cruel treatment he had received at the hands of his townspeople, his patriotism was too strong to permit him to accept their offer. The English manufacturers, however, adopted his loom. Then it was, and only then, that Lyons, threatened to be beaten out of the field, adopted it with eagerness; and before long the Jacquard machine was employed in nearly all kinds of weaving. The result proved that the fears of the workpeople had been entirely unfounded. Instead of diminishing employment, the Jacquard loom increased it at least tenfold. The number of persons occupied in the manufacture of figured goods in Lyons, was stated by M. Léon Faucher to have been 60,000 in 1833; and that number has since been considerably increased.

As for Jacquard himself, the rest of his life passed peacefully, excepting that the workpeople who dragged him along the quay to drown him were shortly after found eager to bear him in triumph along the same route in celebration of his birthday. But his modesty would not permit him to take part in such a demonstration. The Municipal Council of Lyons proposed to him that he should devote himself to improving his machine for the benefit of the local industry, to which Jacquard agreed in consideration of a moderate pension, the amount of which was fixed by himself. After perfecting his invention accordingly, he retired at sixty to end his days at Oullins, his father's native place. It was there that he received, in 1820, the decoration of the Legion of Honour; and it was there that he died and was buried in 1834. A statue was erected to his memory, but his relatives remained in poverty; and twenty years after his death, his two nieces were under the necessity of selling for a few hundred francs the gold medal bestowed upon their uncle by Louis XVIII. 'Such,' says a French writer, 'was the gratitude of the manufacturing interest of Lyons to the man to whom it owes so large a portion of its splendour.'

It would be easy to extend the martyrology of inventors, and to cite the names of other equally distinguished men who have, without any corresponding advantage to themselves, contributed to the industrial progress of the age – for it has too often happened that genius has planted the tree, of which patient dullness has gathered the fruit; but we will confine ourselves for the present to a brief account of an inventor of comparatively recent date, by way of illustration of the difficulties and privations which it is so frequently the lot of mechanical genius to surmount. We allude to Joshua Heilmann, the inventor of the combing-machine.

Heilmann was born in 1796 at Mulhouse, the principal seat of the

59

Alsace cotton manufacture. His father was engaged in that business; and Joshua entered his office at fifteen. He remained there for two years, employing his spare time in mechanical drawing. He afterwards spent two years in his uncle's banking-house in Paris, prosecuting the study of mathematics in the evenings. He became a student at the Conservatoire des Arts et Métiers, where he attended the lectures, and studied the machines in the museum. He also took practical lessons in turning from a toymaker. After some time, thus diligently occupied, he returned to Alsace, to superintend the construction of the machinery for the new factory at Vieux-Thann, which was shortly finished and set to work. The operations of the manufactory were, however, seriously affected by a commercial crisis which occurred, and it passed into other hands, on which Heilmann returned to his family at Mulhouse.

He had in the meantime been occupying much of his leisure with inventions, more particularly in connection with the weaving of cotton and the preparation of the staple for spinning. One of his earliest contrivances was an embroidering-machine, in which twenty needles were employed, working simultaneously; and he succeeded in accomplishing his object after about six months' labour. One of his most ingenious contrivances was his loom for weaving simultaneously two pieces of velvet or other piled fabric, united by the pile common to both, with a knife and traversing apparatus for separating the two fabrics when woven. But by far the most beautiful and ingenious of his inventions was the combing-machine, the history of which we now proceed shortly to describe.

Heilmann had for some years been diligently studying the contrivance of a machine for combing long-stapled cotton, the ordinary carding-machine being found ineffective in preparing the raw material for spinning, especially the finer sort of yarn, besides causing considerable waste. To avoid these imperfections, the cotton-spinners of Alsace offered a prize of 5,000 francs for an improved combing-machine, and Heilmann immediately proceeded to compete for the reward. He was not stimulated by the desire of gain, for he was comparatively rich, having acquired a considerable fortune by his wife. It was a saying of his that 'one will never accomplish great things who is constantly asking himself, how much gain will this bring me?' What mainly impelled him was the irrepressible instinct of the inventor, who no sooner has a mechanical problem set before him than he feels impelled to undertake its solution. The problem in this case was, however, much more difficult than he had anticipated.

While still struggling with poverty and difficulties, Heilmann's wife died, believing her husband ruined; and shortly after he proceeded to England and settled for a time at Manchester, still labouring at his machine. He had a model made for him by the eminent machine-makers, Sharpe, Roberts & Co.; but still he could not make it work satisfactorily, and he was at length brought almost to the verge of despair. He returned to France to visit his family, still pursuing his idea, which had obtained complete possession of his mind. While sitting by his hearth one evening, meditating upon the hard fate of inventors and the misfortunes in which their families so often become involved, he found himself almost unconsciously watching his daughters combing their long hair and drawing it out at full length between their fingers. The thought suddenly struck him that if he could successfully imitate in a machine the process of combing out the longest hair and forcing back the short by reversing the action of the comb, it might serve to extricate him from his difficulty.

Upon this idea he proceeded, introduced the apparently simple but really most intricate process of machine-combing, and after great labour he succeeded in perfecting the invention. The singular beauty of the process can only be appreciated by those who have witnessed the machine at work, when the similarity of its movements to that of combing the hair, which suggested the invention, is at once apparent. The machine has been described as 'acting with almost the delicacy of touch of the human fingers'. It combs the lock of cotton *at both ends*, places the fibres exactly parallel with each other, separates the long from the short, and unites the long fibres in one sliver and the short ones in another. In fine, the machine not only acts with the delicate accuracy of the human fingers, but apparently with the delicate intelligence of the human mind.

The chief commercial value of the invention consisted in its rendering the commoner sorts of cotton available for fine spinning. The manufacturers were thereby enabled to select the most suitable fibres for high-priced fabrics, and to produce the finer sorts of yarn in much larger quantities. It became possible by its means to make thread so fine that a length of 334 miles might be spun from a single pound weight of the prepared cotton, and, worked up into the finer sorts of lace, the original shilling's worth of cotton-wool, before it passed into the hands of the consumer, might thus be increased to the value of between £300 and £400 sterling.

The beauty and utility of Heilmann's invention were at once appreciated by the English cotton-spinners. Six Lancashire firms united and purchased the patent for cotton-spinning for England for the sum of £30,000; the wool-spinners paid the same sum for the privilege of applying the process to wool; and the Messrs Marshall, of Leeds, £20,000 for the privilege of applying it to flax. Thus wealth suddenly flowed in upon poor Heilmann at last. But he did not live to enjoy it. Scarcely had his long labours been crowned by success than he died, and his son, who had shared in his privations, shortly followed him.

It is at the price of lives such as these that the wonders of civilization are achieved.

3. Three Great Potters: Palissy, Böttgher, Wedgwood

It so happens that the history of pottery furnishes some of the most remarkable instances of patient perseverance to be found in the whole range of biography. Of these we select three of the most striking, as exhibited in the lives of Bernard Palissy, the Frenchman; Johann Friedrich Böttgher, the German; and Josiah Wedgwood, the Englishman.

Bernard Palissy is supposed to have been born in the south of France, in the diocese of Agen, about the year 1510. His father was probably a worker in glass, to which trade Bernard was brought up. His parents were poor people – too poor to give him the benefit of any school education. 'I had no other books,' said he afterwards, 'than heaven and earth, which are open to all.' He learnt, however, the art of glass-painting, to which he added that of drawing, and afterwards reading and writing.

When about eighteen years old, the glass trade becoming decayed, Palissy left his father's house, with his wallet on his back, and he went out into the world to search whether there was any place in it for him. He first travelled towards Gascony, working at his trade where he could find employment, and occasionally occupying part of his time in land-measuring. Then he travelled northwards, sojourning for various periods at different places in France, Flanders, and Lower Germany.

Thus Palissy occupied about ten more years of his life, after which he married, and ceased from his wanderings, settling down to practise glass-painting and land-measuring at the small town of Saintes, in the Lower Charente. Probably he felt capable of better things than drudging in an employment so precarious as glass-painting; and hence he was induced to turn his attention to the kindred art of painting and enamelling earthenware. Yet on this subject he was wholly ignorant; for he had never seen earth baked before he began his operations.

It was the sight of an elegant cup of Italian manufacture – most probably one of Luca della Robbia's make – which first set Palissy athinking about the new art. At first he could merely guess the materials

63

of which the enamel was composed; and he proceeded to try all manner of experiments to ascertain what they really were. He pounded all the substances which he supposed were likely to produce it. Then he bought common earthen pots, broke them into pieces, and, spreading his compounds over them, subjected them to the heat of a furnace which he erected for the purpose of baking them. His experiments failed; and the results were broken pots and a waste of fuel, drugs, time, and labour.

For many successive months and years Palissy pursued his experiments. The first furnace having proved a failure, he proceeded to erect another out of doors. There he burnt more wood, spoiled more drugs and pots, and lost more time, until poverty stared him and his family in the face. 'Thus,' said he, 'I fooled away several years, with sorrow and sighs, because I could not at all arrive at my intention.' In the intervals of his experiments he occasionally worked at his former callings, painting on glass, drawing portraits, and measuring land; but his earnings from these sources were very small. At length he was no longer able to carry on his experiments in his own furnace because of the heavy cost of fuel; but he bought more potsherds, broke them up as before into three or four hundred pieces, and, covering them with chemicals, carried them to a tile-work a league and a half distance from Saintes, there to be baked in an ordinary furnace. After the operation he went to see the pieces taken out; and, to his dismay, the whole of the experiments were failures. But though disappointed, he was not yet defeated; for he determined on the very spot to 'begin afresh'.

For two more years he went on experimenting without any satisfactory result, until the proceeds of his survey of the salt-marshes having become nearly spent, he was reduced to poverty again. But he resolved to make a last great effort; and he began by breaking more pots than ever. More than three hundred pieces of pottery covered with his compounds were sent to the glass-furnace; and thither he himself went to watch the results of the baking. Four hours passed, during which he watched; and then the furnace was opened. The material on *one* only of the three hundred pieces of potsherd had melted, and it was taken out to cool. As it hardened, it grew white – white and polished! The piece of potsherd was covered with white enamel, described by Palissy as 'singularly beautiful!' and beautiful it must no doubt have been in his eyes after all his weary waiting. He ran home with it to his wife, feeling himself, as he expressed it, quite a new creature. But the prize was not yet won – far from it. The partial success of this intended last effort merely had the effect of luring him on to a succession of further experiments and failures.

In order that he might complete the invention, which he now believed to be at hand, he resolved to build for himself a glass-furnace near his dwelling, where he might carry on his operations in secret. He proceeded to build the furnace with his own hands, carrying the bricks from the brick-field upon his back. He was bricklayer, labourer, and all. From seven to eight more months passed. At last the furnace was built and ready for use. Palissy had in the meantime fashioned a number of vessels of clay in readiness for the laying on of the enamel. After being subjected to a preliminary process of baking, they were covered with the enamel compound, and again placed in the furnace for the grand crucial experiment. Although his means were nearly exhausted, Palissy had been for some time accumulating a great store of fuel for the final effort; and he thought it was enough. At last the fire was lit, and the operation proceeded. All day he sat by the furnace, feeding it with fuel. He sat there watching and feeding all through the long night. But the enamel did not melt. The sun rose upon his labours. His wife brought him a portion of the scanty morning meal – for he would not stir from the furnace, into which he continued from time to time to heave more fuel. The second day passed, and still the enamel did not melt. The sun set, and another night passed. The pale, haggard, unshorn, baffled yet not beaten Palissy sat by his furnace eagerly looking for the melting of the enamel. A third day and night passed – a fourth, a fifth, and even a sixth – yes, for six long days and nights did the unconquerable Palissy watch and toil, fighting against hope; and still the enamel would not melt.

It then occurred to him that there might be some defect in the materials for the enamel – perhaps something wanting in the flux; so he set to work to pound and compound fresh materials for a new experiment. Thus two or three more weeks passed. But how to buy more pots? – for those which he had made with his own hands for the purposes of the first experiment were by long baking irretrievably spoilt for the purposes of a second. His money was now all spent; but he could borrow. His character was still good, though his wife and the neighbours thought him foolishly wasting his means in futile experiments. Nevertheless he succeeded. He borrowed sufficient from a friend to enable him to buy more fuel and more pots, and he was again ready for a further experiment. The pots were covered with the new compound, placed in the furnace, and the fire was again lit.

It was the last and most desperate experiment of the whole. The fire blazed up; the heat became intense; but still the enamel did not melt. The fuel began to run short! How to keep up the fire? There were the garden palings: these would burn. They must be sacrificed rather than that the great experiment should fail. The garden palings were pulled up and cast into the furnace. They were burnt in vain! The enamel had not yet melted. Ten minutes more heat might do it. Fuel must be had at whatever cost. There remained the household furniture and shelving. A crashing noise was heard in the house; and amidst the screams of his wife and children, who now feared Palissy's reason was giving way, the tables were seized, broken up, and heaved into the furnace. The enamel had not melted yet! There remained the shelving. Another noise of the wrenching of timber was heard within the house; and the shelves were torn down and hurled after the furniture into the fire. Wife and children then rushed from the house, and went frantically through the town, calling out that poor Palissy had gone mad, and was breaking up his very furniture for firewood!

For an entire month his shirt had not been off his back, and he was utterly worn out – wasted with toil, anxiety, watching, and want of food. He was in debt, and seemed on the verge of ruin. But he had at length mastered the secret; for the last great burst of heat had melted the enamel. The common brown household jars, when taken out of the furnace after it had become cool, were found covered with a white glaze! For this he could endure reproach, contumely, and scorn, and wait patiently for the opportunity of putting his discovery into practice as better days came round.

Palissy next hired a potter to make some earthen vessels after designs which he furnished; while he himself proceeded to model some medallions in clay for the purpose of enamelling them. But how to maintain himself and his family until the wares were made and ready for sale? Fortunately there remained one man in Saintes who still believed in the integrity, if not in the judgement, of Palissy – an inn-keeper, who agreed to feed and lodge him for six months, while he went on with his manufacture.

Palissy next erected an improved furnace, but he was so unfortunate as to build part of the inside with flints. When it was heated, these flints cracked and burst, and the spiculae were scattered over the pieces of pottery, sticking to them. Though the enamel came out right, the work was irretrievably spoilt, and thus six more months' labour was lost. Persons were found willing to buy the articles at a low price, notwithstanding the injury they had sustained; but Palissy would not sell them, considering that to have done so would be to 'decry and abase his honour'; and so he broke in pieces the entire batch.

At this stage of his affairs, Palissy became melancholy and almost helpless, and seems to have all but broken down. He wandered gloomily about the fields near Saintes, his clothes hanging in tatters, and himself worn to a skeleton. In a curious passage in his writings he describes how that the calves of his legs had disappeared and were no longer able with the help of garters to hold up his stockings, which fell about his heels when he walked. The family continued to reproach him for his recklessness, and his neighbours cried shame upon him for his obstinate folly. So he returned for a time to his former calling; and after about a year's diligent labour, during which he earned bread for his household and somewhat recovered his character among his neighbours, he again resumed his darling enterprise.

At last, after about sixteen years' labour, Palissy took heart and called himself potter. These sixteen years had been his term of apprenticeship to the art; during which he had wholly to teach himself, beginning at the very beginning. He was now able to sell his wares and thereby maintain his family in comfort. But he never rested satisfied with what he had accomplished. He proceeded from one step of improvement to another; always aiming at the greatest perfection possible. He studied natural objects for patterns, and with such success that the great Buffon spoke of him as 'so great a naturalist as Nature only can produce'. His ornamental pieces are now regarded as rare gems in the cabinets of virtuosi, and sell at almost fabulous prices. The ornaments on them are for the most part accurate models from life, of wild animals, lizards, and plants, found in the fields about Saintes, and tastefully combined as ornaments into the texture of a plate or vase. When Palissy had

67

reached the height of his art he styled himself 'Ouvrier de Terre et Inventeur des Rustics Figulines'.

The life of John Frederick Böttgher, the inventor of hard porcelain, presents a remarkable contrast to that of Palissy; though it also contains many points of singular and almost romantic interest. Böttgher was born at Schleiz, in the Voightland, in 1685, and at twelve years of age was placed apprentice with an apothecary at Berlin. He seems to have been early fascinated by chemistry, and occupied most of his leisure in making experiments. These for the most part tended in one direction – the art of converting common metals into gold. At the end of several years, Böttgher pretended to have discovered the universal solvent of the alchemists, and professed that he had made gold by its means. He exhibited its powers before his master, the apothecary Zörn, and by some trick or other succeeded in making him and several other witnesses believe that he had actually converted copper into gold.

The news spread abroad that the apothecary's apprentice had discovered the grand secret, and crowds collected about the shop to get a sight of the wonderful young 'gold-cook'. The king himself expressed a wish to see and converse with him, and when Frederick I was presented with a piece of the gold pretended to have been converted from copper, he was so dazzled with the prospect of securing an infinite quantity of it – Prussia being then in great straits for money – that he determined to secure Böttgher and employ him to make gold for him within the strong fortress of Spandau. But the young apothecary, suspecting the king's intention, and probably fearing detection, at once resolved on flight, and he succeeded in getting across the frontier into Saxony.

A reward of a thousand thalers was offered for Böttgher's apprehension, but in vain. He arrived at Wittenberg, and appealed for protection to the Elector of Saxony, Frederick Augustus I (King of Poland), surnamed 'the strong'. Frederick was himself very much in want of money at the time, and he was overjoyed at the prospect of obtaining gold in any quantity by the aid of the young alchemist. Böttgher was accordingly conveyed in secret to Dresden, accompanied by a royal escort. He had scarcely left Wittenberg when a battalion of Prussian grenadiers appeared before the gates demanding the gold-maker's extradition. But it was too late: Böttgher had already arrived in Dresden, where he was lodged in the Golden House, and treated with every consideration, though strictly watched and kept under guard.

The Elector, however, must needs leave him there for a time, having to depart forthwith to Poland, then almost in a state of anarchy. But, impatient for gold, he wrote to Böttgher from Warsaw, urging him to communicate the secret, so that he himself might practise the art of commutation. The young 'gold-cook', thus pressed, forwarded to Frederick a small phial containing 'a reddish fluid', which, it was asserted, changed all metals, when in a molten state, into gold. This important phial was taken in charge by the Prince Fürst von Fürsten-burg, who, accompanied by a regiment of Guards, hurried with it to Warsaw. Arrived there, it was determined to make immediate trial of the process. The king and the prince locked themselves up in a secret chamber of the palace, girt themselves about with leather aprons, and like true 'gold-cooks' set to work melting copper in a crucible and afterwards applying to it the red fluid of Böttgher. But the result was unsatisfactory; for notwithstanding all that they could do, the copper obstinately remained copper. On referring to the alchemist's instructions, however, the king found that, to succeed with the process, it was necessary that the fluid should be used 'in great purity of heart': and as His Majesty was conscious of having spent the evening in very bad company he attributed the failure of the experiment to that cause. A second trial was followed by no better results, and then the king became furious; for he had confessed and received absolution before beginning the second experiment.

Frederick Augustus now resolved on forcing Böttgher to disclose the golden secret, as the only means of relief from his urgent pecuniary difficulties. The alchemist, hearing of the royal intention, again determined to fly. He succeeded in escaping his guard, and, after three days' travel, arrived at Ens in Austria, where he thought himself safe. The agents of the Elector were, however, at his heels; they had tracked him to the 'Golden Stag', which they surrounded, and seizing him in his bed, notwithstanding his resistance and appeals to the Austrian authorities for help, they carried him by force to Dresden. From this time he was more strictly watched than ever, and he was shortly after transferred to the strong fortress of Köningstein. It was communicated to him that the royal exchequer was completely empty, and that ten regiments of Poles in arrears of pay were waiting for his gold. The king himself visited him, and told him in a severe tone that if he did not at once proceed to make gold, he would be hung! (*'Thu mir zurecht, Böttgher, sonst lass ich dich hangen.'*)

Years passed, and still Böttgher made no gold; but he was not hung. It was reserved for him to make a far more important discovery than the conversion of copper into gold, namely, the conversion of clay into porcelain. Some rare specimens of this ware had been brought by the Portuguese from China, which were sold for more than their weight in gold. Böttgher was first induced to turn his attention to the subject by Walter von Tschirnhaus, a maker of optical instruments, also an alchemist. Tschirnhaus was a man of education and distinction, and was held in much esteem by Prince Fürstenburg as well as by the Elector. He very sensibly said to Böttgher, still in fear of the gallows: 'If you can't make gold, try and do something else; make porcelain.'

The alchemist acted on the hint, and began his experiments, working night and day. He prosecuted his investigations for a long time with great assiduity, but without success. At length some red clay, brought to him for the purpose of making his crucibles, set him on the right track. He found that this clay, when submitted to a high temperature, became vitrified and retained its shape; and that its texture resembled that of porcelain, excepting in colour and opacity. He had in fact accidentally discovered red porcelain, and he proceeded to manufacture it and sell it as porcelain.

Böttgher was, however, well aware that the white colour was an essential property of true porcelain; and he therefore prosecuted his experiments in the hope of discovering the secret. Several years thus passed, but without success; until again accident stood his friend, and helped him to a knowledge of the art of making white porcelain. One day, in the year 1707, he found his perruque unusually heavy, and asked of his valet the reason. The answer was, that it was owing to the powder with which the wig was dressed, which consisted of a kind of earth then much used for hair powder. Böttgher's quick imagination immediately seized upon the idea. This white earthy powder might possibly be the very earth of which he was in search – at all events the opportunity must not be let slip of ascertaining what it really was. He was rewarded for his painstaking care and watchfulness, for he found, on experiment, that the principal ingredient of the hair-powder consisted of *kaolin*, the want of which had so long formed an insuperable difficulty in the way of his inquiries.

The discovery, in Böttgher's intelligent hands, led to great results, and proved of far greater importance than the discovery of the philosopher's stone would have been. In October 1707 he presented his first piece of porcelain to the Elector, who was greatly pleased with it; and it was resolved that Böttgher should be furnished with the means necessary for perfecting his invention. Having obtained a skilled workman from Delft, he began to *turn* porcelain with great success. He now entirely abandoned alchemy for pottery, and inscribed over the door of his workshop this distich:

> *Es machte Gott, der grosse Schöpfer,*
> *Aus einem Goldmacher einen Töpfer.*

Böttgher, however, was still under strict surveillance, for fear lest he should communicate his secret to others or escape the Elector's control. The new workshop and furnaces which were erected for him, were guarded by troops night and day, and six superior officers were made responsible for the personal security of the potter.

Böttgher's further experiments with his new furnaces proving very successful, and the porcelain which he manufactured being found to fetch large prices, it was next determined to establish a Royal Manufactory of porcelain. The manufacture of delft ware was known to have greatly enriched Holland. Why should not the manufacture of porcelain equally enrich the Elector? Accordingly, a decree went forth, dated 23 January 1710, for the establishment of 'a large manufactory of porcelain' at the Albrechtsburg in Meissen. In this decree, which was translated into Latin, French and Dutch, and distributed by the Ambassadors of the Elector at all the European Courts, Frederick Augustus set forth that to promote the welfare of Saxony, which had suffered much through the Swedish invasion, he had 'directed his attention to the subterranean treasures (*unterirdischen Schätze*)' of the country, and having employed some able persons in the investigation, they had succeeded in manufacturing 'a sort of red vessel (*eine Art rother Gefässe*) far superior to the Indian terra sigillata'; as also 'coloured ware and plates (*buntes Geschirr und Tafeln*) which may be cut, ground, and polished, and are quite equal to Indian vessels', and finally that 'specimens of white porcelain (*Proben von weisem Porzellan*)' had already been obtained, and it was hoped that this quality, too, would soon be manufactured in considerable quantities.

It has been stated in German publications that Böttgher, for the great services rendered by him to the Elector and to Saxony, was made Manager of the Royal Porcelain Works, and further promoted to the dignity of Baron. Doubtless he deserved these honours; but his treatment was of an altogether different character, for it was shabby, cruel, and inhuman. Two royal officials, named Matthieu and Nehmitz, were put over his head as directors of the factory, while he himself only held the position of foreman of potters, and at the same time was detained as the king's prisoner. During the erection of the factory at Meissen, while his assistance was still indispensable, he was conducted by soldiers to and from Dresden; and even after the works were finished, he was locked up nightly in his room. All this preyed upon his mind, and in repeated letters to the king he sought to obtain mitigation of his fate. Some of these letters are very touching. 'I will devote my whole soul to the art of making porcelain,' he writes on one occasion. 'I will do more than any inventor ever did before; only give me liberty, liberty!'

Böttgher at last fell seriously ill, and in May 1713 his dissolution was hourly expected. The king, alarmed at losing so valuable a slave, now gave him permission to take carriage exercise under a guard; and, having somewhat recovered, he was allowed occasionally to go to Dresden. In a letter written by the king in April 1714 Böttgher was promised his full liberty; but the offer came too late. Broken in body and mind, alternately working and drinking, though with occasional gleams of nobler intention, and suffering under constant ill-health, the result of his enforced confinement, Böttgher lingered on for a few years more, until death freed him from his sufferings on 13 March 1719 in the thirty-fifth year of his age. He was buried *at night* – as if he had been a dog – in the Johannis Cemetery of Meissen. Such was the treatment, and such the unhappy end, of one of Saxony's greatest benefactors.

The career of Josiah Wedgwood, the English potter, was less chequered and more prosperous than that of either Palissy or Böttgher, and his lot was cast in happier times. Down to the middle of the eighteenth century England was behind most other nations of the first order in Europe in respect of skilled industry. Although there were many potters in Staffordshire – and Wedgwood himself belonged to a numerous clan of potters of the same name – their productions were of the rudest kind, for the most part only plain brown ware, with the pattern scratched in while the clay was wet. The principal supply of the better articles of earthenware came from Delft in Holland, and of drinking stone pots from Cologne. Two foreign potters, the brothers Elers from Nuremberg, settled for a time in Staffordshire, and introduced an improved manufacture, but they shortly after removed to Chelsea, where they confined themselves to the manufacture of ornamental pieces. No porcelain capable of resisting a scratch with a hard point had yet been made in England; and for a long time the 'white ware' made in Staffordshire was not white, but of a dirty cream colour. Such, in a few words, was the condition of the pottery manufacture when Josiah Wedgwood was born at Burslem in 1730. By the time that he died, sixty-four years later, it had become completely changed. By his energy, skill, and genius, he established the trade upon a new and solid foundation; and, in the words of his epitaph, 'converted a rude and inconsiderable manufacture into an elegant art and an important branch of national commerce'.

Josiah Wedgwood was one of those indefatigable men who from time to time spring from the ranks of the common people, and by their energetic character not only practically educate the working population in habits of industry, but by the example of diligence and perseverance which they set before them, largely influence the public activity in all directions, and contribute in a great degree to form the national character. He was, like Arkwright, the youngest of a family of thirteen children. His grandfather and granduncle were both potters, as was also his father, who died when he was a mere boy, leaving him a patrimony of twenty pounds. He had learned to read and write at the village school; but on the death of his father he was taken from it and set to work as a 'thrower' in a small pottery carried on by his elder brother. There he began life, his working life, to use his own words, 'at the lowest round of the ladder', when only eleven years old.

When he had completed his apprenticeship with his brother, Josiah joined partnership with another workman, and carried on a small business in making knife-hafts, boxes, and sundry articles for domestic

73

use. Another partnership followed, when he proceeded to make melon table plates, green pickle leaves, candlesticks, snuff boxes, and such like articles; but he made comparatively little progress until he began business on his own account at Burslem in the year 1759. There he diligently pursued his calling, introduced new articles to the trade, and gradually extending his business. What he chiefly aimed at was to manufacture cream-coloured ware of a better quality than was then produced in Staffordshire as regarded shape, colour, glaze, and durability. To understand the subject thoroughly, he devoted his leisure to the study of chemistry; and he made numerous experiments on fluxes, glazes, and various sorts of clay. Being a close inquirer and accurate observer, he noticed that a certain earth containing silica, which was black before calcination, became white after exposure to the heat of a furnace. This fact, observed and pondered on, led to the idea of mixing silica with the red powder of the potteries, and to the discovery that the mixture becomes white when calcined. He had but to cover this material with a vitrification of transparent glaze, to obtain one of the most important products of fictile art – that which, under the name of English earthenware, was to attain the greatest commercial value and become of the most extensive utility.

Wedgwood was for some time much troubled by his furnaces, though nothing like to the same extent that Palissy was; and he overcame his difficulties in the same way – by repeated experiments and unfaltering perseverance. His first attempts at making porcelain for table use were a succession of disastrous failures – the labours of months being often destroyed in a day. It was only after a long series of trials, in the course of which he lost time, money, and labour, that he arrived at the proper sort of glaze to be used; but he would not be denied, and at last he conquered success through patience. The improvement of pottery became his passion, and was never lost sight of for a moment. Even when he had mastered his difficulties, and become a prosperous man – manufacturing white stone ware and cream-coloured ware in large quantities for home and foreign use – he went forward perfecting his manufactures, until his example extending in all directions, the action of the entire district was stimulated, and a great branch of British industry was eventually established on firm foundations. He aimed throughout at the highest excellence, declaring his determination 'to give over manufacturing any article, whatsoever it might be, rather than to degrade it'.

The result of Wedgwood's labours was, that the manufacture of pottery, which he found in the very lowest conditions, became one of the staples of England; and instead of importing what we needed for home use from abroad, we became large exporters to other countries, supplying them with earthenware even in the face of enormous prohibitory duties on articles of British produce.

4. Application and Perseverance

Fortune has often been blamed for her blindness; but fortune is not so blind as men are. Those who look into practical life will find that fortune is usually on the side of the industrious, as the winds and waves are on the side of the best navigators. In the pursuit of even the highest branches of human inquiry the commoner qualities are found the most useful – such as common sense, attention, application, and perseverance. Genius may not be necessary, though even genius of the highest sort does not disdain the use of these ordinary qualities. The very greatest men have been among the least believers in the power of genius, and as worldly wise and persevering as successful men of the commoner sort. Some have even defined genius to be only common sense intensified. A distinguished teacher and president of a college spoke of it as the power of making efforts. John Foster held it to be the power of lighting one's own fire. Buffon said of genius 'it is patience'.

Newton's was unquestionably a mind of the very highest order, and yet, when asked by what means he had worked out his extraordinary discoveries, he modestly answered, 'By always thinking unto them.' At another time he thus expressed his method of study: 'I keep the subject continually before me, and wait till the first dawnings open slowly by little and little into a full and clear light.' It was in Newton's case, as in every other, only by diligent application and perseverance that his great reputation was achieved. Even his recreation consisted in change of study, laying down one subject to take up another. To Dr Bentley he said: 'If I have done the public any service, it is due to nothing but industry and patient thought.' So Kepler, another great philosopher, speaking of his studies and his progress, said: 'As in Virgil, *Fama mobilitate viget, vires acquirit eundo*, so it was with me, that the diligent thought on these things was the occasion of still further thinking; until at last I brooded with the whole energy of my mind upon the subject.'

The extraordinary results effected by dint of sheer industry and perseverance, have led many distinguished men to doubt whether the gift of genius be so exceptional an endowment as it is usually supposed to be. Thus Voltaire held that it is only a very slight line of separation that divides the man of genius from the man of ordinary mould. Beccaria was even of opinion that all men might be poets and orators, and Reynolds that they might be painters and sculptors. If this were really so, that stolid Englishman might not have been so very far wrong after all, who, on Canova's death, inquired of his brother whether it was 'his intention to carry on the business'! Locke, Helvetius and Diderot believed that all men have an equal aptitude for genius, and that what some are able to effect, under the laws which regulate the operations of the intellect, must also be within the reach of others who, under like circumstances, apply themselves to like pursuits. But while admitting to the fullest extent the wonderful achievements of labour and recognizing the fact that men of the most distinguished genius have invariably been found the most indefatigable workers, it must nevertheless be sufficiently obvious that, without the original endowment of heart and brain, no amount of labour, however well applied, could have produced a Shakespeare, a Newton, a Beethoven, or a Michael Angelo.

Dalton, the chemist, repudiated the notion of his being 'a genius', attributing everything which he had accomplished to simple industry and accumulation. John Hunter said of himself, 'My mind is like a beehive; but full as it is of buzz and apparent confusion, it is yet full of order and regularity, and food collected with incessant industry from the choicest of nature.' We have, indeed, but to glance at the biographies of great men to find that the most distinguished inventors, artists, thinkers, and workers of all kinds, owe their success, in a great measure, to their indefatigable industry and application.

Progress, however, of the best kind, is comparatively slow. Great results cannot be achieved at once; and we must be satisfied to advance in life as we walk, step by step. De Maistre says that 'to know *how to wait* is the great secret of success'. We must sow before we can reap, and often have to wait long, content meanwhile to look patiently forward in hope; the fruit best worth waiting for often ripening the slowest. But 'time and patience', says the Eastern proverb, 'change the mulberry leaf to satin'.

To wait patiently, however, men must work cheerfully. Cheerfulness is an excellent working quality, imparting great elasticity to the character. Sydney Smith, when labouring as a parish priest at Foston-le-Clay, in Yorkshire – though he did not feel himself to be in his proper element – went cheerfully to work in the firm determination to do his best. 'I am resolved,' he said, 'to like it and reconcile myself to it, which is more manly than to feign myself above it, and to send up complaints by the post of being thrown away, and being desolate, and such like trash.' So Dr Hook, when leaving Leeds for a new sphere of labour, said, 'Wherever I may be, I shall, by God's blessing, do with my might what my hand findeth to do; and if I do not find work, I shall make it.'

One of the most cheerful and courageous, because one of the most hopeful of workers, was Carey, the missionary. When in India, it was no uncommon thing for him to weary out three pundits, who officiated as his clerks, in one day, he himself taking rest only in change of employment. Carey, the son of a shoemaker, was supported in his labours by Ward, the son of a carpenter, and Marsham, the son of a weaver. By their labours, a magnificent college was erected at Seram-pore; sixteen flourishing stations were established; the Bible was trans-lated into sixteen languages, and the seeds were sown of a beneficent moral revolution in British India. Carey was never ashamed of the humbleness of his origin. On one occasion, when at the Governor-General's table he overheard an officer opposite him asking another, loud enough to be heard, whether Carey had not once been a shoemaker: 'No, sir,' exclaimed Carey immediately; 'only a cobbler.'

It was a maxim of Dr Young the philosopher that 'Any man can do what any other man has done'; and it is unquestionable that he himself never recoiled from any trials to which he determined to subject himself. It is related of him, that the first time he mounted a horse, he was in company with the grandson of Mr Barclay of Ury, the well-known sportsman; when the horseman who preceded them leapt a high fence, Young wished to imitate him, but fell off his horse in the attempt. Without saying a word, he remounted, made a second effort, and was again unsuccessful, but this time he was not thrown further than on to the horse's neck, to which he clung. At the third trial, he succeeded, and cleared the fence.

The accidental destruction of Sir Isaac Newton's papers, by his little dog 'Diamond' upsetting a lighted taper upon his desk, by which the elaborate calculations of many years were in a moment destroyed, is a well-known anecdote, and need not be repeated: it is said that the loss caused the philosopher such profound grief that it seriously injured his health, and impaired his understanding. An accident of a somewhat similar kind happened to the MS. of Mr Carlyle's first volume of his *French Revolution*. He had lent the MS. to a literary neighbour to peruse. By some mischance, it had been left lying on the parlour floor, and became forgotten. Weeks ran on, and the historian sent for his work, the printers being loud for 'copy'. Inquiries were made, and it was found that the maid-of-all-work, finding what she conceived to be a bundle of waste paper on the floor, had used it to light the kitchen and parlour fires with! Such was the answer returned to Mr Carlyle; and his feelings may be imagined. There was, however, no help for him but to set resolutely to work to re-write the book; and he turned to and did it. He had no draft, and was compelled to rake up from his memory facts, ideas, and expressions, which had been long dismissed.

The lives of eminent inventors are eminently illustrative of the same quality of perseverance. George Stephenson, when addressing young men, was accustomed to sum up his best advice to them in the words, 'Do as I have done – persevere.' He had worked at the improvement of his locomotive for some fifteen years before achieving his decisive victory at Rainhill; and Watt was engaged for some thirty years upon the condensing-engine before he brought it to perfection. But there are equally striking illustrations of perseverance to be found in every other branch of science, art and industry. Perhaps one of the most interesting is that connected with the disentombment of the Nineveh marbles, and the discovery of the long-lost cuneiform or arrow-headed character in which the inscriptions on them are written – a kind of writing which had been lost to the world since the period of the Macedonian conquest of Persia.

An intelligent cadet of the East India Company, stationed at Kermanshah, in Persia, had observed the curious cuneiform inscriptions on the old monuments in the neighbourhood – so old that all historical traces of them had been lost – and amongst the inscriptions which he copied was that on the celebrated rock of Behistun – a perpendicular rock rising abruptly some 1,700 feet from the plain, the lower part bearing inscriptions for the space of about 300 feet in three languages – Persian, Scythian and Assyrian. Comparison of the known with the unknown, of the language which survived with the language that had been lost, enabled this cadet to acquire some knowledge of the cuneiform character, and even to form an alphabet. Mr (afterwards Sir Henry) Rawlinson sent his tracings home for examination. No professors in colleges as yet knew anything of the cuneiform character; but there was a ci-devant clerk of the East India House – a modest unknown man of the name of Norris – who had made this little understood subject his study, to whom the tracings were submitted; and so accurate was his knowledge, that, though he had never seen the Behistun rock, he pronounced that the cadet had not copied the puzzling inscription with proper exactness. Rawlinson, who was still in the neighbourhood of the rock, compared his copy with the original, and found that Norris was right; and by further comparison and careful study the knowledge of the cuneiform writing was thus greatly advanced.

But to make the learning of these two self-taught men of avail, a third labourer was necessary in order to supply them with material for the exercise of their skill. Such a labourer presented himself in the person of Austen Layard, originally an articled clerk in the office of a London solicitor. One would scarcely have expected to find in these three men, a cadet, an India House clerk, and a lawyer's clerk, the discoverers of a forgotten language, and of the buried history of Babylon; yet it was so. Layard was a youth of only twenty-two, travelling in the East, when he was possessed with a desire to penetrate the regions beyond the Euphrates. Accompanied by a single companion, trusting to his arms for protection, and, what was better, to his cheerfulness, politeness, and chivalrous bearing, he passed safely amidst tribes at deadly war with each other; and, after the lapse of many years, with comparatively slender means at his command, but aided by application and persever-ance, resolute will and purpose, and almost sublime patience – borne up throughout by his passionate enthusiasm for discovery and research – he succeeded in laying bare and digging up an amount of historical treasures, the like of which has probably never before been collected by the industry of any one man.

The career of the Comte de Buffon presents another remarkable illustration of the power of patient industry, as well as of his own saying, that 'Genius is patience'. Notwithstanding the great results achieved by him in natural history, Buffon, when a youth, was regarded as of mediocre talents. His mind was slow in forming itself, and slow in reproducing what it had acquired. He was also constitutionally indolent; and being born to good estate, it might be supposed that he would indulge his liking for ease and luxury. Instead of which, he early formed the resolution of denying himself pleasure, and devoting himself to study and self-culture. Regarding time as a treasure that was limited, and finding that he was losing many hours by lying abed in the morning, he determined to break himself of the habit. He struggled hard against it for some time, but failed in being able to rise at the hour he had fixed. He then called his servant, Joseph, to his help, and promised him the reward of a crown every time that he succeeded in getting him up before six. At first, when called, Buffon declined to rise – pleaded that he was ill, or pretended anger at being disturbed; and on the Count at length getting up, Joseph found that he had earned nothing but reproaches for having permitted his master to lie abed contrary to his express orders. At length the valet determined to earn his crown; and again and again he forced Buffon to rise, notwithstanding his entreaties, expostulations, and threats of immediate discharge from his service. One morning Buffon was unusually obstinate, and Joseph found it necessary to resort to the extreme measure of dashing a basin of ice-cold water under the bed-clothes, the effect of which was instantaneous. By the persistent use of such means, Buffon at length conquered his habit; and he was accustomed to say that he owed to Joseph three or four volumes of his Natural History.

For forty years of his life, Buffon worked every morning at his desk from nine till two, and again in the evening from five till nine. His diligence was so continuous and so regular that it became habitual. His biographer has said of him, 'Work was his necessity; his studies were the charm of his life; and towards the last term of his glorious career he frequently said that he still hoped to be able to consecrate to them a few more years.' He was a most conscientious worker, always studying to give the reader his best thoughts, expressed in the very best manner. He was never wearied with touching and retouching his compositions, so that his style may be pronounced almost perfect. He wrote the *Epoques de la Nature* not fewer than eleven times before he was satisfied with it; although he had thought over the work about fifty years. He was a thorough man of business, most orderly in everything; and he was accustomed to say that genius without order lost three-fourths of its power.

Literary life affords abundant illustrations of the same power of perseverance; and perhaps no career is more instructive, viewed in this light, than that of Sir Walter Scott. His admirable working qualities were trained in the lawyer's office, where he pursued for many years a sort of drudgery scarcely above that of a copying clerk. His daily dull routine made his evenings, which were his own, all the more sweet; and he generally devoted them to reading and study. He himself attributed to his prosaic office discipline that habit of steady, sober diligence, in which mere literary men are so often found wanting. As a copying clerk he was allowed 3d. for every page containing a certain number of words; and he sometimes, by extra work, was able to copy as many as 120 pages in twenty-four hours, thus earning some 30s.; out of which he would occasionally purchase an odd volume, otherwise beyond his means.

During his later life Scott was wont to pride himself upon being a man of business, and he averred, in contradiction to what he called the cant of sonneteers, that there was no necessary connection between genius and an aversion or contempt for the common duties of life. On the contrary, he was of opinion that to spend some fair portion of every day in any matter-of-fact occupation was good for the higher faculties themselves in the upshot. While afterwards acting as clerk to the Court of Session in Edinburgh, he performed his literary work chiefly before breakfast, attending the court during the day, where he authenticated registered deeds and writings of various kinds. On the whole, says Lockhart, 'it forms one of the most remarkable features in his history, that throughout the most active period of his literary career, he must have devoted a large proportion of his hours, during half at least of every year, to the conscientious discharge of professional duties'. It was a principle of action which he laid down for himself, that he must earn his living by business, and not by literature.

His punctuality was one of the most carefully cultivated of his habits, otherwise it had not been possible for him to get through so enormous an amount of literary labour. He made it a rule to answer every letter received by him on the same day, except where inquiry and deliberation were requisite. Nothing else could have enabled him to keep abreast with the flood of communications that poured in upon him and sometimes put his good nature to the severest test. It was his practice to rise by five o'clock, and light his own fire. He shaved and dressed with deliberation, and was seated at his desk by six o'clock, with his papers arranged before him in the most accurate order, his works of reference marshalled round him on the floor, while at least one favourite dog lay watching his eye, outside the line of books. Thus by the time the family assembled for breakfast, between nine and ten, he had done enough – to use his own words – to break the neck of the day's work. But with all his diligent and indefatigable industry, and his immense knowledge, the result of many years' patient labour, Scott always spoke with the greatest diffidence of his own powers. On one occasion he said, 'Throughout every part of my career I have felt pinched and hampered by my own ignorance.'

The lives of second-rate literary men furnish equally remarkable illustrations of the powers of perseverance. John Britton, author of *The Beauties of England and Wales*, and of many valuable architectural works, was born in a miserable cot in Kingston, Wiltshire. His father had been a baker and maltster, but was ruined in trade and became insane while Britton was yet a child. The boy received very little schooling, but a great deal of bad example, which happily did not corrupt him. He was early in life set to labour with an uncle, a tavern-keeper in Clerkenwell, under whom he bottled, corked, and binned wine for more than five years. His health failing him, his uncle turned him adrift in the world, with only two guineas, the fruits of his five years' service, in his pocket. During the next seven years of his life he endured many vicissitudes and hardships. Travelling on foot to Bath, he there obtained an engagement as a cellarman, but shortly after we find him back in the metropolis again almost penniless, shoeless, and shirtless. He succeeded, however, in obtaining employment as a cellarman at the London Tavern, where it was his duty to be in the cellar from seven in the morning until eleven at night. His health broke down under his confinement in the dark, added to the heavy work; and he then engaged himself, at fifteen shillings a week, to an attorney – for he had been diligently cultivating the art of writing during the few spare minutes that he could call his own. Then he shifted to another office, at the advanced wages of twenty shillings a week, still reading and studying. At twenty-eight he was able to write a book, which he

83

published under the title of *The Enterprising Adventures of Pizarro*; and from that time until his death, during a period of about fifty-five years, Britton was occupied in laborious literary occupation. The number of his published works is not fewer than eighty-seven; the most important being *The Cathedral Antiquities of England*, in fourteen volumes, a truly magnificent work; itself the best monument of John Britton's indefatigable industry.

Loudon, the landscape gardener, was a man of somewhat similar character, possessed of an extraordinary working power. The son of a farmer near Edinburgh, he was early inured to work. His skill in drawing plans and making sketches of scenery induced his father to train him for a landscape gardener. During his apprenticeship he sat up two whole nights every week to study; yet he worked harder during the day than any labourer. In the course of his night studies he learnt French, and before he was eighteen he translated a life of Abelard for an encyclopaedia. He was so eager to make progress in life, that when only twenty, while working as a gardener in England, he wrote down in his note-book, 'I am now twenty years of age, and perhaps a third part of my life has passed away, and yet what have I done to benefit my fellow men?' an unusual reflection for a youth of only twenty. From French he proceeded to learn German, and rapidly mastered that language. Having taken a large farm, for the purpose of introducing Scotch improvements in the art of agriculture, he shortly succeeded in realizing a considerable income. The continent being thrown open at the end of the war, he travelled abroad for the purpose of inquiring into the system of gardening and agriculture in other countries. He twice repeated his journeys, and the results were published in his encyclopaedias, which are among the most remarkable works of their kind – distinguished for the immense mass of useful matter which they contain, collected by an amount of industry and labour which has rarely been equalled.

The career of Samuel Drew is not less remarkable than any of those which we have cited. His father was a hard-working labourer of the parish of St Austell, in Cornwall. Though poor, he contrived to send his two sons to a penny-a-week school in the neighbourhood. Jabez, the elder, took delight in learning, and made great progress in his lessons; but Samuel, the younger, was a dunce, notoriously given to mischief and playing truant. At ten he was apprenticed to a shoemaker, and while in this employment he endured much hardship – living, as he used to say, 'like a toad under a harrow'. When about seventeen, before his apprenticeship was out, he ran away, intending to enter on board a man-of-war; but sleeping in a hay-field at night cooled him a little, and he returned to his trade.

Drew next removed to the neighbourhood of Plymouth to work at his shoemaking business, and while at Cawsand he won a prize for cudgel-playing, in which he seems to have been an adept. While living there, he had nearly lost his life in a smuggling exploit which he had joined, partly induced by the love of adventure and partly by the love of gain, for his regular wages were not more than eight shillings a week.

This was a very unpromising beginning of a life; and yet this same Drew, scapegrace, orchard-robber, shoemaker, cudgel-player, and smuggler, outlived the recklessness of his youth, and became distinguished as a minister of the Gospel and a writer of good books. Happily, before it was too late, the energy which characterized him was turned into a more healthy direction, and rendered him as eminent in usefulness as he had before been in wickedness. His father again took him back to St Austell, and found employment for him as a journeyman shoemaker. Speaking of himself, about that time, Drew afterwards said, 'The more I read, the more I felt my own ignorance; and the more I felt my ignorance the more invincible became my energy to surmount it. Every leisure moment was now employed in reading one thing or another. Having to support myself by manual labour, my time for reading was but little, and to overcome this disadvantage, my usual method was to place a book before me while at meat, and at every repast I read five or six pages.' The perusal of Locke's *Essay on the Understanding* gave the first metaphysical turn to his mind. 'It awakened me from my stupor,' said he, 'and induced me to form a resolution to abandon the grovelling views which I had been accustomed to entertain.'

Drew began business on his own account, with a capital of a few shillings; but his character for steadiness was such that a neighbouring miller offered him a loan, which was accepted, and, success attending his industry, the debt was repaid at the end of a year. He started with a determination to 'owe no man anything', and he held to it in the midst of many privations. Often he went to bed supperless, to avoid rising in debt. His ambition was to achieve independence by industry and

85

economy, and in this he gradually succeeded. In the midst of incessant labour, he sedulously strove to improve his mind, studying astronomy, history, and metaphysics.

Added to his labours in shoemaking and metaphysics, Drew became a local preacher and a class leader. He took an eager interest in politics, and his shop became a favourite resort with the village politicians. And when they did not come to him, he went to them to talk over public affairs. This so encroached upon his time that he found it necessary sometimes to work until midnight to make up for the hours lost during the day.

His literary taste first took the direction of poetical composition; and from some of the fragments which have been preserved, it appears that his speculations as to the immateriality and immortality of the soul had their origin in these poetical musings. His study was the kitchen, where his wife's bellows served him for a desk; and he wrote amidst the cries and cradlings of his children. Various pamphlets from his pen shortly appeared in rapid succession, and a few years later, while still working at shoemaking, he wrote and published his admirable *Essay on the Immateriality and Immortality of the Human Soul*, which he sold for twenty pounds, a great sum in his estimation at the time. The book went through many editions, and is still prized.

Drew was in no wise puffed up by his success, as many young writers are, but, long after he had become celebrated as a writer, used to be seen sweeping the street before his door, or helping his apprentice to carry in the winter's coals. Towards the close of his career, he said of himself – 'Raised from one of the lowest stations in society, I have endeavoured through life to bring my family into a state of respectability, by honest industry, frugality, and a high regard for my moral character. Divine providence has smiled on my exertions, and crowned my wishes with success.'

Joseph Hume pursued a very different career, but worked in an equally persevering spirit. He was a man of moderate parts, but of great industry and unimpeachable honesty of purpose. The motto of his life was 'Perseverance', and well he acted up to it. His father dying while he was a mere child, his mother opened a small shop in Montrose, and toiled hard to maintain her family and bring them up respectably. Joseph she put apprentice to a surgeon, and educated for the medical profession. Having got his diploma, he made several voyages to India, as ship's surgeon, and afterwards obtained a cadetship in the Company's service. None worked harder, or lived more temperately, than he did; and, securing the confidence of his superiors, who found him a capable man in the performance of his duty, they gradually promoted him to higher offices. In 1803 he was with the division of the army under General Powell, in the Mahratta war; and the interpreter having died, Hume, who had meanwhile studied and mastered the native languages, was appointed in his stead. He was next made chief of the medical staff. But as if this were not enough to occupy his full working power, he undertook in addition the offices of paymaster and postmaster, and filled them satisfactorily. He also contracted to supply the commissariat, which he did with advantage to the army and profit to himself.

But Joseph Hume was not a man to enjoy the fruits of his industry in idleness. Work and occupation had become necessary for his comfort and happiness. To make himself fully acquainted with the actual state of his own country, and the condition of the people, he visited every town in the kingdom which then enjoyed any degree of manufacturing celebrity. He afterwards travelled abroad for the purpose of obtaining a knowledge of foreign states. Returned to England, he entered Parliament in 1812, and continued a member of that assembly, with a short interruption, for a period of about thirty-four years. His first recorded speech was on the subject of public education, and throughout his long and honourable career he took an active and earnest interest in that and all other questions calculated to elevate and improve the condition of the people – criminal reform, savings-banks, free trade, economy and retrenchment, extended representation, and such like measures, all of which he indefatigably promoted. Whatever subject he undertook, he worked at with all his might. He was not a good speaker, but what he said was believed to proceed from the lips of an honest, single-minded, accurate man.

5. Helps and Opportunities: Scientific Pursuits

Accident does very little towards the production of any great result in life. Though sometimes what is called 'a happy hit' may be made by a bold venture, the common highway of steady industry and application is the only safe road to travel. It is said of the landscape painter Wilson, that when he had nearly finished a picture in a tame, correct manner, he would step back from it, his pencil fixed at the end of a long stick, and after gazing earnestly on the work, he would suddenly walk up and by a few bold touches give a brilliant finish to the painting. But it will not do for every one who would produce an effect, to throw his brush at the canvas in the hope of producing a picture. The capability of putting in these last vital touches is acquired only by the labour of a life; and the probability is, that the artist who has not carefully trained himself beforehand, in attempting to produce a brilliant effect at a dash, will only produce a blotch.

Sedulous attention and painstaking industry always mark the true worker. The greatest men are not those who 'despise the day of small things', but those who improve them most carefully. Michael Angelo was one day explaining to a visitor at his studio, what he had been doing at a statue since his previous visit. 'I have retouched this part – polished that – softened this feature – brought out that muscle – given some expression to this lip, and more energy to that limb.' 'But these are trifles,' remarked the visitor. 'It may be so,' replied the sculptor, 'but recollect that trifles make perfection, and perfection is no trifle.' So it was said of Nicolas Poussin, the painter, that the rule of his conduct was, that 'whatever was worth doing at all was worth doing well'; and when asked, late in life, by his friend Vigneul de Marville, by what means he had gained so high a reputation among the painters of Italy, Poussin emphatically answered, 'Because I have neglected nothing.'

Although there are discoveries which are said to have been made by accident, if carefully inquired into, it will be found that there has really been very little that was accidental about them. For the most part, these so-called accidents have only been opportunities carefully improved by genius. The fall of the apple at Newton's feet has often been quoted in proof of the accidental character of some discoveries. But Newton's whole mind had already been devoted for years to the laborious and patient investigation of the subject of gravitation; and the circumstance of the apple falling before his eyes was suddenly apprehended only as genius could apprehend it, and served to flash upon him the brilliant discovery then opening to his sight. In like manner, the brilliantly coloured soap-bubbles blown from a common tobacco pipe – though 'trifles light as air' in most eyes – suggested to Dr Young his beautiful theory of 'interferences', and led to his discovery relating to the diffraction of light. Although great men are popularly supposed only to deal with great things, men such as Newton and Young were ready to detect the significance of the most familiar and simple facts; their greatness consisting mainly in their wise interpretation of them.

The difference between men consists, in a great measure, in the intelligence of their observation. Many before Galileo had seen a suspended weight swing before their eyes with a measured beat; but he was the first to detect the value of the fact. One of the vergers in the cathedral at Pisa, after replenishing with oil a lamp which hung from the roof, left it swinging to and fro; and Galileo, then a youth of only eighteen, noting it attentively, conceived the idea of applying it to the measurement of time. Fifty years of study and labour, however, elapsed before he completed the invention of his pendulum – the importance of which, in the measurement of time and in astronomical calculations, can scarcely be overrated. In like manner, Galileo, having casually heard that one Lippershey, a Dutch spectacle-maker, had presented to Count Maurice of Nassau an instrument by means of which distant objects appeared nearer to the beholder, addressed himself to the cause of such a phenomenon, which led to the invention of the telescope, and proved the beginning of the modern science of astronomy. Discoveries such as these could never have been made by a negligent observer, or by a mere passive listener.

While Captain (afterwards Sir Samuel) Brown was occupied in studying the construction of bridges, with the view of contriving one of a cheap description to be thrown across the Tweed, near which he lived, he was walking in his garden one dewy autumn morning, when he saw a tiny spider's net suspended across his path. The idea immediately occurred to him, that a bridge of iron ropes or chains might be constructed in like manner, and the result was the invention of his suspension bridge. So James Watt, when consulted about the mode of carrying water by pipes under the Clyde, along the unequal bed of the river, turned his attention one day to the shell of a lobster presented at table; and from that model he invented an iron tube, which, when laid down, was found effectually to answer the purpose. Sir Isambard Brunel took his first lessons in forming the Thames Tunnel from the tiny shipworm: he saw how the little creature perforated the wood with its well-armed head, first in one direction and then in another, till the archway was complete, and then daubed over the roof and sides with a kind of varnish; and by copying this work exactly on a large scale, Brunel was at length enabled to construct his shield and accomplish his great engineering work.

It is the close observation of little things which is the secret of success in business, in art, in science; and in every pursuit in life. Human knowledge is but an accumulation of small facts, made by successive generations of men, the little bits of knowledge and experience carefully treasured up by them growing at length into a mighty pyramid. Though many of these facts and observations seemed in the first instance to have but slight significance, they are all found to have their eventual uses, and to fit into their proper places. Even many speculations seemingly remote, turn out to be the basis of results the most obviously practical.

When Franklin made his discovery of the identity of lightning and electricity, it was sneered at, and people asked, 'Of what use is it?' To which his reply was, 'What is the use of a child? It may become a man!' When Galvani discovered that a frog's leg twitched when placed in contact with different metals, it could scarcely have been imagined that so apparently insignificant a fact could have led to important results. Yet therein lay the germ of the electric telegraph, which binds the intelligence of continents together, and, probably before many years have elapsed, will 'put a girdle round the globe'. So too, little bits of stone and fossil, dug out of the earth, intelligently interpreted, have issued in the science of geology and the practical operations of mining, in which large capitals are invested and vast numbers of persons profitably employed.

It is said that the Marquis of Worcester's attention was first accidentally directed to the subject of steam power by the tight cover of a vessel containing hot water having been blown off before his eyes, when confined a prisoner in the Tower. He published the results of his observations in his *Century of Inventions*, which formed a sort of text-book for inquirers into the powers of steam for a time, until Savery, Newcomen, and others, applying it to practical purposes, brought the steam-engine to the state in which Watt found it when called upon to repair a model of Newcomen's engine, which belonged to the University of Glasgow. This accidental circumstance was an opportunity for Watt, which he was not slow to improve; and it was the labour of his life to bring the steam-engine to perfection.

This art of seizing opportunities and turning even accidents to account, bending them to some purpose, is a great secret of success. Dr Johnson has defined genius to be 'a mind of large general powers accidentally determined in some particular direction'. Men who are resolved to find a way for themselves will always find opportunities enough; and if they do not lie ready to their hand, they will make them. It is not those who have enjoyed the advantages of colleges, museums, and public galleries that have accomplished the most for science and art; nor have the greatest mechanics and inventors been trained in mechanics' institutes. Necessity, oftener than facility, has been the mother of invention; and the most prolific school of all has been the school of difficulty. Some of the very best workmen have had the most indifferent tools to work with. But it is not tools that make the workman, but the trained skill and perseverance of the man himself. Indeed it is proverbial that the bad workman never yet had a good tool. Some one asked Opie by what wonderful process he mixed his colours. 'I mix them with my brains, sir,' was his reply. It is the same with every workman who would excel. Ferguson made marvellous things – such as his wooden clock, that accurately measured the hours – by means of a common penknife, a tool in everybody's hand; but then everybody is not a Ferguson. A pan of water and two thermometers were the tools by which Dr Black discovered latent heat; and a prism, a lens, and a sheet of pasteboard enabled Newton to unfold the composition of light and the origin of colours. An eminent foreign *savant* once called upon Dr Wollaston, and requested to be shown over his laboratories in which science had been enriched by so many important discoveries, when the doctor took him into a little study, and, pointing to an old tea-tray on the table, containing a few watch-glasses, test papers, a small balance, and a blowpipe, said, 'There is all the laboratory that I have!'

Stothard learnt the art of combining colours by closely studying butterflies' wings: he would often say that no one knew what he owed to these tiny insects. A burnt stick and a barn door served Wilkie in lieu of pencil and canvas. Bewick first practised drawing on the cottage walls of his native village, which he covered with his sketches in chalk; and Benjamin West made his first brushes out of the cat's tail. Ferguson laid himself down in the fields at night in a blanket, and made a map of the heavenly bodies by means of a thread with small beads on it stretched between his eye and the stars. Franklin first robbed the thundercloud of its lightning by means of a kite made with two cross sticks and a silk handkerchief. Watt made his first model of the condensing steam-engine out of an old anatomist's syringe, used to inject the arteries previous to dissection. Gifford worked his first problems in mathematics, when a cobbler's apprentice, upon small scraps of leather, which he beat smooth for the purpose; whilst Rittenhouse, the astronomer, first calculated eclipses on his plough handle.

The most ordinary occasions will furnish a man with opportunities or suggestions for improvement, if he be but prompt to take advantage of them. Professor Lee was attracted to the study of Hebrew by finding a Bible in that tongue in a synagogue, while working as a common carpenter at the repairs of the benches. He became possessed with a desire to read the book in the original, and, buying a cheap second-hand copy of a Hebrew grammar, he set to work and learnt the language for himself. As Edmund Stone said to the Duke of Argyle, in answer to His Grace's inquiry how he, a poor gardener's boy, had contrived to be able to read Newton's *Principia* in Latin, 'One needs only to know the twenty-four letters of the alphabet in order to learn everything else that one wishes.' Application and perseverance, and the diligent improvement of opportunities, will do the rest.

Sir Walter Scott found opportunities for self-improvement in every pursuit, and turned even accidents to account. Thus it was in the discharge of his functions as a writer's apprentice that he first visited the Highlands, and formed those friendships among the surviving heroes of 1745 which served to lay the foundation of a large class of his works. Later in life, when employed as a quartermaster of the Edinburgh Light Cavalry, he was accidentally disabled by the kick of a horse, and confined for some time to his house; but Scott was a sworn enemy to idleness, and he forthwith set his mind to work. In three days he had composed the first canto of *The Lay of the Last Minstrel*, which he shortly after finished – his first great original work.

The attention of Dr Priestley, the discoverer of so many gases, was accidentally drawn to the subject of chemistry through his living in the neighbourhood of a brewery. When visiting the place one day, he noted the peculiar appearances attending the extinction of lighted chips in the gas floating over the fermented liquor. He was forty years old at the time, and he knew nothing of chemistry. He consulted books to ascertain the cause, but they told him little, for as yet nothing was known on the subject. Then he began to experiment, with some rude apparatus of his own contrivance. The curious results of his first experiments led to others, which in his hands shortly became the science of pneumatic chemistry. About the same time Scheele was obscurely working in the same direction in a remote Swedish village; and he discovered several new gases, with no more effective apparatus at his command than a few apothecaries' phials and pigs' bladders.

Sir Humphry Davy, when an apothecary's apprentice, performed his first experiments with instruments of the rudest description. He extemporized the greater part of them himself, out of the motley materials which chance threw in his way – the pots and pans of the kitchen, and the phials and vessels of his master's surgery. It happened that a French ship was wrecked off the Land's End, and the surgeon escaped, bearing with him his case of instruments, amongst which was an old-fashioned glyster apparatus; this article he presented to Davy, with whom he had become acquainted. The apothecary's apprentice received it with great exultation, and forthwith employed it as a part of a pneumatic apparatus which he contrived, afterwards using it to perform the duties of an air-pump in one of his experiments on the nature and sources of heat.

In like manner Professor Faraday, Sir Humphry Davy's scientific successor, made his first experiments in electricity by means of an old bottle, while he was still a working bookbinder. And it is a curious fact that Faraday was first attracted to the study of chemistry by hearing one of Sir Humphry Davy's lectures on the subject at the Royal Institution. A gentleman, who was a member, calling one day at the shop where Faraday was employed in binding books, found him poring over the article 'Electricity' in an encyclopaedia placed in his hands to bind. The gentleman, having made inquiries, found that the young bookbinder was curious about such subjects, and gave him an order of admission to the Royal Institution, where he attended a course of four lectures delivered by Sir Humphry. He took notes of them, which he showed to the lecturer, who acknowledged their scientific accuracy, and was surprised when informed of the humble position of the reporter. Faraday then expressed his desire to devote himself to the prosecution of chemical studies, from which Sir Humphry at first endeavoured to dissuade him: but the young man persisting, he was at length taken into the Royal Institution as an assistant; and eventually the mantle of the brilliant apothecary's boy fell upon the worthy shoulders of the equally brilliant bookbinder apprentice.

The words which Davy entered in his note-book, when about twenty years of age, working in Dr Beddoes' laboratory at Bristol, were eminently characteristic of him: 'I have neither riches, nor power, nor birth to recommend me; yet if I live, I trust I shall not be of less service to mankind and my friends, than if I had been born with all these advantages.' Davy possessed the capability, as Faraday does, of devoting the whole power of his mind to the practical and experimental investigation of a subject in all its bearings; and such a mind will rarely fail, by dint of mere industry and patient thinking, in producing results of the highest order. Coleridge said of Davy, 'There is an energy and elasticity in his mind, which enables him to seize on and analyse all questions, pushing them to their legitimate consequences. Every subject in Davy's mind has the principle of vitality. Living thoughts spring up like turf under his feet.' Davy, on his part, said of Coleridge, whose abilities he greatly admired, 'With the most exalted genius, enlarged views, sensitive heart, and enlightened mind, he will be the victim of a want of order, precision, and regularity.'

The great Cuvier was a singularly accurate, careful, and industrious observer. When a boy, he was attracted to the subject of natural history by the sight of a volume of Buffon which accidentally fell in his way. He at once proceeded to copy the drawings, and to colour them after the descriptions given in the text. While still at school, one of his teachers made him a present of Linnaeus's *System of Nature*; and for more than ten years this constituted his library of natural history. At eighteen he was offered the situation of tutor in a family residing near Fécamp, in Normandy. Living close to the sea-shore, he was brought face to face with the wonders of marine life. Strolling along the sands one day, he observed a stranded cuttle-fish. He was attracted by the curious object, took it home to dissect, and thus began the study of the molluscae, in the pursuit of which he achieved so distinguished a reputation. About this time Cuvier became known to the learned Abbé Teissier, who wrote to Jessieu and other friends in Paris on the subject of the young naturalist's inquiries, in terms of such high commendation, that Cuvier was requested to send some of his papers to the Society of Natural History; and he was shortly after appointed assistant-superintendent at the Jardin des Plantes. In the letter written by Teissier to Jessieu, introducing the young naturalist to his notice, he said, 'You remember that it was I who gave Delambre to the Academy in another branch of science: this also will be a Delambre.' We need scarcely add that the prediction of Teissier was more than fulfilled.

Watt taught himself chemistry and mechanics while working at his trade of a mathematical-instrument maker, at the same time that he was learning German from a Swiss dyer. Stephenson taught himself arithmetic and mensuration while working as an engineman during the night shifts; and when he could snatch a few moments in the intervals allowed for meals during the day, he worked his sums with a bit of chalk upon the sides of the colliery wagons. Dalton's industry was the habit of his life. He began from his boyhood, for he taught a little village-school when he was only about twelve years old – keeping the school in winter, and working upon his father's farm in summer. He would sometimes urge himself and his companions to study by the stimulus of a bet, though bred a Quaker; and on one occasion, by his satisfactory solution of a problem, he won as much as enabled him to buy a winter's store of candles. He continued his meteorological observations until a day or two before he died – having made and recorded upwards of 200,000 in the course of his life.

With perseverance, the very odds and ends of time may be worked up into results of the greatest value. Dr Mason Good translated

Lucretius while riding in his carriage in the streets of London, going the round of his patients. Dr Darwin composed nearly all his works in the same way while driving about in his 'sulky' from house to house in the country – writing down his thoughts on little scraps of paper, which he carried about with him for the purpose. Hale wrote his *Contemplations* while travelling on circuit. Dr Burney learnt French and Italian while travelling on horseback from one musical pupil to another in the course of his profession. Kirke White learnt Greek while walking to and from a lawyer's office; and we personally know of a man of eminent position who learnt Latin and French while going messages as an errand-boy in the streets of Manchester.

Daguesseau, one of the great Chancellors of France, by carefully working up his odd bits of time, wrote a bulky and able volume in the successive intervals of waiting for dinner, and Madame de Genlis composed several of her charming volumes while waiting for the princess to whom she gave her daily lessons. Elihu Burritt attributed his first success in self-improvement, not to genius, which he disclaimed, but simply to the careful employment of those invaluable fragments of time called 'odd moments'. While working and earning his living as a blacksmith, he mastered some eighteen ancient and modern languages, and twenty-two European dialects.

What a solemn and striking admonition to youth is that inscribed on the dial at All Souls, Oxford– *Pereunt et imputantur* – the hours perish, and are laid to our charge. Time is the only little fragment of Eternity that belongs to man; and, like life, it can never be recalled. 'In the dissipation of worldly treasure,' says Jackson of Exeter, 'the frugality of the future may balance the extravagance of the past; but who can say, "I will take from minutes tomorrow to compensate for those I have lost today"?' Melancthon noted down the time lost by him, that he might thereby reanimate his industry, and not lose an hour. Time was the estate out of which these great workers, and all other workers, formed that rich treasury of thoughts and deeds which they have left to their successors.

The mere drudgery undergone by some men in carrying on their undertakings has been something extraordinary, but the drudgery they regarded as the price of success. Addison amassed as much as three folios of manuscript materials before he began his *Spectator*. Newton wrote his *Chronology* fifteen times over before he was satisfied with it; and Gibbon wrote out his *Memoir* nine times. Hale studied for many years at the rate of sixteen hours a day, and when wearied with the study of the law he would recreate himself with philosophy and the study of the mathematics. Hume wrote thirteen hours a day while preparing his *History of England*. Montesquieu, speaking of one part of his writings, said to a friend, 'You will read it in a few hours; but I assure you it has cost me so much labour that it has whitened my hair.'

The practice of writing down thoughts and facts for the purpose of holding them fast and preventing their escape into the dim regions of forgetfulness, has been much resorted to by thoughtful and studious men. Lord Bacon left behind him many manuscripts entitled 'Sudden thoughts set down for use'. Erskine made great extracts from Burke; and Eldon copied Coke upon Littleton twice over with his own hand so that the book became, as it were, part of his own mind. The late Dr Pye Smith, when apprenticed to his father as a bookbinder, was accustomed to make copious memoranda of all the books he read, with extracts and criticisms. This indomitable industry in collecting materials distinguished him through life, his biographer describing him as 'always at work, always in advance, always accumulating'. These note-books afterwards proved, like Richter's 'quarries', the great storehouse from which he drew his illustrations.

The same practice characterized the eminent John Hunter who adopted it for the purpose of supplying the defects of memory; and he was accustomed thus to illustrate the advantages which one derives from putting one's thoughts in writing: 'It resembles,' he said, 'a tradesman taking stock, without which he never knows either what he possesses or in what he is deficient.' John Hunter – whose observation was so keen that Abernethy was accustomed to speak of him as 'the Argus-eyed' – furnished an illustrious example of the power of patient industry. He received little or no education till he was about twenty years of age, and it was with difficulty that he acquired the arts of reading and writing. He worked for some years as a common carpenter at Glasgow, after which he joined his brother William, who had settled in London as a lecturer and anatomical demonstrator. John entered his dissecting-room as an assistant, but soon shot ahead of his brother, partly by virtue of his great natural ability, but mainly by reason of his

97

patient application and indefatigable industry. He was one of the first in this country to devote himself assiduously to the study of comparative anatomy, and the objects he dissected and collected took the eminent Professor Owen no less than ten years to arrange. The collection contains some twenty thousand specimens, and is the most precious treasure of the kind that has ever been accumulated by the industry of one man. Hunter used to spend every morning from sunrise until eight o'clock in his museum; and throughout the day he carried on his extensive private practice, performed his laborious duties as surgeon to St George's Hospital and deputy surgeon-general to the army, delivered lectures to students, and superintended a school of practical anatomy at his own house, finding leisure, amidst all, for elaborate experiments on the animal economy, and the composition of various works of great scientific importance. To find time for this gigantic amount of work, he allowed himself only four hours of sleep at night, and an hour after dinner. When once asked what method he had adopted to insure success in his undertakings, he replied, 'My rule is, deliberately to consider, before I commence, whether the thing be practicable. If it be not practicable, I do not attempt it. If it be practicable, I can accomplish it if I give sufficient pains to it; and having begun, I never stop till the thing is done. To this rule I owe all my success.'

Ambrose Paré, the great French surgeon, was another illustrious instance of close observation, patient application, and indefatigable perseverance. He was the son of a barber at Laval, in Maine, where he was born in 1509. His parents were too poor to send him to school, but they placed him as foot-boy with the curé of the village, hoping that under that learned man he might pick up an education for himself. But the curé kept him so busily employed in grooming his mule and in other menial offices that the boy found no time for learning. While in his service, it happened that the celebrated lithotomist, Cotot, came to Laval to operate on one of the curé's ecclesiastical brethren. Paré was present at the operation, and was so much interested by it that he is said to have from that time formed the determination of devoting himself to the art of surgery.

Leaving the curé's household service, Paré apprenticed himself to a barber-surgeon named Vialot, under whom he learnt to let blood, draw teeth, and perform the minor operations. After four years' experience of this kind, he went to Paris to study at the school of anatomy and surgery, meanwhile maintaining himself by his trade of a barber. He afterwards succeeded in obtaining an appointment as assistant at the Hôtel Dieu, where his conduct was so exemplary, and his progress so marked, that the chief surgeon, Goupil, entrusted him with the charge of the patients whom he could not himself attend to. After the usual course of instruction, Paré was admitted to a master barber-surgeon, and shortly after was appointed to a charge with the French army under Montmorenci in Piedmont. Paré was not a man to follow in the ordinary ruts of his profession, but brought the resources of an ardent and original mind to bear upon his daily work, diligently thinking out for himself the rationale of diseases and their befitting remedies. Before his time the wounded suffered much more at the hands of their surgeons than they did at those of their enemies. To stop bleeding from gunshot wounds the barbarous expedient was resorted to of dressing them with boiling oil. Haemorrhage was also stopped by searing the wounds with a red-hot iron; and when amputation was necessary, it was performed with a red-hot knife. At first Paré treated wounds according to the approved methods; but, fortunately, on one occasion, running short of boiling oil, he substituted a mild and emollient application. He was in great fear all night lest he should have done wrong in adopting this treatment; but was greatly relieved next morning on finding his patients comparatively comfortable, while those whose wounds had been treated in the usual way were writhing in torment. Such was the casual origin of one of Paré's greatest improvements in the treatment of gunshot wounds; and he proceeded to adopt the emollient treatment in all future cases. Another still more important improvement was his employment of the ligature in tying arteries to stop haemorrhage, instead of the actual cautery. Paré, however, met with the usual fate of innovators and reformers. His practice was denounced by his surgical brethren as dangerous, unprofessional, and empirical; and the older surgeons banded themselves together to resist its adoption. They reproached him for his want of education, more especially for his ignorance of Latin and Greek; and they assailed him with quotations from ancient writers, which he was unable either to verify or refute. But the best answer to his assailants was the success of his practice.

After three years' active service as army-surgeon, Paré returned to

Paris with such a reputation that he was at once appointed surgeon in ordinary to the King. When Metz was besieged by the Spanish army, under Charles V, the garrison suffered heavy loss, and the number of wounded was very great. The surgeons were few and incompetent, and probably slew more by their bad treatment than the Spaniards did by the sword. The Duke of Guise, who commanded the garrison, wrote to the King imploring him to send Paré to his help. The courageous surgeon at once set out, and, after braving many dangers (to use his own words, 'd'estre pendu, estranglé ou mis en pièces'), he succeeded in passing the enemy's lines, and entered Metz in safety. The Duke, the generals, and the captains gave him an affectionate welcome; while the soldiers, when they heard of his arrival, cried, 'We no longer fear dying of our wounds; our friend is among us.' In the following year Paré was in like manner with the besieged in the town of Hesdin, which shortly fell before the Duke of Savoy, and he was taken prisoner. But having succeeded in curing one of the enemy's chief officers of a serious wound, he was discharged without ransom, and returned in safety to Paris.

Harvey was as indefatigable a labourer as any we have named. He spent not less than eight long years of investigation and research before he published his views of the circulation of the blood. He repeated and verified his experiments again and again, probably anticipating the opposition he would have to encounter from the profession on making known his discovery. The tract in which he at length announced his views was a modest one – but simple, perspicuous, and conclusive. It was nevertheless received with ridicule, as the utterance of a crack-brained impostor. For some time he did not make a single convert, and gained nothing but contumely and abuse. He had called in question the revered authority of the ancients; and it was even averred that his views were calculated to subvert the authority of the Scriptures and undermine the very foundations of morality and religion. His little practice fell away, and he was left almost without a friend. This lasted for some years, until the great truth, held fast by Harvey amidst all his adversity, and which had dropped into many thoughtful minds, gradually ripened by further observation, and after a period of about twenty-five years, it became generally recognized as an established scientific truth.

The difficulties encountered by Dr Jenner in promulgating and establishing his discovery of vaccination as a preventive of small-pox were even greater than those of Harvey. Many, before him, had witnessed the cow-pox and had heard of the report current among the milkmaids in Gloucestershire, that whoever had taken that disease was secure against small-pox. It was a trifling, vulgar rumour, supposed to have no significance whatever; and no one had thought it worthy of investigation, until it was accidentally brought under the notice of Jenner. He was a youth, pursuing his studies at Sodbury, when his attention was arrested by the casual observation made by a country girl who came to his master's shop for advice. The small-pox was mentioned, when the girl said, 'I can't take that disease, for I have had cow-pox.' The observation immediately riveted Jenner's attention, and he forthwith set about inquiring and making observations on the subject. His professional friends, to whom he mentioned his views as to the prophylactic virtues of cow-pox, laughed at him, and even threatened to expel him from their society, if he persisted in harassing them with the subject. In London he was so fortunate as to study under John Hunter, to whom he communicated his views. The advice of the anatomist was thoroughly characteristic: 'Don't think, but *try*; be patient, be accurate.' Jenner's courage was supported by the advice, which conveyed to him the true art of philosophical investigation. He went back to the country to practise his profession and make observations and experiments, which he continued to pursue for a period of twenty years. His faith in his discovery was so implicit that he vaccinated his own son on three several occasions. At length he published his views in a quarto of about seventy pages, in which he gave the details of twenty-three cases of successful vaccination of individuals, to whom it was found afterwards impossible to communicate the small-pox either by contagion or inoculation. It was in 1798 that this treatise was published; though he had been working out his ideas since the year 1775, when they had begun to assume a definite form.

How was the discovery received? First with indifference, then with active hostility. Jenner proceeded to London to exhibit to the profession the process of vaccination and its results; but not a single medical man could be induced to make trial of it, and after fruitlessly waiting for nearly three months, he returned to his native village. He was even caricatured and abused for his attempt to 'bestialize' his species by the introduction into their systems of diseased matter from the cow's udder. Vaccination was denounced from the pulpit as 'diabolical'. It was averred that vaccinated children became 'ox-faced', that abscesses broke out to 'indicate sprouting horns', and that the countenance was gradually 'transmuted into the visage of a cow, the voice into the bellowing of bulls'. Vaccination, however, was a truth, and notwithstanding the violence of the opposition, belief in it spread slowly. In one village, where a gentleman tried to introduce the practice, the first persons who permitted themselves to be vaccinated were absolutely pelted and driven into their houses if they appeared out of doors. Two ladies of title – Lady Ducie and the Countess of Berkeley (to their honour be it remembered) – had the courage to vaccinate their children; and the prejudices of the day were at once broken through. The medical profession gradually came round, and there were several who even sought to rob Dr Jenner of the merit of the discovery, when its importance came to be recognized. Jenner's cause at last triumphed, and he was publicly honoured and rewarded. In his prosperity he was as modest as he had been in his obscurity. He was invited to settle in London, and told that he might command a price of £10,000 a year. But his answer was, 'No! In the morning of my days I have sought the sequestered and lowly paths of life – the valley, and not the mountain – and now, in the evening of my days, it is not meet for me to hold myself up as an object for fortune and for fame.' During Jenner's own lifetime the practice of vaccination became adopted all over the civilized world; and when he died, his title as a benefactor of his kind was recognized far and wide. Cuvier has said, 'If vaccine were the only discovery of the epoch, it would serve to render it illustrious for ever; yet it knocked twenty times in vain at the doors of the Academies.'

Not less patient, resolute, and persevering was Sir Charles Bell in the prosecution of his discoveries relating to the nervous system. Previous to his time, the most confused notions prevailed as to the functions of the nerves and this branch of study was little more advanced than it had been in the times of Democritus and Anaxagoras three thousand years before. Sir Charles Bell, in the valuable series of papers the publication of which was commenced in 1821, took an entirely original view of the subject, based upon a long series of careful, accurate, and oft-repeated experiments. Elaborately tracing the development of the nervous system up from the lowest order of animated being, to man – the lord of the animal kingdom – he displayed it, to use his own words, 'as plainly as if it were written in our mother-tongue'. His discovery consisted in the fact, that the spinal nerves are double in their function, and arise by double roots from the spinal marrow – volition being conveyed by that part of the nerves springing from the one root, and sensation by the other. The subject occupied the mind of Sir Charles Bell for a period of forty years, when, in 1840, he laid his last paper before the Royal Society. As in the cases of Harvey and Jenner, when he had lived down the ridicule and opposition with which his views were first received, and their truth came to be recognized, numerous claims for priority in making the discovery were set up at home and abroad. Like them, too, he lost practice by the publication of his papers; and he left it on record that, after every step in his discovery, he was obliged to work harder than ever to preserve his reputation as a practitioner. The great merits of Sir Charles Bell were, however, at length fully recognized; and Cuvier himself, when on his death-bed, finding his face distorted and drawn to one side, pointed out the symptom to his attendants as a proof of the correctness of Sir Charles Bell's theory.

The life of Sir William Herschel affords another remarkable illustration of the force of perseverance in another branch of science. His father was a poor German musician, who brought up his four sons to the same calling. William came over to England to seek his fortune, and he joined the band of the Durham Militia, in which he played the oboe. The regiment was lying at Doncaster, where Dr Miller first became acquainted with Herschel, having heard him perform a solo on the violin in a surprising manner. The doctor entered into conversation with the youth, and was so pleased with him, that he urged him to leave the militia and take up his residence at his house for a time. Herschel did so, and while at Doncaster was principally occupied in violin-playing at concerts, availing himself of the advantages of Dr Miller's library to study in his leisure hours. A new organ having been built for the parish church of Halifax, an organist was advertised for, on which Herschel applied for the office, and was selected. Leading the wandering life of an artist, he was next attracted to Bath, where he played in the

Pump-room band, and also officiated as organist in the Octagon chapel. Some recent discoveries in astronomy having arrested his mind, and awakened in him a powerful spirit of curiosity, he sought and obtained from a friend a loan of a two-foot Gregorian telescope. So fascinated was the poor musician by the science, that he even thought of purchasing a telescope, but the price asked by the London optician was so alarming, that he determined to make one.

Herschel succeeded, after long and painful labour, in completing a five-foot reflector, with which he had the gratification of observing the ring and satellites of Saturn. Not satisfied with his triumph, he proceeded to make other instruments in succession, of seven, ten, and even twenty feet. In constructing the seven-foot reflector, he finished no fewer than two hundred specula before he produced one that would bear any power that was applied to it – a striking instance of the persevering laboriousness of the man. While gauging the heavens with his instruments, he continued patiently to earn his bread by piping to the fashionable frequenters of the Pump-room. So eager was he in his astronomical observations, that he would steal away from the room during an interval of the performance, give a little turn at his telescope, and contentedly return to his oboe. Thus working away, Herschel discovered the Georgium Sidus, the orbit and rate of motion of which he carefully calculated, and sent the result to the Royal Society, when the humble oboe player found himself at once elevated from obscurity to fame. He was shortly after appointed Astronomer Royal, and by the kindness of George III was placed in a position of honourable competency for life.

The career of William Smith, the father of English geology, though perhaps less known, is not less interesting and instructive as an example of patient and laborious effort, and the diligent cultivation of opportunities. He was born in 1769, the son of a yeoman farmer at Churchill, in Oxfordshire. His father dying when he was but a child, he received a very sparing education at the village school, and even that was to a considerable extent interfered with by his wandering and somewhat idle habits as a boy. His mother having married a second time, he was taken in charge by an uncle, also a farmer, by whom he was brought up. Though the uncle was by no means pleased with the boy's love of wandering about, collecting 'poundstones', 'pundips', and other stony curiosities which lay scattered about the adjoining land, he yet enabled him to purchase a few of the necessary books wherewith to instruct himself in the rudiments of geometry and surveying; for the boy was already destined for the business of a land-surveyor. One of his marked characteristics, even as a youth, was the accuracy and keenness of his observations; and what he once clearly saw he never forgot. He began to draw, attempted to colour, and practised the arts of mensuration and surveying, all without regular instruction; and by his efforts in self-culture, he shortly became so proficient that he was taken on as assistant to a local surveyor of ability in the neighbourhood. In carrying on his business he was constantly under the necessity of traversing Oxfordshire and the adjoining counties. One of the first things he seriously pondered over was the position of the various soils and strata that came under his notice on the lands which he surveyed or travelled over; more especially the position of the red earth in regard to the lias and superincumbent rocks. The surveys of numerous collieries which he was called upon to make gave him further experience; and already, when only twenty-three years of age, he contemplated making a model of the strata of the earth.

While engaged in levelling for a proposed canal in Gloucestershire, the idea of a general law occurred to him relating to the strata of that district. He conceived that the strata lying above the coal were not laid horizontally, but inclined, and in one direction, towards the east; resembling, on a large scale, 'the ordinary appearance of superposed slices of bread and butter'. The correctness of this theory he shortly after confirmed by observations of the strata in two parallel valleys, the 'red ground', 'lias', and 'freestone' or 'oolite', being found to come down in an eastern direction, and to sink below the level, yielding place to the next in succession. He was shortly enabled to verify the truth of his views on a larger scale, having been appointed to examine personally into the management of canals in England and Wales. During his journeys, which extended from Bath to Newcastle-on-Tyne, returning by Shropshire and Wales, his keen eyes were never idle for a moment. He rapidly noted the aspect and structure of the country through which he passed with his companions, treasuring up his observations for future use. His geologic vision was so acute, that, though the road along which he passed from York to Newcastle in the post chaise was from five to fifteen miles distant from the hills of chalk and oolite on the east, he was satisfied as to their nature, by their contours and relative position, and their ranges on the surface in relation to the lias and 'red ground' occasionally seen on the road.

The general results of his observation seem to have been these. He noted that the rocky masses of country in the western parts of England generally inclined to the east and south-east; and the red sandstones and marls above the coal measures passed beneath the lias, clay, and limestone; that these again passed beneath the sands, yellow limestones and clays, forming the table-land of the Cotswold Hills, while these in turn passed beneath the great chalk deposits occupying the eastern parts of England. He further observed, that each layer of clay, sand, and limestone held its own peculiar classes of fossils; and pondering much on these things, he at length came to the then unheard-of conclusion, that each distinct deposit of marine animals, in these several strata, indicated a distinct sea-bottom, and that each layer of clay, sand, chalk, and stone marked a distinct epoch of time in the history of the earth.

This idea took firm possession of his mind, and he could talk and think of nothing else. At canal boards, at sheep-shearings, at county meetings, and at agricultural associations, 'Strata Smith', as he came to be called, was always running over with the subject that possessed him. He had indeed made a great discovery, though he was as yet a man utterly unknown in the scientific world. He proceeded to project a map of the stratification of England; but was for some time deterred from proceeding with it, being fully occupied in carrying out the works of the Somerset coal canal, which engaged him for a period of about six years.

One day, when looking over the cabinet collection of fossils belonging to the Rev. Samuel Richardson, at Bath, Smith astonished his friend by suddenly disarranging his classification, and rearranging the fossils in their stratigraphical order, saying: 'These came from the blue lias, these from the over-lying sand and freestone, these from the fuller's earth, and these from the Bath building stone.' A new light flashed upon Mr Richardson's mind, and he shortly became a convert to and believer in William Smith's doctrine. The geologists of the day were not, however, so easily convinced; and it was scarcely to be tolerated that an unknown land-surveyor should pretend to teach them the science of geology. But William Smith had an eye and mind to penetrate deep beneath the skin of the earth; he saw its very fibre and skeleton, as it were, divined its organization. His knowledge of the strata in the neighbourhood of Bath was so accurate, that one evening, when dining at the house of the Rev. Joseph Townsend, he dictated to Mr Richardson the different strata according to their order of succession in descending order, twenty-three in number, commencing with the chalk and descending in continuous series down to the coal, below which the strata was not then sufficiently determined. To this was added a list of the more remarkable fossils which had been gathered in the several layers of rock. This was printed and extensively circulated in 1801.

He next determined to trace out the strata through districts as remote from Bath as his means would enable him to reach. For years he journeyed to and fro, sometimes on foot, sometimes on horseback, riding on the tops of stage coaches, often making up by night-travelling the time he had lost by day, so as not to fail in his ordinary business arrangements. When he was professionally called away to any distance from home – as, for instance, when travelling from Bath to Holkham, in Norfolk, to direct the irrigation and drainage of Mr Coke's land in that county – he rode on horseback, making frequent detours from the road to note the geological features of the country which he traversed.

For several years he was thus engaged in his journeys to distant quarters in England and Ireland, to the extent of upwards of ten thousand miles yearly; and it was amidst this incessant and laborious travelling that he contrived to commit to paper his fast-growing generalizations on what he rightly regarded as a new science. No observation, howsoever trivial it might appear, was neglected, and no opportunity of collecting fresh facts was overlooked. Whenever he could, he possessed himself of records of borings, natural and artificial sections, drew them to a constant scale of eight yards to the inch, and coloured them up. Of his keenness of observation take the following illustration. When making one of his geological excursions about the country near Woburn, as he was drawing near to the foot of the Dunstable chalk hills, he observed to his companion, 'If there be any broken ground about the foot of these hills, we may find *sharks' teeth*'; and they had not proceeded far before they picked up six from the white bank of a new fence-ditch. As he afterwards said of himself, 'The habit of observation crept on me, gained a settlement in my mind, became a constant associate of my life, and started up in activity at the first thought of a journey; so that I generally went off well prepared with maps, and sometimes with contemplations on its objects, or on those on the road, reduced to writing before it commenced. My mind was, therefore, like the canvas of a painter, well prepared for the first and best impressions.'

Notwithstanding his courageous and indefatigable industry, many circumstances contributed to prevent the promised publication of William Smith's *Map of the Strata of England and Wales*, and it was not until 1814 that he was enabled, by the assistance of some friends, to give to the world the fruits of his twenty years' incessant labour. To prosecute his inquiries, and collect the extensive series of facts and observations requisite for his purpose, he had to expend the whole of the profits of his professional labours during that period; and he even sold off his small property to provide the means of visiting remoter parts of the island. Meanwhile he had entered on a quarrying speculation near Bath, which proved unsuccessful, and he was under the necessity of selling his geological collection (which was purchased by the British Museum), his furniture and library, reserving only his papers, maps, and sections which were useless save to himself. He bore his losses and misfortunes with exemplary fortitude; and, amidst all, he went on working with cheerful courage and untiring patience. He died at Northampton, in August 1839, while on his way to attend the meeting of the British Association at Birmingham.

It is difficult to speak in terms of too high praise of the first geological map of England, which we owe to the industry of this courageous man of science. The genius of the Oxfordshire surveyor did not fail to be duly recognized and honoured by men of science during his lifetime. In 1831 the Geological Society of London awarded him the Wollaston medal, 'in consideration of his being a great original discoverer in English geology, and especially for his being the first in this country to discover and to teach the identification of strata, and to determine their succession by means of their embedded fossils'. William Smith, in his simple, earnest way, gained for himself a name as lasting as the science he loved so well.

Hugh Miller was a man of like observant faculties, who studied literature as well as science with zeal and success. The book in which he has told the story of his life, *My School and Schoolmasters*, is extremely interesting, and calculated to be eminently useful. It is the history of the formation of a truly noble character in the humblest condition of life, and inculcates most powerfully the lessons of self-help, self-respect, and self-dependence. While Hugh was but a child, his father, who was a sailor, was drowned at sea, and he was brought up by his widowed mother. He had a school training after a sort, but his best teachers were the boys with whom he played, the men amongst whom he worked, the friends and relatives with whom he lived. He read much and miscellaneously, and picked up odd sorts of knowledge from many quarters – from workmen, carpenters, fishermen and sailors, and, above all, from the old boulders strewed along the shores of the Cromarty Firth. With a big hammer which had belonged to his great-grandfather, an old buccaneer, the boy went about chipping the stones, and accumulating specimens of mica, porphyry, garnet, and such like. Sometimes he had a day in the woods, and there, too, the boy's attention was excited by the peculiar geological curiosities which came in his way. While searching among the rocks on the beach, he was sometimes asked, in irony, by the farm servants who came to load their carts with sea-weed, whether he 'was gettin' siller in the stanes', but was so unlucky as never to be able to answer in the affirmative. When of a suitable age he was apprenticed to the trade of his choice – that of a working stonemason; and he began his labouring career in a quarry looking out upon the Cromarty Firth. This quarry proved one of his best schools. The remarkable geological formations which it displayed awakened his curiosity. The bar of deep-red stone beneath, and the bar of pale-red clay above, were noted by the young quarryman, who even in such unpromising subjects found matter for observation and reflection. Where other men saw nothing, he detected analogies, differences, and peculiarities, which set him athinking. He simply kept his eyes and his mind open; was sober, diligent, and persevering; and this was the secret of his intellectual growth.

His curiosity was excited and kept alive by the curious organic remains, principally of old and extinct species of fishes, ferns, and ammonites, which were revealed along the coast by the washings of the waves, or were exposed by the stroke of his mason's hammer. He never lost sight of the subject; but went on accumulating observations and comparing formations, until at length, many years afterwards, when no longer a working mason, he gave to the world his highly interesting work on the Old Red Sandstone, which at once established his reputation as a scientific geologist. But this work was the fruit of long years of patient observation and research. As he modestly states in his autobiography, 'The only merit to which I lay claim in the case is that of patient research – a merit in which whoever wills may rival or surpass me; and this humble faculty of patience, when rightly developed, may lead to more extraordinary developments of idea than even genius itself.'

John Brown, the eminent English geologist, was, like Miller, a stonemason in his early life, serving an apprenticeship to the trade at Colchester, and afterwards working as a journeyman mason at Norwich. He began business as a builder on his own account at Colchester, where by frugality and industry he secured a competency. It was while working at his trade that his attention was first drawn to the study of fossils and shells; and he proceeded to make a collection of them, which afterwards grew into one of the finest in England. His researches along the coast of Essex, Kent, and Sussex brought to light some magnificent remains of the elephant and rhinoceros, the most valuable of which were presented by him to the British Museum.

Sir Roderick Murchison discovered at Thurso, in Scotland, a profound geologist, in the person of a baker there, named Robert Dick. When Sir Roderick called upon him at the bakehouse in which he baked and earned his bread, Robert Dick delineated to him, by means of flour upon the board, the geographical phenomena of his native county, pointing out the imperfections in the existing maps, which he had ascertained by travelling over the country in his leisure hours. On further inquiry, Sir Roderick ascertained that the humble individual before him was not only a capital baker and geologist, but a first-rate botanist. 'I found,' said the President of the Geographical Society, 'to my great humiliation that the baker knew infinitely more of botanical science, ay, ten times more, than I did, and that there were only some twenty or thirty specimens of flowers which he had not collected. Some he had obtained as presents, some he had purchased, but the greater portion had been accumulated by his industry, in his native county of Caithness; and the specimens were all arranged in the most beautiful order, with their scientific names affixed.'

6. Workers in Art

Excellence in art, as in everything else, can only be achieved by dint of painstaking labour. There is nothing less accidental than the painting of a fine picture or the chiselling of a noble statue. Every skilled touch of the artist's brush or chisel, though guided by genius, is the product of unremitting study.

Sir Joshua Reynolds was such a believer in the force of industry, that he held that artistic excellence, 'however expressed by genius, taste, or the gift of heaven, may be acquired'. Writing to Barry he said, 'Whoever is resolved to excel in painting, or indeed any other art, must bring all his mind to bear upon that one object from the moment that he rises till he goes to bed.' And on another occasion he said, 'Those who are resolved to excel must go to their work, willing or unwilling, morning, noon, and night: they will find it no play, but very hard labour.' But although diligent application is no doubt absolutely necessary for the achievement of the highest distinction in art, it is equally true that without the inborn genius no amount of mere industry, however well applied, will make an artist. The gift comes by nature, but it is preferred by self-culture, which is of more avail than all the imparted education of the schools.

Some of the greatest artists have had to force their way upward in the face of poverty and manifold obstructions. Illustrious instances will at once flash upon the reader's mind. Claude Lorraine, the pastrycook; Tintoretto, the dyer; the two Caravaggios, the one a colour-grinder, the other a mortar-carrier at the Vatican; Salvator Rosa, the associate of bandits; Giotto, the peasant boy; Zingaro, the gipsy; Cavedone, turned out of doors to beg by his father; Canova, the stone-cutter; these, and many other well-known artists, succeeded in achieving distinction by severe study and labour, under circumstances the most adverse.

Nor have the most distinguished artists of our own country been born in a position of life more than ordinarily favourable to the culture of artistic genius. Gainsborough and Bacon were the sons of cloth-workers; Barry was an Irish sailor boy, and Maclise a banker's apprentice at Cork; Opie and Romney, like Inigo Jones, were carpenters; West was the son of a small Quaker farmer in Pennsylvania; Northcote was a watchmaker, Jackson a tailor, and Etty a printer; Reynolds, Wilson, and Wilkie were the sons of clergymen; Lawrence was the son of a publican, and Turner of a barber. Several of our painters, it is true, originally had some connection with art, though in a very humble way – such as Flaxman, whose father sold plaster casts; Bird, who ornamented tea-trays; Martin, who was a coach-painter; Wright and Gilpin, who were ship-painters; Chantrey, who was a carver and gilder; and David Cox, Stanfield, and Roberts, who were scene-painters.

It was not by luck or accident that these men achieved distinction, but by sheer industry and hard work. Though some achieved wealth, yet this was rarely, if ever, the ruling motive. Indeed, no mere love of money could sustain the efforts of the artist in his early career of self-denial and application. The pleasure of the pursuit has always been its best reward; the wealth which followed but an accident. Many noble-minded artists have preferred following the bent of their genius to chaffering with the public for terms. Spagnoletto verified in his life the beautiful fiction of Xenophon, and after he had acquired the means of luxury, preferred withdrawing himself from their influence, and voluntarily returned to poverty and labour. When Michael Angelo was asked his opinion respecting a work which a painter had taken great pains to exhibit for profit, he said, 'I think that he will be a poor fellow so long as he shows such an extreme eagerness to become rich.'

Like Sir Joshua Reynolds, Michael Angelo was a great believer in the force of labour; and he held that there was nothing which the imagination conceived, that could not be embodied in marble, if the hand were made vigorously to obey the mind. He was himself one of the most indefatigable of workers; and he attributed his power of studying for a greater number of hours than most of his contemporaries to his spare habits of living.

Titian, also, was an indefatigable worker. His celebrated 'Pietro Martire' was eight years in hand, and his 'Last Supper' seven. In his letter to Charles V he said, 'I sent your Majesty the "Last Supper" after working at it almost daily for seven years – *dopo sette anni lavorandovi quasi continuamente*'. Few think of the patient labour and long training involved in the greatest works of the artist. They seem easy and quickly accomplished, yet with how great difficulty has this ease been acquired. 'You charge me fifty sequins,' said the Venetian nobleman to the sculptor, 'for a bust that cost you only ten days' labour.' 'You forget,' said the artist, 'that I have been thirty years learning to make that bust in ten days.' Once when Domenichino was blamed for his slowness in finishing a picture which was bespoken, he made answer, 'I am continually painting it within myself'. It was eminently characteristic of the industry of the late Sir Augustus Callcott, that he made not fewer than forty separate sketches in the composition of his famous picture of 'Rochester'. This constant repetition is one of the main conditions of success in art, as in life itself.

Richard Wilson, when a mere child, indulged himself with tracing figures of men and animals on the walls of his father's house, with a burnt stick. He first directed his attention to portrait painting; but when in Italy, calling one day at the house of Zucarelli, and growing weary with waiting, he began painting the scene on which his friend's chamber window looked. When Zucarelli arrived, he was so charmed with the picture, that he asked if Wilson had not studied landscape, to which he replied that he had not. 'Then, I advise you,' said the other, 'to try; for you are sure of great success.' Wilson adopted the advice, studied and worked hard, and became our first great English landscape painter.

Sir Joshua Reynolds, when a boy, forgot his lessons, and took pleasure only in drawing, for which his father was accustomed to rebuke him. The boy was destined for the profession of physic, but his strong instinct for art could not be repressed, and he became a painter. Gainsborough went sketching, when a schoolboy, in the woods of Sudbury; and at twelve he was a confirmed artist; he was a keen observer and a hard worker – no picturesque feature of any scene he had once looked upon escaping his diligent pencil. William Blake, a hosier's son, employed himself in drawing designs on the backs of his father's shop-bills, and making sketches on the counter. Edward Bird, when a child only three or four years old, would mount a chair and draw figures on the walls, which he called French and English soldiers. A box of colours was purchased for him, and his father, desirous of turning his love of art to account, put him apprentice to a maker of tea-trays! Out of this trade he gradually raised himself, by study and labour, to the rank of a Royal Academician.

Hogarth, though a very dull boy at his lessons, took pleasure in making drawings of the letters of the alphabet, and his school exercises were more remarkable for the ornaments with which he embellished them than for the matter of the exercises themselves. In the latter respect he was beaten by all the blockheads of the school, but in his adornments he stood alone. His father put him apprentice to a silversmith, where he learnt to draw, and also to engrave spoons and forks with crests and ciphers. From silver-chasing, he went on to teach himself engraving on copper, principally griffins and monsters and heraldry, in the course of which practice he became ambitious to delineate the varieties of human character. The singular excellence which he reached in this art was mainly the result of careful observation and study. He had the gift, which he sedulously cultivated, of committing to memory the precise features of any remarkable face, and afterwards reproducing them on paper; but if any singularly fantastic form or *outré* face came in his way, he would make a sketch of it on the spot, upon his thumb-nail, and carry it home to expand at his leisure. By this careful storing of his mind, he was afterwards enabled to crowd an immense amount of thought and treasured observation into his works. Hence it is that Hogarth's pictures are so truthful a memorial of the character, the manners, and even the very thoughts of the times in which he lived. When he had conquered all his difficulties and become a famous and thriving man, he loved to dwell upon his early labours and privations, and to fight over again the battle which ended so honourably to him as a man and so gloriously as an artist. 'I remember the time,' said he on one occasion, 'when I have gone moping into the city with scarce a shilling, but as soon as I have received ten guineas there for a plate, I have returned home, put on my sword, and sallied out with all the confidence of a man who had thousands in his pockets.'

'Industry and perseverance' was the motto of the sculptor Banks, which he acted on himself, and strongly recommended to others. His well-known kindness induced many aspiring youths to call upon him and ask for his advice and assistance; and it is related that one day a boy called at his door to see him with this object, but the servant, angry at the loud knock he had given, scolded him and was about sending him away, when Banks, overhearing her, himself went out. The little boy stood at the door with some drawings in his hand. 'What do you want with me?' asked the sculptor. 'I want, sir, if you please, to be admitted to draw at the Academy.' Banks explained that he himself could not procure his admission, but he asked to look at the boy's drawings. Examining them, he said, 'Time enough for the Academy, my little man! go home – mind your schooling – try to make a better drawing of the Apollo – and in a month come again and let me see it.' The boy went home – sketched and worked with redoubled diligence – and, at the end of the month, called again on the sculptor. The drawing was better; but again Banks sent him back, with good advice, to work and study. In a week the boy was again at his door, his drawing much improved; and Banks bid him be of good cheer, for if spared he would distinguish himself. The boy was Mulready; and the sculptor's augury was amply fulfilled.

The fame of Claude Lorraine is partly explained by his indefatigable industry. Born at Champagne, in Lorraine, of poor parents, he was first apprenticed to a pastry-cook. His brother, who was a wood-carver, afterwards took him into his shop to learn that trade. Having there shown indications of artistic skill, a travelling dealer persuaded the brother to allow Claude to accompany him to Italy. He assented, and the young man reached Rome, where he was shortly after engaged by Agostino Tassi, the landscape painter, as his house-servant. In that capacity Claude first learnt landscape painting, and in course of time he began to produce pictures. We next find him making the tour of Italy, France and Germany, occasionally resting by the way to paint landscapes, and thereby replenish his purse. On returning to Rome he found an increasing demand for his works, and his reputation at length became European. He was unwearied in the study of nature in her various aspects. It was his practice to spend a great part of his time in closely copying builders, bits of ground, trees, leaves, and such like, which he finished in detail, keeping the drawings by him in store for the purpose of introducing them in his studied landscapes. He also gave close attention to the sky, watching it for whole days from morning till night, and noting the various changes occasioned by the passing clouds, and the increasing and waning light. By this constant practice he acquired, although it is said very slowly, such a mastery of hand and eye as eventually secured for him the first rank among landscape painters.

Turner, who has been styled 'the English Claude', pursued a career of like laborious industry. He was destined by his father for his own trade of a barber, which he carried on in London, until one day the sketch which the boy had made of a coat of arms on a silver salver having attracted the notice of a customer whom his father was shaving, the latter was urged to allow his son to follow his bias, and he was eventually permitted to follow art as a profession. Like all young artists, Turner had many difficulties to encounter, and they were all the greater that his circumstances were so straitened. But he was always willing to work, and to take pains with his work, no matter how humble it might be. He was glad to hire himself out at half-a-crown a night to wash in skies in Indian ink upon other people's drawings, getting his supper into the bargain. He aimed at learning as well as living; always doing his best, and never leaving a drawing without having made a step in advance upon his previous work. A man who thus laboured was sure to do much; and his growth in power and grasp of thought was, to use Ruskin's words, 'as steady as the increasing light of sunrise'. But Turner's genius needs no panegyric; his best monument is the noble gallery of pictures bequeathed by him to the nation, which will ever be the most lasting memorial of his fame.

To reach Rome, the capital of the fine arts, is usually the highest ambition of the art student. But the journey to Rome is costly, and the student is often poor. With a will resolute to overcome difficulties, Rome may, however, at last be reached. Thus François Perrier, an early French painter, in his eager desire to visit the Eternal City, consented to act as guide to a blind vagrant. After long wanderings he reached the Vatican, studied and became famous. Not less enthusiasm was displayed by Jacques Callot in his determination to visit Rome. Having set out without means, he was soon reduced to great straits; but falling in with a band of gipsies, he joined their company, and wandered about with them from one fair to another, sharing in their numerous adventures. During this remarkable journey Callot picked up much of that extraordinary knowledge of figure, feature and character which he afterwards reproduced, sometimes in such exaggerated forms, in his wonderful engravings.

When Callot at length reached Florence, a gentleman, pleased with his ingenious ardour, placed him with an artist to study; but he was not satisfied to stop short of Rome, and we find him shortly on his way thither. At Rome he made the acquaintance of Porigi and Thomassin, who, on seeing his crayon sketches, predicted for him a brilliant career as an artist. But a friend of Callot's family having accidentally encountered him, took steps to compel the fugitive to return home. By this time he had acquired such a love of wandering that he could not rest; so he ran away a second time, and a second time he was brought back by his elder brother, who caught him at Turin. At last the father, seeing resistance was in vain, gave his reluctant consent to Callot's prosecuting his studies at Rome. Thither he went accordingly; and this time he remained diligently studying design and engraving for several years, under competent masters. On his way back to France, he was encouraged by Cosimo II to remain at Florence, where he studied and worked for several years more. On the death of his patron he returned to his family at Nancy, where, by the use of his burin and needle, he shortly acquired both wealth and fame.

Still more romantic and adventurous was the career of Benvenuto Cellini, the marvellous gold-worker, painter, sculptor, engraver, engineer, and author. His life, as told by himself, is one of the most extraordinary autobiographies ever written. Giovanni Cellini, his father, was one of the Court musicians to Lorenzo de Medici at Florence; and his highest ambition concerning his son Benvenuto was that he should become an expert player on the flute. But Giovanni, having lost his appointment, found it necessary to send his son to learn some trade, and he was apprenticed to a goldsmith. The boy had already displayed a love of drawing and of art; and, applying himself to his business, he soon became a dexterous workman. Having got mixed up in a quarrel with some of the townspeople, he was banished for six months, during which period he worked with a goldsmith at Siena, gaining further experience in jewellery and gold-working.

His father still insisting on his becoming a flute-player, Benvenuto continued to practise on the instrument, though he detested it. His chief pleasure was in art, which he pursued with enthusiasm. Returning to Florence, he carefully studied the designs of Leonardo da Vinci and Michael Angelo; and, still further to improve himself in gold-working, he went on foot to Rome, where he met with a variety of adventures. He returned to Florence with the reputation of being a most expert worker in the precious metals, and his skill was soon in great request. But being of an irascible temper, he was constantly getting into scrapes, and was frequently under the necessity of flying for his life. Thus he fled from Florence in the disguise of a friar, again taking refuge at Siena, and afterwards at Rome.

During his second residence in Rome, Cellini met with extensive patronage, and he was taken into the Pope's service in the double capacity of goldsmith and musician. He was constantly studying and improving himself by acquaintance with the works of the best masters. He mounted jewels, finished enamels, engraved seals, and designed and executed works in gold, silver, and bronze, in such a style as to excel all other artists. Whenever he heard of a goldsmith who was famous in any particular branch, he immediately determined to surpass him. Thus it was that he rivalled the medals of one, the enamels of another, and the jewellery of a third; in fact, there was not a branch of his business that he did not feel impelled to excel in.

Among the statues executed by Cellini, the most important are the silver figure of Jupiter, executed at Paris for Francis I, and the Perseus, executed in bronze for the Grand Duke Cosimo of Florence. He also executed statues in marble of Apollo, Hyacinthus, Narcissus, and Neptune. The extraordinary incidents connected with the casting of the Perseus were peculiarly illustrative of the remarkable character of the man.

The Grand Duke having expressed a decided opinion that the model, when shown to him in wax, could not possibly be cast in bronze, Cellini was immediately stimulated by the predicted impossibility, not only to attempt, but to do it. He first made the clay model, baked it, and covered it with wax, which he shaped into the perfect form of a statue. Then coating the wax with a sort of earth, he baked the second covering, during which the wax dissolved and escaped, leaving the space between the two layers for the reception of the metal. To avoid disturbance, the latter process was conducted in a pit dug immediately under the furnace, from which the liquid metal was to be introduced by pipes and apertures into the mould prepared for it.

Cellini had purchased and laid in several loads of pine-wood, in anticipation of the process of casting, which now began. The furnace was filled with pieces of brass and bronze, and the fire was lit. The resinous pine-wood was soon in such a furious blaze, that the shop took fire, and part of the roof was burnt; while at the same time the wind blowing and the rain falling on the furnace kept down the heat, and prevented the metals from melting. For hours Cellini struggled to keep up the heat, continually throwing in more wood, until at length he became so exhausted and ill, that he feared he should die before the statue could be cast. He was forced to leave to his assistants the pouring in of the metal when melted, and betook himself to his bed. While those about him were condoling with him in his distress, a workman suddenly entered the room, lamenting that 'poor Benvenuto's work was irretrievably spoiled!' On hearing this, Cellini immediately sprang from his bed and rushed to the workshop, where he found the fire so much gone down that the metal had again become hard.

Sending across to a neighbour for a load of young oak which had been more than a year in drying, he soon had the fire blazing again and the metal melting and glittering. The wind was, however, still blowing with fury, and the rain falling heavily; so, to protect himself, Cellini had some tablets with pieces of tapestry and old clothes brought to him, behind which he went on hurling wood into the furnace. A mass of pewter was thrown in upon the other metal, and by stirring, sometimes with iron and sometimes with long poles, the whole soon became completely melted. At this junction, when the trying moment was close at hand, a terrible noise as of a thunderbolt was heard, and a glittering of fire flashed before Cellini's eyes. The cover of the furnace had burst, and the metal began to flow! Finding that it did not run with the proper velocity, Cellini rushed into the kitchen, bore away every piece of copper and pewter that it contained – some two hundred porringers, dishes, and kettles of different kinds – and threw them into the furnace. Then at length the metal flowed freely, and thus the splendid statue of Perseus was cast.

The divine fury of genius in which Cellini rushed to his kitchen and stripped it of its utensils for the purposes of his furnace will remind the reader of the like act of Palissy in breaking up his furniture for the purpose of baking his earthenware. Excepting, however, in their enthusiasm, no two men could be less alike in character. Cellini was an Ishmael against whom, according to his own account, every man's hand was turned. But about his extraordinary skill as a workman, and his genius as an artist, there cannot be two opinions.

Much less turbulent was the career of Nicolas Poussin, a man as pure and elevated in his ideas of art as he was in his daily life and distinguished alike for his vigour of intellect, his rectitude of character, and his noble simplicity. He was born in a very humble station, at Andeleys, near Rouen, where his father kept a small school. A country painter, much pleased with his sketches, besought his parents not to thwart him in his tastes. The painter agreed to give Poussin lessons, and he soon made such progress that his master had nothing more to teach him. Becoming restless, and desirous of further improving himself, Poussin, at the age of eighteen, set out for Paris, painting sign-boards on his way for a maintenance.

At Paris a new world of art opened before him, exciting his wonder and stimulating his emulation. He worked diligently in many studios, drawing, copying, and painting pictures. After a time he resolved, if possible, to visit Rome, and set out on his journey; but he only succeeded in getting as far as Florence, and again returned to Paris. At length Poussin succeeded in reaching Rome. There he diligently studied the old masters, and especially the ancient statues, with whose perfection he was greatly impressed. For some time he lived with the sculptor Duquesnoi, as poor as himself, and assisted him in modelling figures after the antique. With him he carefully measured some of the most celebrated statues in Rome, more particularly the 'Antinous': and it is supposed that this practice exercised considerable influence on the formation of his future style. At the same time he studied anatomy, practised drawing from the life, and made a great store of sketches of postures and attitudes of people whom he met, carefully reading at his leisure such standard books on art as he could borrow from his friends.

During all this time he remained very poor, satisfied to be continually improving himself. He was glad to sell his pictures for whatever they would bring. One, of a prophet, he sold for eight livres; and another, the 'Plague of the Philistines', he sold for 60 crowns − a picture afterwards bought by Cardinal de Richelieu for a thousand. To add to his troubles, he was stricken by a cruel malady, during the helplessness occasioned by which the Chevalier del Posso assisted him with money. For this gentleman Poussin afterwards painted the 'Rest in the Desert', a fine picture, which far more than repaid the advances made during his illness.

The brave man went on toiling and learning through suffering. Still aiming at higher things, he went to Florence and Venice, enlarging the range of his studies. The fruits of his conscientious labour at length appeared in the series of great pictures which he now began to produce – his 'Death of Germanicus', followed by 'Extreme Unction', the 'Testament of Eudamidas', the 'Manna', and the 'Abduction of the Sabines'. The monotony and the quiet of Rome were suited to his taste, and, provided he could earn a moderate living by his brush, he had no wish to leave it.

But his fame now extended beyond Rome, and repeated invitations were sent him to return to Paris. He was offered the appointment of principal painter to the King. At first he hesitated; quoted the Italian proverb, *Chi sta bene non si muove*; said he had lived fifteen years in Rome, married a wife there, and looked forward to dying and being buried there. Urged again, he consented, and while in Paris, he painted some of his greatest works – his 'Saint Xavier', the 'Baptism', and the 'Last Supper'. He was kept constantly at work. At first he did whatever he was asked to do, such as designing frontispieces for the royal books, more particularly a Bible and a Virgil, cartoons for the Louvre, and designs for tapestry; but at length he expostulated: 'It is impossible for me,' he said to M. de Chanteloup, 'to work at the same time at frontispieces for books, at a Virgin, at a picture of the Congregation of St Louis, at the various designs for the gallery, and, finally, at designs for the royal tapestry. I have only one pair of hands and a feeble head, and can neither be helped nor can my labours be lightened by another.'

The career of Ary Scheffer furnishes one of the best examples in modern times of a like high-minded devotion to art. Born at Dordrecht, the son of a German artist, he early manifested an aptitude for drawing and painting, which his parents encouraged. His father dying while he was still young, his mother resolved, though her means were but small, to remove the family to Paris, in order that her son might obtain the best opportunities for instruction. There young Scheffer was placed with Guérin the painter. But his mother's means were too limited to permit him to devote himself exclusively to study. She had sold the few jewels she possessed, and refused herself every indulgence, in order to forward the instruction of her other children. Under such circumstances, it was natural that Ary should wish to help her; and by the time he was eighteen years of age he began to paint small pictures of simple subjects, which met with a ready sale at moderate prices. He also practised portrait painting, at the same time gathering experience and earning honest money. He gradually improved in drawing, colouring, and composition. The 'Baptism' marked a new epoch in his career, and from that point he went on advancing, until his fame culminated in his pictures illustrative of 'Faust', his 'Francesca da Rimini', 'Christ the Consoler', the 'Holy Women', 'St Monica and St Augustin', and many other noble works.

One of the artists whom Scheffer most admired was Flaxman; and he once said to a friend, 'If I have unconsciously borrowed from any one in the design of the "Francesca", it must have been from something I had seen among Flaxman's drawings.' John Flaxman was the son of a humble seller of plaster casts in New Street, Covent Garden. When a child, he was such an invalid that it was his custom to sit behind his father's shop counter propped by pillows, amusing himself with drawing and reading.

Like all youthful efforts, his first designs were crude. The proud father one day showed some of them to Roubilliac the sculptor, who turned from them with a contemptuous 'pshaw!' But the boy had the right stuff in him; he had industry and patience; and he continued to labour incessantly at his books and drawings. He then tried his young powers in modelling figures in plaster of Paris, wax and clay. Some of these early works are still preserved, not because of their merit, but because they are curious as the first healthy efforts of patient genius. It was long before the boy could walk, and he only learnt to do so by hobbling along upon crutches. At length he became strong enough to walk without them.

At fifteen Flaxman entered a pupil at the Royal Academy. Notwithstanding his retiring disposition, he soon became known among the students, and great things were expected of him. Nor were their expectations disappointed: in his fifteenth year he gained the silver prize, and next year he became a candidate for the gold one. Everybody prophesied that he would carry off the medal, for there was none who surpassed him in ability and industry. Yet he lost it, and the gold medal was adjudged to a pupil who was not afterwards heard of. This failure on the part of the youth was really of service to him; for defeats do not long cast down the resolute-hearted, but only serve to call forth their real powers. 'Give me time,' said he to his father, 'and I will yet produce works that the Academy will be proud to recognize.' He redoubled his efforts, spared no pains, designed and modelled incessantly, and made steady if not rapid progress. But meanwhile poverty threatened his father's household; the plaster-cast trade yielded a very bare living; and young Flaxman, with resolute self-denial, curtailed his hours of study, and devoted himself to helping his father in the humble details of his business. He laid aside his Homer to take up the plaster-trowel. He was willing to work in the humblest department of the trade so that his father's family might be supported, and the wolf kept from the door. To this drudgery of his art he served a long apprenticeship; but it did him good. It familiarized him with steady work, and cultivated in him the spirit of patience. The discipline may have been hard, but it was wholesome.

At length, in the year 1782, when twenty-seven years of age, he quitted his father's roof and rented a small house and studio in Wardour Street, Soho; and what was more he married – Ann Denman was the name of his wife – and a cheerful, bright-souled, noble woman she was. He believed that in marrying her he should be able to work with an intenser spirit; for, like him, she had a taste for poetry and art; and besides was an enthusiastic admirer of her husband's genius. Yet when Sir Joshua Reynolds – himself a bachelor – met Flaxman shortly after his marriage, he said to him, 'So, Flaxman, I am told you are married; if so, sir, I tell you you are ruined for an artist.' Flaxman went straight home, sat down beside his wife, took her hand in his, and said, 'Ann, I am ruined for an artist.' 'How so, John? How has it happened? and who has done it?' 'It happened,' he replied, 'in the church, and Ann Denman has done it.' He then told her of Sir Joshua's remark – whose opinion was well known, and had often been expressed, that if students would excel they must bring the whole powers of their mind to bear upon their art, from the moment they rose until they went to bed; and also, that no man could be a *great* artist unless he studied the grand works of Raffaelle, Michael Angelo and others, at Rome and Florence. 'And I,' said Flaxman, drawing up his little figure to its full height, '*I* would be a great artist.' 'And a great artist you shall be,' said his wife, 'and visit Rome too, if that be really necessary to make you great.' 'But how?' asked Flaxman. '*Work and economize*,' rejoined the brave wife; 'I will never have it said that Ann Denman ruined John Flaxman for an artist.' And so it was determined by the pair that the journey to Rome was to be made when their means would admit. 'I will go to Rome,' said Flaxman, 'and show the President that wedlock is for a man's good rather than his harm; and you, Ann, shall accompany me.'

Patiently and happily the affectionate couple plodded on during five years in their humble little home in Wardour Street, always with the long journey to Rome before them. It was never lost sight of for a moment, and not a penny was uselessly spent that could be saved towards the necessary expenses. They said no word to any one about their project; solicited no aid from the Academy, but trusted only to their own patient labour and love to pursue and achieve their object.

At length Flaxman and his wife, having accumulated sufficient store of savings, set out for Rome. Arrived there, he applied himself diligently to study, maintaining himself, like other poor artists, by making copies from the antique. English visitors sought his studio, and gave him commissions; and it was then that he composed his beautiful designs illustrative of Homer, Aeschylus, and Dante. The price paid for them was moderate – only fifteen shillings apiece; but Flaxman worked for art as well as money; and the beauty of the designs brought him other friends and patrons. He executed 'Cupid and Aurora' for the munificent Thomas Hope, and the 'Fury of Athamas' for the Earl of Bristol. He then prepared to return to England, his taste improved and cultivated by careful study; but before he left Italy the Academies of Florence and Carrara recognized his merit by electing him a member.

His fame preceded him to London, where he soon found abundant employment. While at Rome he had been commissioned to execute his famous monument in memory of Lord Mansfield, and it was erected in the north transept of Westminster Abbey shortly after his return. It stands there in majestic grandeur, a monument to the genius of Flaxman himself – calm, simple, and severe. No wonder that Banks, the sculptor, then in the heyday of his fame, exclaimed when he saw it, 'This little man cuts us all out!'

When the members of the Royal Academy heard of Flaxman's return, and especially when they had an opportunity of seeing and admiring his portrait-statue of Mansfield, they were eager to have him enroled among their number. He allowed his name to be proposed in the candidates' list of associates, and was immediately elected. Shortly after, he appeared in an entirely new character. The little boy who had begun his studies behind the plaster-cast-seller's shop-counter in New Street, Covent Garden, was now a man of high intellect and recognized supremacy in art, to instruct students, in the character of Professor of Sculpture to the Royal Academy! And no man better deserved to fill that distinguished office; for none is so able to instruct others as he who, for himself and by his own efforts, has learnt to grapple with and overcome difficulties.

Chantrey was a more robust man, somewhat rough, but hearty in his demeanour; proud of his successful struggle with the difficulties which beset him in early life; and, above all, proud of his independence. He was born a poor man's child, at Norton, near Sheffield. His father dying when he was a mere boy, his mother married again. Young Chantrey used to drive an ass laden with milk-cans across its back into the neighbouring town of Sheffield, and there serve his mother's customers with milk. Such was the humble beginning of his industrial career; and it was by his own strength that he rose from that position, and achieved the highest eminence as an artist. Not taking kindly to his step-father, the boy was sent to trade, and was first placed with a grocer in Sheffield. The business was very distasteful to him; but, passing a carver's shop window one day, his eye was attracted by the glittering articles it contained, and, charmed with the idea of being a carver, he begged to be released from the grocery business with that object. His friends consented, and he was bound apprentice to the carver and gilder for seven years. His new master, besides being a carver in wood, was also a dealer in prints and plaster models; and Chantrey at once set about imitating both, studying with great industry and energy. All his spare hours were devoted to drawing, modelling, and self-improvement, and he often carried his labours far into the night. Before his apprentice-ship was out – at the age of twenty-one – he paid over to his master the whole wealth which he was able to muster – a sum of £50 – to cancel his indentures, determined to devote himself to the career of an artist.

for he was exceedingly taciturn and habitually modest – when the committee of the Scott Monument offered a prize for the best design. The competitors were numerous – including some of the greatest names in classical architecture; but the design unanimously selected was that of George Kemp, who was working at Kilwinning Abbey in Ayrshire, many miles off, when the letter reached him intimating the decision of the committee. Poor Kemp! Shortly after this event he met an untimely death, and did not live to see the first result of his indefatigable industry and self-culture embodied in stone – one of the most beautiful and appropriate memorials ever erected to literary genius.

John Gibson was another artist full of a genuine enthusiasm and love for his art, which placed him high above those sordid temptations which urge meaner natures to make time the measure of profit. He was born at Gyffn, near Conway, in North Wales – the son of a gardener. He early showed indications of his talent by the carvings in wood which he made by means of a common pocket knife; and his father, noting the direction of his talent, sent him to Liverpool and bound him apprentice to a cabinet-maker and wood-carver. He rapidly improved at his trade, and some of his carvings were much admired. He was thus naturally led to sculpture, and when eighteen years old he modelled a small figure of Time in wax, which attracted considerable notice. The Messrs Franceys, sculptors, of Liverpool, having purchased the boy's indentures, took him as their apprentice for six years, during which his genius displayed itself in many original works. From thence he proceeded to London, and afterwards to Rome; and his fame became European.

Robert Thorburn, the Royal Academician, like John Gibson, was born of poor parents. His father was a shoemaker at Dumfries. Besides Robert there were two other sons; one of whom is a skilful carver in wood. One day a lady called at the shoemaker's and found Robert, then a mere boy, engaged in drawing upon a stool which served him for a table. The boy was diligent, painstaking, staid and silent, mixing little with his companions and forming but few intimacies. About the year 1830, some gentlemen of the town provided him with the means of proceeding to Edinburgh, where he was admitted a student at the Scottish Academy. There he had the advantage of studying under competent masters, and the progress which he made was rapid. From Edinburgh he removed to London, where, we understand, he had the advantage of being introduced to notice under the patronage of the Duke of Buccleuch. We need scarcely say, however, that of whatever use patronage may have been to Thorburn in giving him an introduction to the best circles, patronage of no kind could have made him the great artist that he unquestionably is, without native genius and diligent application.

Noel Paton, the well-known painter, began his artistic career at Dunfermline and Paisley, as a drawer of patterns for tablecloths and muslin embroidered by hand: meanwhile working diligently at higher subjects, including the drawing of the human figure. He worked his way step by step, slowly yet surely; but he remained unknown until the exhibition of the prize cartoons painted for the Houses of Parliament, when his picture of the 'Spirit of Religion' (for which he obtained one of the first prizes) revealed him to the world as a genuine artist; and the works which he has since exhibited – such as the 'Reconciliation of Oberon and Titania', 'Home', and 'The Bluidy Tryste' – have shown a steady advance in artistic power and culture.

Another striking exemplification of perseverance and industry in the cultivation of art in humble life is presented in the career of James Sharples, a working blacksmith at Blackburn. He was born at Wakefield in Yorkshire, in 1825, one of a family of thirteen children. His father was a working ironfounder, and removed to Bury to follow his business. The boys received no school education, but were all sent to work as soon as they were able; and at about ten James was placed in a foundry, where he was employed for about two years as smithy-boy. After that he was sent into the engine-shop where his father worked as engine-smith. The boy's employment was to heat and carry rivets for the boiler-makers. An incident occurred in the course of his employment among the boiler-makers which first awakened in him the desire to learn drawing. He had occasionally been employed by the foreman to hold the chalked line with which he made the designs of boilers upon the floor of the workshop; and on such occasions the foreman was accustomed to hold the line, and direct the boy to make the necessary dimensions. James soon became so expert at this as to be of considerable service to the foreman; and in his leisure hours at home his great delight was to practise drawing designs of boilers upon his mother's floor.

Encouraged by his elder brother, he began to practise figure and landscape drawing, making copies of lithographs, but as yet without any knowledge of the rules of perspective and the principles of light and shade. He worked on, however, and gradually acquired expertness in copying. At sixteen he entered the Bury Mechanics' Institution in order to attend the drawing class, taught by an amateur who followed the trade of a barber. There he had a lesson a week during three months. The teacher recommended him to obtain from the library Burnet's *Practical Treatise on Painting*; but as he could not yet read with ease, he was under the necessity of getting his mother, and sometimes his elder brother, to read passages from the book for him while he sat by and listened. Feeling hampered by his ignorance of the art of reading, and eager to master the contents of Burnet's book, he ceased attending the drawing class at the Institute after the first quarter, and devoted himself to learning reading and writing at home. In this he soon succeeded; and when he again entered the Institute and took out 'Burnet' a second time, he was not only able to read it, but to make written extracts for further use. So ardently did he study the volume, that he used to rise at four o'clock in the morning to read it and copy out passages; after which he went to the foundry at six, worked until six and sometimes eight in the evening, and returned home to enter with fresh zest upon the study of Burnet, which he continued often until a late hour. Parts of his nights were also occupied in drawing and making copies of drawings. On one of these – a copy of Leonardo da Vinci's 'Last Supper' – he spent an entire night. He went to bed indeed, but his mind was so engrossed with the subject that he could not sleep, and rose again to resume his pencil.

He next proceeded to try his hand at painting in oil, for which purpose he procured some canvas from a draper, stretched it on a frame, coated it over with white lead, and began painting on it with colours bought from a house-painter. But his work proved a total failure; for the canvas was rough and knotty, and the paint would not dry. In his extremity he applied to his old teacher, the barber, from whom he first learnt that prepared canvas was to be had, and that there were colours and varnishes made for the special purposes of oil-painting. As soon, therefore, as his means would allow, he bought a small stock of the necessary articles and began afresh – his amateur master showing him how to paint; and the pupil succeeded so well that he excelled the master's copy. His first picture was a copy from an engraving called 'Sheep-shearing', and was afterwards sold by him for half-a-crown. Aided by a shilling *Guide to Oil-painting*, he went on working in his leisure hours, and gradually acquired a better knowledge of his materials. He made his own easel and palette, palette-knife, and paint-chest; he bought his paint, brushes and canvas, as he could raise the money by working overtime.

Thus assiduously working and studying, James Sharples steadily advanced in his knowledge of the principles of art, and acquired great facility in its practice. Some eighteen months after the expiry of his apprenticeship he painted a portrait of his father, which attracted considerable notice in the town; as also did the picture of 'The Forge', which he finished soon after. His success in portrait-painting obtained for him a commission from the foreman of the shop to paint a family group, and Sharples executed it so well that the foreman not only paid him the agreed price of eighteen pounds, but thirty shillings to boot. While engaged on this group, he ceased to work at the foundry, and he had thoughts of giving up his trade altogether and devoting himself exclusively to painting. He proceeded to paint several pictures, amongst others a head of Christ, an original conception, life-size, and a view of Bury; but not obtaining sufficient employment at portraits to occupy his time, or give him the prospect of a steady income, he had the good sense to resume his leather apron, and go on working at his honest trade of a blacksmith; employing his leisure hours in engraving his picture of 'The Forge', since published. He was induced to commence the engraving by the following circumstance. A Manchester picture-dealer, to whom he showed the painting, let drop the observation, that in the hands of a skilful engraver it would make a very good print. Sharples immediately conceived the idea of engraving it himself, though altogether ignorant of the art.

It would be beside our purpose to enter upon any criticism of 'The Forge' as an engraving, its merits having been already fully recognized by the art journals. The execution of the work occupied Sharples's leisure evening hours during a period of five years; and it was only when he took the plate to the printer that he for the first time saw an engraved plate produced by any other man. To this unvarnished picture of industry and genius we add one other trait, and it is a domestic one. 'I have been married seven years,' says he, 'and during that time my greatest pleasure, after I had finished my daily labour at the foundry, has been to resume my pencil or graver, frequently until a late hour in the evening, my wife meanwhile sitting by my side and reading to me from some interesting book' – a simple but beautiful testimony to the thorough common sense as well as the genuine right-heartedness of this most interesting and deserving workman.

The same industry and application which we have found to be necessary in order to acquire excellence in painting and sculpture are equally required in the sister art of music – the one being the poetry of form and colour, the other of the sounds of nature. Handel was an indefatigable and constant worker; he was never cast down by defeat, but his energy seemed to increase the more that adversity struck him. When a prey to his mortifications as an insolvent debtor, he did not give way for a moment, but in one year produced his 'Saul', 'Israel', the music for Dryden's 'Ode', his 'Twelve Grand Concertos', and the opera of 'Jupiter in Argos', among the finest of his works. As his biographer says of him, 'He braved everything, and, by his unaided self, accomplished the work of twelve men.'

Haydn, speaking of his art, said, 'It consists in taking up a subject and pursuing it.' 'Work,' said Mozart, 'is my chief pleasure.' Beethoven's favourite maxim was, 'The barriers are not erected which can say to aspiring talents and industry, "Thus far and no farther."' When Moscheles submitted his score of 'Fidelio' for the pianoforte to Beethoven, the latter found written at the bottom of the last page, 'Finis, with God's help.' Beethoven immediately wrote underneath, 'O man! help thyself!' This was the motto of his artistic life. John Sebastian Bach said of himself, 'I was industrious; whoever is equally sedulous, will be equally successful.' But there is no doubt that Bach was born with a passion for music, which formed the mainspring of his industry, and was the true secret of his success. When a mere youth, his elder brother, wishing to turn his abilities in another direction, destroyed a collection of studies which the young Sebastian, being denied candles, had copied by moonlight; proving the strong natural bent of the boy's genius. Of Meyerbeer, Bayle thus wrote from Milan in 1820: 'He is a man of some talent, but no genius; he lives solitary, working fifteen hours a day at music.' Years passed, and Meyerbeer's hard work fully brought out his genius, as displayed in his 'Roberto', 'Huguenots', 'Prophète', and other works, confessedly amongst the greatest operas which have been produced in modern times.

Although musical composition is not an art in which Englishmen have as yet greatly distinguished themselves, their energies having for the most part taken other and more practical directions, we are not without native illustrations of the power of perseverance in this special pursuit. Arne was an upholsterer's son, intended by his father for the legal profession; but his love of music was so great, that he could not be withheld from pursuing it. While engaged in an attorney's office, his means were very limited, but, to gratify his tastes, he was accustomed to borrow a livery and go into the gallery of the Opera, then appropriated to domestics. Unknown to his father he made great progress with the violin, and the first knowledge his father had of the circumstance was when accidentally calling at the house of a neighbouring gentleman, to his surprise and consternation he found his son playing the leading instrument with a party of musicians. This incident decided the fate of Arne. His father offered no further opposition to his wishes; and the world thereby lost a lawyer, but gained a musician of much taste and delicacy of feeling, who added many valuable works to our stores of English music.

The career of William Jackson, author of *The Deliverance of Israel*, an oratorio which has been successfully performed in the principal towns of his native county of York, furnishes an interesting illustration of the triumph of perseverance over difficulties in the pursuit of musical science. He was the son of a miller at Masham, a little town situated in the valley of the Yore, in the north-west corner of Yorkshire. Musical taste seems to have been hereditary in the family, for his father played the fife in the band of the Masham Volunteers, and was a singer in the parish choir. His grandfather also was leading singer and ringer at Masham Church; and one of the boy's earliest musical treats was to be present at the bell-pealing on Sunday mornings. During the service, his wonder was still more excited by the organist's performance on the barrel-organ, the doors of which were thrown open behind to let the sound fully into the church, by which the stops, pipes, barrels, staples, keyboard, and jacks were fully exposed to the wonderment of the little boys sitting in the gallery behind, and to none more than our young musician. At eight years of age he began to play upon his father's old fife, which, however, would not sound D; but his mother remedied the difficulty by buying for him a one-keyed flute; and shortly after a gentleman presented him with a flute with four silver keys. As the boy made no progress with his 'book learning', being fonder of cricket, fives and boxing than of his school lessons – the village schoolmaster giving him up as 'a bad job' – his parents sent him off to a school at Pateley Bridge. While there he found congenial society in a club of village choral singers at Brighouse Gate, and with them he learnt the solfaing gamut on the old English plan. He was thus well drilled in the reading of music, in which he soon became a proficient. His progress astonished the club, and he returned home full of musical ambition. He now learnt to play upon his father's old piano, but with little melodious result; and he became eager to possess a finger-organ, but had no means of procuring one. About this time a neighbouring parish clerk had purchased, for an insignificant sum, a small disabled barrel-organ, which had gone the circuit of the northern counties with a show. The clerk tried to revive the tones of the instrument, but failed; at last he bethought him that he would try the skill of young Jackson, who had succeeded in making some alterations and improvements in the hand-organ of the parish church. He accordingly brought it to the lad's house in a donkey cart, and in a short time the instrument was repaired, and played over its old tunes again, greatly to the owner's satisfaction.

The thought now haunted the youth that he could make a barrel-organ, and he determined to do so. His father and he set to work, and though without practice in carpentering, yet, by dint of hard labour and after many failures, they at last succeeded; and an organ was constructed which played ten tunes very decently, and the instrument was generally regarded as a marvel in the neighbourhood. Young Jackson was now frequently sent for to repair old church organs, and to put new music upon the barrels which he added to them. All this he accomplished to the satisfaction of his employers, after which he proceeded with the construction of a four-stop finger-organ, adapting to it the keys of an old harpsichord.

A village band having been set on foot at Masham, young Jackson joined it, and was ultimately appointed leader. He played all the instruments by turns, and thus acquired a considerable practical knowledge of his art: he also composed numerous tunes for the band. A new finger-organ having been presented to the parish church, he was appointed the organist. In 1839 he published his first anthem – 'For joy let fertile valleys sing'; and in the following year he gained the first prize from the Huddersfield Glee Club, for his 'Sisters of the Lea'. His other anthem, 'God be merciful to us', and the 103rd Psalm, written for a double chorus and orchestra, are well known. In the midst of these minor works, Jackson proceeded with the composition of his oratorio – 'The Deliverance of Israel from Babylon'. His practice was, to jot down a sketch of the ideas as they presented themselves to his mind, and to write them out in score in the evenings, after he had left his work in the candle-shop. His oratorio was published in parts in the course of 1844–5, and he published the last chorus on his twenty-ninth birthday. Mr Jackson eventually settled as a professor of music at Bradford, where he contributed in no small degree to the cultivation of the musical taste of that town and its neighbourhood. Some years since he had the honour of leading his fine company of Bradford choral singers before Queen Victoria at Buckingham Palace; on which occasion, as well as at the Crystal Palace, some choral pieces of his composition were performed with great effect.

Such is a brief outline of the career of a self-taught musician, whose life affords but another illustration of the power of self-help, and the force of courage and industry in enabling a man to surmount and overcome early difficulties and obstructions of no ordinary kind.

7. Industry and the Peerage

The blood of all men flows from equally remote sources; and though some are unable to trace their line directly beyond their grandfathers, all are nevertheless justified in placing at the head of their pedigree the great progenitors of the race, as Lord Chesterfield did when he wrote, 'ADAM *de Stanhope* – EVE *de Stanhope*.' No class is ever long stationary. The mighty fall, and the humble are exalted. New families take the place of the old, who disappear among the ranks of the common people. Burke's *Vicissitudes of Families* strikingly exhibits this rise and fall of families, and shows that the misfortunes which overtake the rich and noble are greater in proportion than those which overwhelm the poor.

The great bulk of our peerage is comparatively modern, so far as titles go; but it is not the less noble that it has been recruited to so large an extent from the ranks of honourable industry. In olden times, the wealth and commerce of London, conducted as it was by energetic and enterprising men, was a prolific source of peerages. Thus, the earldom of Cornwallis was founded by Thomas Cornwallis, the Cheapside merchant; that of Essex by William Capel, the draper; and that of Craven by William Craven, the merchant tailor. The modern Earl of Warwick is not descended from the 'King-maker', but from William Greville, the woolstapler; whilst the modern dukes of Northumberland find their head, not in the Percys, but in Hugh Smithson, a respectable London apothecary. The founders of the families of Dartmouth, Radnor, Ducie and Pomfret were respectively a skinner, a silk manufacturer, a merchant tailor, and a Calais merchant; whilst the founders of the peerages of Tankerville, Dormer and Coventry were mercers. The ancestors of Earl Romney, and Lord Dudley and Ward, were goldsmiths and jewellers; and Lord Dacre's was a banker in the reign of Charles I, as Lord Overstone is in that of Queen Victoria. Edward Osborne, the founder of the Dukedom of Leeds, was apprentice to William Hewet, a rich clothworker of London Bridge, whose only daughter he courageously rescued from drowning, by leaping into the Thames after her, and eventually married. Among other peerages founded by trade are those of Fitzwilliam, Leigh, Petre, Cowper, Darnley, Hill and Carrington. The founders of the houses of Foley and Normanby were remarkable men in many respects, and, as furnishing striking examples of energy of character, the story of their lives is worthy of preservation.

The father of Richard Foley, the founder of the family, was a small yeoman living in the neighbourhood of Stourbridge in the time of Charles I. That place was then the centre of the iron manufacture of the Midland districts, and Richard was brought up to work at one of the branches of the trade – that of nail-making. He was thus a daily observer of the great labour and loss of time caused by the clumsy process then adopted for dividing the rods of iron in the manufacture of nails. It appeared that the Stourbridge nailers were gradually losing their trade in consequence of the importation of nails from Sweden, by which they were undersold in the market. It became known that the Swedes were enabled to make their nails so much cheaper by the use of splitting mills and machinery, which had completely superseded the laborious process of preparing the rods for nail-making then practised in England.

Richard Foley, having ascertained this much, determined to make himself master of the process. He suddenly disappeared from the neighbourhood of Stourbridge, and was not heard of for several years. No one knew whither he had gone, not even his own family; for he had not informed them of his intention, lest he should fail. He had little or no money in his pocket, but contrived to get to Hull, where he engaged himself on board a ship bound for a Swedish port, and worked his passage there. The only article of property which he possessed was his fiddle, and on landing in Sweden he begged and fiddled his way to the Dannemora mines, near Uppsala. He was received into the works, to every part of which he had access; and he seized the opportunity thus afforded him of storing his mind with observations, and mastering, as he thought, the mechanism of iron splitting.

Returned to England, he communicated the results of his voyage to Mr Knight and another person at Stourbridge, who had sufficient confidence in him to advance the requisite funds for the purpose of erecting buildings and machinery for splitting iron by the new process. But when set to work, to the great vexation and disappointment of all, and especially of Richard Foley, it was found that the machinery would not act – at all events it would not split the bars of iron. Again Foley disappeared. He had again set out for Sweden, accompanied by his fiddle as before, and found his way to the iron works, where he was joyfully welcomed by the miners; and, to make sure of their fiddler, they this time lodged him in the very splitting-mill itself. He now carefully examined the works, and soon discovered the cause of his failure. He made drawings or tracings of the machinery as well as he could, though this was a branch of art quite new to him; and after remaining at the place long enough to enable him to verify his observations, and to impress the mechanical arrangements clearly and vividly on his mind, he again left the miners, reached a Swedish port, and took ship for England. A man of such purpose could not but succeed. Arrived amongst his surprised friends, he now completed his arrangements, and the results were entirely successful. By his skill and his industry he soon laid the foundations of a large fortune, at the same time that he restored the business of an extensive district. He himself continued, during his life, to carry on his trade, aiding and encouraging all works of benevolence in his neighbourhood.

William Petty, the founder of the house of Lansdowne, was a man of like energy and public usefulness in his day. He was the son of a clothier in humble circumstances, at Romsey, in Hampshire, where he was born in 1623. In his boyhood he obtained a tolerable education at the grammar school of his native town: after which he determined to improve himself by study at the University of Caen, in Normandy. Whilst there he contrived to support himself unassisted by his father, carrying on a sort of small pedlar's trade with 'a little stock of merchandise'. Returning to England, he had himself bound apprentice to a sea captain, who 'drubbed him with a rope's end' for the badness of his sight. He left the navy in disgust, taking to the study of medicine. When at Paris he engaged in dissection, during which time he also drew diagrams for Hobbes, who was then writing his treatise on Optics. He was reduced to such poverty that he subsisted for two or three weeks entirely on walnuts. But again he began to trade in a small way, turning an honest penny, and he was enabled shortly to return to England with money in his pocket. Being of an ingenious mechanical turn, we find him taking out a patent for a letter-copying machine. He began to write upon the arts and sciences, and practised chemistry and physic with such success that his reputation shortly became considerable. Associating with men of science, the project of forming a Society for its prosecution was discussed, and the first meetings of the infant Royal Society were held at his lodgings. At Oxford he acted for a time as deputy to the anatomical professor there, who had a great repugnance to dissection. In 1652 his industry was rewarded by the appointment of physician to the army in Ireland, whither he went; and whilst there he was the medical attendant of three successive lords-lieutenant, Lambert, Fleetwood, and Henry Cromwell. Large grants of forfeited land having been awarded to the Puritan soldiery, Petty observed that the lands were very inaccurately measured; and in the midst of his many avocations he undertook to do the work himself. His appointments became so numerous and lucrative that he was charged by the envious with corruption, and removed from them all; but he was again taken into favour at the Restoration.

Petty was a most indefatigable contriver, inventor, and organizer of industry. One of his inventions was a double-bottomed ship, to sail against wind and tide. He published treatises on dyeing, on naval philosophy, on woollen cloth manufacture, on political arithmetic, and many other subjects. He founded iron works, opened lead mines, and commenced a pilchard fishery and a timber trade; in the midst of which he found time to take part in the discussions of the Royal Society, to which he largely contributed. He left an ample fortune to his sons, the eldest of whom was created Baron Shelburne.

Another family, ennobled by invention and trade in our own day, is that of Strutt of Belper. Their patent of nobility was virtually secured by Jedediah Strutt in 1758, when he invented his machine for making ribbed stockings, and thereby laid the foundations of a fortune which the subsequent bearers of the name have largely increased and nobly employed. The father of Jedediah was a farmer and maltster, who did but little for the education of his children; yet they all prospered. Jedediah was the second son, and when a boy assisted his father in the work of the farm. At an early age he exhibited a taste for mechanics, and introduced several improvements in the rude agricultural implements of the period. On the death of his uncle he succeeded to a farm at Blackwall, near Normanton, long in the tenancy of the family, and shortly after he married Miss Wollatt, the daughter of a Derby hosier. Having learned from his wife's brother that various unsuccessful attempts had been made to manufacture ribbed stockings, he proceeded to study the subject with a view to effect what others had failed in accomplishing. He accordingly obtained a stocking-frame, and after mastering its construction and mode of action, he proceeded to introduce new combinations, by means of which he succeeded in effecting a variation in the plain looped-work of the frame, and was thereby enabled to turn out 'ribbed' hosiery. Having secured a patent for the improved machine, he removed to Derby, and there entered largely on the manufacture of ribbed stockings, in which he was very successful. He afterwards joined Arkwright, of the merits of whose invention he fully satisfied himself, and found the means of securing his patent, as well as erecting a large cotton-mill at Cranford, in Derbyshire. After the expiry of the partnership with Arkwright, the Strutts erected extensive cotton-mills at Milford, near Belper, which worthily gives its title to the present head of the family. The sons of the founder were, like their father, distinguished for their mechanical ability. Thus William Strutt, the eldest, is said to have invented a self-acting mule, the success of which was only prevented by the mechanical skill of that day being unequal to its manufacture. Edward, the son of William, was a man of eminent mechanical genius, having early discovered the principle of suspension-wheels for carriages: he had a wheel-barrow and two carts made on the principle, which were used on his farm near Belper. It may be added that the Strutts have throughout been distinguished for their noble employment of the wealth which their industry and skill have brought them; that they have sought in all ways to improve the moral and social condition of the work-people in their employment; and that they have been liberal donors in every good cause – of which the presentation, by Mr Joseph Strutt, of the beautiful park or Arboretum at Derby, as a gift to the townspeople for ever, affords only one of many illustrations.

No less industry and energy have been displayed by the many brave men, both in present and past times, who have earned the peerage by their valour on land and at sea. Not to mention the older feudal lords, whose tenure depended upon military service, and who so often led the van of the English armies in great national encounters, we may point to Nelson, St Vincent, and Lyons – to Wellington, Hill, Hardinge,

Clyde, and many more in recent times, who have nobly earned their rank by their distinguished services. But plodding industry has far oftener worked its way to the peerage by the honourable pursuit of the legal profession than by any other. No fewer than seventy British peerages, including two dukedoms, have been founded by successful lawyers. Mansfield and Erskine were, it is true, of noble family; but the latter used to thank God that out of his own family he did not know a lord.

Lord Lyndhurst's father was a portrait painter, and that of St Leonards a perfumer and hairdresser in Burlington Street. Young Edward Sugden was originally an errand-boy in the office of the late Mr Groom, of Henrietta Street, Cavendish Square, a certificated conveyancer; and it was there that the future Lord Chancellor of Ireland obtained his first notions of law. The origin of the late Lord Tenterden was perhaps the humblest of all, nor was he ashamed of it; for he felt that the industry, study, and application, by means of which he achieved his eminent position, were entirely due to himself. It is related of him, that on one occasion he took his son Charles to a little shed, then standing opposite the western front of Canterbury Cathedral, and, pointing it out to him, said, 'Charles, you see this little shop; I have brought you here on purpose to show it you. In that shop your grandfather used to shave for a penny: that is the proudest reflection of my life.' When a boy, Lord Tenterden was a singer in the Cathedral, and it is a curious circumstance that his destination in life was changed by a disappointment. When he and Mr Justice Richards were going the Home Circuit together, they went to service in the Cathedral; and on Richards commending the voice of a singing man in the choir, Lord Tenterden said, 'Ah, that is the only man I ever envied! When at school in this town, we were candidates for a chorister's place, and he obtained it.'

Not less remarkable was the rise, to the same distinguished office of Lord Chief Justice, of the rugged Kenyon and the robust Ellenborough; nor was he a less notable man who recently held the same office – the astute Lord Campbell, late Lord Chancellor of England, son of a parish minister in Fifeshire. For many years he worked hard as a reporter for the press, while diligently preparing himself for the practice of his profession. It is said of him, that at the beginning of his career he was accustomed to walk from county town to county town when on circuit, being as yet too poor to afford the luxury of posting.

There have been other illustrious instances of Lord Chancellors who have plodded up the steep of fame and honour with equal energy and success. The career of the late Lord Eldon is perhaps one of the most remarkable examples. He was the son of a Newcastle coal-fitter; a mischievous rather than a studious boy; a great scapegrace at school, and the subject of many terrible thrashings – for orchard-robbing was one of the favourite exploits of the future Lord Chancellor. But by this time his eldest son William (afterwards Lord Stowell), who had gained a scholarship at Oxford, wrote to his father, 'Send Jack up to me, I can do better for him.' John was sent up to Oxford accordingly, where, by his brother's influence and his own application, he succeeded in obtaining a fellowship. He married and lost his fellowship, and at the same time shut himself out from preferment in the Church. He accordingly turned his attention to the study of the law.

John Scott came up to London, and took a small house in Cursitor Lane, where he settled down to the study of the law. He worked with great diligence and resolution; rising at four every morning and studying till late at night, binding a wet towel round his head to keep himself awake. When at length called to the bar, he waited long for employment. His first year's earnings amounted to only nine shillings. For four years he assiduously attended the London Courts and the Northern Circuit, with little better success. Even in his native town, he seldom had other than pauper cases to defend. The results were indeed so discouraging, that he had almost determined to relinquish his chance of London business, and settle down in some provincial town as a country barrister. But as he had escaped being a grocer, a coal-fitter, and a country parson, so did he also escape being a country lawyer.

An opportunity at length occurred which enabled John Scott to exhibit the large legal knowledge which he had so laboriously acquired. In a case in which he was engaged, he urged a legal point against the wishes both of the attorney and client who employed him. The Master of the Rolls decided against him, but on an appeal to the House of Lords, Lord Thurlow reversed the decision on the very point that Scott had urged. On leaving the House that day, a solicitor tapped him on the shoulder and said, 'Young man, your bread and butter's cut for life.' It was in the dull but unflinching drudgery of the early part of his career that he laid the foundation of his future success. He won his spurs by perseverance, knowledge, and ability, diligently cultivated. He was successively appointed to the offices of solicitor and attorney-general, and rose steadily upwards to the highest office that the Crown had to bestow – that of Lord Chancellor of England, which he held for a quarter of a century.

Henry Bickersteth was the son of a surgeon at Kirkby Lonsdale, in Westmorland, and was himself educated to that profession. As a student at Edinburgh, he distinguished himself by the steadiness with which he worked, and the application which he devoted to the science of medicine. Returned to Kirkby Lonsdale, he took an active part in his father's practice; but he had no liking for the profession, and grew discontented with the obscurity of a country town. He went on, nevertheless, diligently improving himself, and engaged on speculations in the higher branches of physiology. In conformity with his own wish, his father consented to send him to Cambridge, where it was his intention to take a medical degree with the view of practising in the metropolis. Close application to his studies, however, threw him out of health, and, with a view of re-establishing his strength, he accepted the appointment of travelling physician to Lord Oxford. While abroad he mastered Italian, and acquired a great admiration for Italian literature, but no greater liking for medicine than before. On the contrary, he determined to abandon it; but returning to Cambridge, he took his degree; and that he worked hard may be inferred from the fact that he was senior wrangler of his year. Disappointed in his desire to enter the army, he turned to the bar, and entered a student of the Inner Temple. He worked as hard at law as he had done at medicine. Writing to his father, he said, 'Everybody says to me, "You are certain of success in the end – only persevere"; and though I don't well understand how this is to happen, I try to believe it as much as I can, and I shall not fail to do everything in my power.' At twenty-eight he was called to the bar, and had every step in life yet to make. His means were straitened, and he lived upon the contributions of his friends. For years he studied and waited. Still no business came. He stinted himself in recreation, in clothes, and even in the necessaries of life; struggling on indefatigably through all. Writing home, he 'confessed that he hardly knew how he should be able to struggle on till he had fair time and opportunity to establish himself'. After three years' waiting, still without success, he wrote to his friends that rather than be a burden upon them longer, he was willing to give the matter up and return to Cambridge, 'where he was sure of support and some profit'. The friends at home sent him another small remittance, and he persevered. Business gradually came in. Acquitting himself creditably in small matters, he was at length entrusted with cases of greater importance. He was a man who never missed an opportunity, nor allowed a legitimate chance of improvement to escape him. His unflinching industry soon began to tell upon his fortunes; a few more years and he was not only enabled to do without assistance from home, but he was in a position to pay back with interest the debts which he had incurred. The clouds had dispersed, and the after career of Henry Bickersteth was one of honour, of emolument, and of distinguished fame. He ended his career as Master of the Rolls, sitting in the House of Peers as Baron Langdale. His life affords only another illustration of the power of patience, perseverance, and conscientious working, in elevating the character of the individual, and crowning his labours with the most complete success.

8. Energy and Courage

There is a famous speech recorded of an old Norseman, thoroughly characteristic of the Teuton. 'I believe neither in idols nor demons,' said he, 'I put my sole trust in my own strength of body and soul.' The ancient crest of a pickaxe with the motto of 'Either I will find a way or make one', was an expression of the same sturdy independence which to this day distinguishes the descendants of the Northmen. Indeed, nothing could be more characteristic of the Scandinavian mythology than that it had a god with a hammer. A man's character is seen in small matters; and from even so slight a test as the mode in which a man wields a hammer, his energy may in some measure be inferred. Thus an eminent Frenchman hit off in a single phrase the characteristic quality of the inhabitants of a particular district, in which a friend of his proposed to settle and buy land. 'Beware,' said he, 'of making a purchase there; I know the men of that department; the pupils who come from it to our veterinary school at Paris *do not strike hard upon the anvil*; they want energy; and you will not get a satisfactory return on any capital you may invest there.' A fine and just appreciation of character, indicating the thoughtful observer; and strikingly illustrative of the fact that it is the energy of the individual men that gives strength to a State, and confers a value even upon the very soil which they cultivate.

The cultivation of this quality is of the greatest importance; resolute determination in the pursuit of worthy objects being the foundation of all true greatness of character. Energy enables a man to force his way through irksome drudgery and dry details and carries him onward and upward in every station in life. It accomplishes more than genius, with not one-half the disappointment and peril. It is not eminent talent that is required to ensure success in any pursuit, so much as purpose – not merely the power to achieve, but the will to labour energetically and perseveringly. Hence energy of will may be defined to be the very central power of character in a man – in a word, it is the Man himself. It gives impulse to his every action, and soul to every effort. True hope is based on it – and it is hope that gives the real perfume to life. There is a fine heraldic motto on a broken helmet in Battle Abbey, 'L'espoir est ma force', which might be the motto of every man's life. 'Woe unto him that is faint-hearted,' says the son of Sirach. There is, indeed, no blessing equal to the possession of a stout heart. Even if a man fail in his efforts, it will be a satisfaction to him to enjoy the consciousness of having done his best. In humble life nothing can be more cheering and beautiful than to see a man combating suffering by patience, triumphing in his integrity, and who, when his feet are bleeding and his limbs failing him, still walks upon his courage.

Hugh Miller said the only school in which he was properly taught was 'that world-wide school in which toil and hardship are the severe but noble teachers'. He who allows his application to falter, or shirks his work on frivolous pretexts, is on the sure road to ultimate failure. Let any task be undertaken as a thing not possible to be evaded and it will soon come to be performed with alacrity and cheerfulness. Charles IX of Sweden was a firm believer in the power of will, even in youth. Laying his hand on the head of his youngest son when engaged on a difficult task, he exclaimed, 'He *shall* do it! he *shall* do it!' The habit of application becomes easy in time, like every other habit. Thus persons with comparatively moderate powers will accomplish much, if they apply themselves wholly and indefatigably to one thing at a time. Fowell Buxton placed his confidence in ordinary means and extraordinary application; realizing the scriptural injunction, 'Whatsoever thy hand findeth to do, do it with all thy might'; and he attributed his own success in life to his practice of 'being a whole man to one thing at a time'.

Nothing that is of real worth can be achieved without courageous working. Man owes his growth chiefly to that active striving of the will, that encounter with difficulty, which we call effort; and it is astonishing to find how often results apparently impracticable are thus made possible. An intense anticipation itself transforms possibility into reality; our desires being often but the precursors of the things which we are capable of performing. On the contrary, the timid and hesitating find everything impossible, chiefly because it seems so.

Whatever theoretical conclusions logicians may have formed as to the freedom of the will, each individual feels that practically he is free to choose between good and evil – that he is not as a mere straw thrown upon the water to mark the direction of the current, but that he has within him the power of a strong swimmer, and is capable of striking out for himself, of buffeting with the waves, and directing to a great extent his own independent course. There is no absolute constraint upon our volitions, and we feel and know that we are not bound, as by a spell, with reference to our actions. It would paralyse all desire of excellence were we to think otherwise. The entire business and conduct of life, with its domestic rules, its social arrangements, and its public institutions, proceed upon the practical conviction that the will is free. Without this where would be responsibility? – and what the advantage of teaching, advising, preaching, reproof, and correction? What were the use of laws, were it not the universal belief, as it is the universal fact, that men obey them or not very much as they individually determine? In every moment of our life, conscience is proclaiming that our will is free. It is the only thing that is wholly ours, and it rests solely with ourselves individually whether we give it the right or the wrong direction. Our habits or our temptations are not our masters, but we of them. Even in yielding, conscience tells us we might resist; and that were we determined to master them, there would not be required for that purpose a stronger resolution than we know ourselves to be capable of exercising.

Buxton held the conviction that a young man might be very much what he pleased, provided he formed a strong resolution and held to it. Writing to one of his sons, he said to him, 'You are now at that period of life in which you must make a turn to the right or the left. You must now give proofs of principle, determination, and strength of mind; or you must sink into idleness, and acquire the habits and character of a desultory, ineffective young man; and if once you fall to that point, you will find it no easy matter to rise again. I am sure that a young man may be very much what he pleases. In my own case it was so ... Much of my happiness, and all my prosperity in life, have resulted from the change I made at your age. If you seriously resolve to be energetic and industrious, depend upon it that you will for your whole life have reason to rejoice that you were wise enough to form and to act upon that determination.' As will, considered without regard to direction, is simply constancy, firmness, perseverance, it will be obvious that everything depends upon right direction and motives. Directed towards the enjoyment of the senses, the strong will may be a demon, and the intellect merely its debased slave; but directed towards good, the strong will is a king, and the intellect the minister of man's highest well-being.

'Where there is a will there is a way', is an old and true saying. He who resolves upon doing a thing, by that very resolution often scales the barriers to it, and secures its achievement. To think we are able, is almost to be so – to determine upon attainment is frequently attainment itself. Thus, earnest resolution has often seemed to have about it almost a savour of omnipotence.

One of Napoleon's favourite maxims was, 'The truest wisdom is a resolute determination.' His life, beyond most others, vividly showed what a powerful and unscrupulous will could accomplish. He threw his whole force of body and mind direct upon his work. Imbecile rulers and the nations they governed went down before him in succession. He was told that the Alps stood in the way of his armies – 'There shall be no Alps,' he said, and the road across the Simplon was constructed, through a district formerly almost inaccessible. 'Impossible,' said he, 'is a word only to be found in the dictionary of fools.' He was a man who toiled terribly; sometimes employing and exhausting four secretaries at a time. He spared no one, not even himself. His influence inspired other men, and put a new life into them. 'I made my generals out of mud,' he said. But all was of no avail; for Napoleon's intense selfishness was his ruin, and the ruin of France, which he left a prey to anarchy. His life taught the lesson that power, however energetically wielded, without beneficence, is fatal to its possessor and its subjects; and that knowledge, or knowingness, without goodness, is but the incarnate principle of Evil.

Our own Wellington was a far greater man. Not less resolute, firm, and persistent, but more self-denying, conscientious, and truly patriotic. Napoleon's aim was 'Glory'; Wellington's watchword, like Nelson's, was 'Duty'. The former word, it is said, does not once occur in his despatches; the latter often, but never accompanied by any high-sounding professions. The greatest difficulties could neither embarrass nor intimidate Wellington; his energy invariably rising in proportion to the obstacles to be surmounted. The patience, the firmness, the resolution, with which he bore through the maddening vexations and gigantic difficulties of the Peninsular campaigns, is, perhaps, one of the sublimest things to be found in history. In Spain, Wellington not only exhibited the genius of the general, but the comprehensive wisdom of the statesman. Though his natural temper was irritable in the extreme, his high sense of duty enabled him to restrain it; and to those about him his patience seemed absolutely inexhaustible. His great character stands untarnished by ambition, by avarice, or any low passion. Though a man of powerful individuality, he yet displayed a great variety of endowment. The equal of Napoleon in generalship, he was as prompt, vigorous, and daring as Clive; as wise a statesman as Cromwell; and as pure and high-minded as Washington. The great Wellington left behind him an enduring reputation, founded on toilsome campaigns won by skilful combination, by fortitude which nothing could exhaust, by sublime daring, and perhaps by still sublimer patience.

Energy usually displays itself in promptitude and decision. When Ledyard the traveller was asked by the African Association when he would be ready to set out for Africa, he immediately answered, 'Tomorrow morning.' Blucher's promptitude obtained for him the cognomen of 'Marshal Forwards' throughout the Prussian army. When John Jervis, afterwards Earl St Vincent, was asked when he would be ready to join his ship, he replied, 'Directly.' And when Sir Colin Campbell, appointed to the command of the Indian army, was asked when he could set out, his answer was, 'Tomorrow' – an earnest of his subsequent success. For it is rapid decision, and a similar promptitude in action, such as taking instant advantage of an enemy's mistakes, that so often win battles.

India has been a great field for the display of British energy. From Clive to Havelock and Clyde there is a long and honourable roll of distinguished names in Indian legislation and warfare – such as Wellesley, Metcalfe, Outram, Edwardes and the Lawrences. Another great but sullied name is that of Warren Hastings – a man of dauntless will and indefatigable industry. His family was ancient and illustrious; but their vicissitudes of fortune and ill-requited loyalty in the cause of the Stuarts brought them to poverty, and the family estate at Daylesford, of which they had been lords of the manor for hundreds of years, at length passed from their hands. The last Hastings of Daylesford had, however, presented the parish living to his second son; and it was in his house, many years later, that Warren Hastings, his grandson, was born.

The boy learnt his letters at the village school, on the same bench with the children of the peasantry. He played in the fields which his fathers had owned; and what the loyal and brave Hastings of Daylesford *had* been, was ever in the boy's thoughts. His young ambition was fired, and it is said that one summer's day, when only seven years old, as he laid him down on the bank of the stream which flowed through the domain, he formed in his mind the resolution that he would yet recover possession of the family lands. It was the romantic vision of a boy; yet he lived to realize it. The dream became a passion, rooted in his very life; and he pursued his determination through youth up to manhood, with that calm but indomitable force of will which was the most striking peculiarity of his character. The orphan boy became one of the most powerful men of his time; he retrieved the fortunes of his line; bought back the old estate, and rebuilt the family mansion.

Sir Charles Napier was another Indian leader of extraordinary courage and determination. He took the right method of inspiring his men with his own heroic spirit. He worked as hard as any private in the ranks. 'The great art of commanding,' he said, 'is to take a fair share of the work. The man who leads an army cannot succeed unless his whole mind is thrown into his work. The more trouble, the more labour must be given; the more danger, the more pluck must be shown, till all is overpowered.' A young officer who accompanied him in his campaign in the Cutchee Hills, once said, 'When I see that old man incessantly on his horse, how can I be idle who am young and strong? I would go into a loaded cannon's mouth if he ordered me.' This remark, when repeated to Napier, he said was ample reward for his toils.

But not less energy and courage have been displayed in India and the East by men of various nations, in other lines of action more peaceful and beneficent than that of war. And while the heroes of the sword are remembered, the heroes of the gospel ought not to be forgotten. From Xavier to Martyn and Williams, there has been a succession of illustrious missionary labourers, working in a spirit of sublime self-sacrifice, without any thought of worldly honour, inspired solely by the hope of seeking out and rescuing the lost and fallen of their race. Borne up by invincible courage and never-failing patience, these men have endured privations, braved dangers, walked through pestilence, and borne all toils, fatigues, and sufferings, yet held on their way rejoicing, glorying even in martyrdom itself. Of these one of the first and most illustrious was Francis Xavier. Born of noble lineage, and with pleasure, power, and honour within his reach, he proved by his life that there are higher objects in the world than rank, and nobler aspirations than the accumulation of wealth. He was a true gentleman in manners and sentiment; brave, honourable, generous; easily led, yet capable of leading; easily persuaded, yet himself persuasive; a most patient, resolute and energetic man. At the age of twenty-two he was earning his living as a public teacher of philosophy at the University of Paris. There Xavier became the intimate friend and associate of Loyola, and shortly afterwards he conducted the pilgrimage of the first little band of proselytes to Rome.

When John III of Portugal resolved to plant Christianity in the Indian territories subject to his influence, Bobadilla was first selected as his missionary; but being disabled by illness, it was found necessary to make another selection, and Xavier was chosen. Repairing his tattered cassock, and with no other baggage than his breviary, he at once started for Lisbon and embarked for the East.

Arrived at Goa, Xavier was shocked at the depravity of the people, settlers as well as natives; for the former had imported the vices without the restraints of civilization, and the latter had only been too apt to imitate their bad example. Passing along the streets of the city, sounding his handbell as he went, he implored the people to send him their children to be instructed. He shortly succeeded in collecting a large number of scholars, whom he carefully taught day by day, at the same time visiting the sick, the lepers, and the wretched of all classes, with the object of assuaging their miseries, and bringing them to the Truth.

On he went, his handbell sounding along the coast of Comorin, among the towns and villages, the temples and the bazaars, summoning the natives to gather about him and be instructed. He had translations made of the Catechism, the Apostles' Creed, the Commandments, the Lord's Prayer, and some of the devotional offices of the Church. Committing these to memory in their own tongue he recited them to the children, until they had them by heart; after which he sent them forth to teach the words to their parents and neighbours. At Cape Comorin he appointed thirty teachers, who, under himself, presided over thirty Christian Churches, though the Churches were but humble, in most cases consisting only of a cottage surmounted by a cross. Thence he passed to Travancore, sounding his way from village to village, baptizing until his hands dropped with weariness, and repeating his formulas until his voice became almost inaudible. According to his own account, the success of his mission surpassed his highest expectations. His pure, earnest, and beautiful life, and the irresistible eloquence of his deeds, made converts wherever he went; and by sheer force of sympathy, those who saw him and listened to him insensibly caught a portion of his ardour.

Other missionaries have followed Xavier in the same field of work, such as Schwartz, Carey and Marshman in India; Gutzlaff and Morrison in China; Williams in the South Seas; Campbell, Moffat and Livingstone in Africa. John Williams, the martyr of Erromanga, was originally apprenticed to a furnishing ironmonger. A casual sermon which he heard gave his mind a serious bias, and he became a Sunday-school teacher. The cause of missions having been brought under his notice at some of his society's meetings, he determined to devote himself to this work. His services were accepted by the London Missionary Society; and his master allowed him to leave the ironmonger's shop before the expiry of his indentures. The islands of the Pacific Ocean were the principal scene of his labours – more particularly Huahine in Tahiti, Raiatea and Raratonga. Like the Apostles, he worked with his hands – at blacksmith work, gardening, shipbuilding; and he endeavoured to teach the islanders the art of civilized life, at the same time that he instructed them in the truths of religion. It was in the course of his indefatigable labours that he was massacred by savages on the shore of Erromanga – none worthier than he to wear the martyr's crown.

The career of Dr Livingstone is one of the most interesting of all. His ancestors were poor but honest Highlanders, and it is related of one of them, renowned in his district for wisdom and prudence, that when on his death-bed he called his children round him and left them these words, the only legacy he had to bequeath – 'In my lifetime,' said he, 'I have searched most carefully through all the traditions I could find of our family, and I never could discover that there was a dishonest man among our forefathers: if, therefore, any of you or your children should take to dishonest ways, it will not be because it runs in our blood;

it does not belong to you: I leave this precept with you – Be honest.' At the age of ten Livingstone was sent to work in a cotton factory near Glasgow as a 'piecer'. With part of his first week's wages he bought a Latin grammar, and began to learn that language, pursuing the study for years at a night school. He would sit up conning his lessons till twelve or later, when not sent to bed by his mother, for he had to be up and at work in the factory every morning by six. In this way he plodded through Virgil and Horace, also reading extensively all books, excepting novels, that came in his way, but more especially scientific works and books of travels. He occupied his spare hours which were but few, in the pursuit of botany, scouring the neighbourhood to collect plants. He even carried on his reading amidst the roar of the factory machinery, so placing the book upon the spinning-jenny which he worked that he could catch sentence after sentence as he passed it. In this way the persevering youth acquired much useful knowledge; and as he grew older, the desire possessed him of becoming a missionary to the heathen. With this object he set himself to obtain a medical education, in order the better to be qualified for the work. At length he finished his medical curriculum, wrote his Latin thesis, passed his examinations, and was admitted a licentiate of the Faculty of Physicians and Surgeons. At first he thought of going to China, but the war then waging with that country prevented his following out the idea; and having offered his services to the London Missionary Society, he was by them sent out to Africa, which he reached in 1840. He had intended to proceed to China by his own efforts; and he says the only pang he had in going to Africa at the charge of the London Missionary Society was, because 'it was not quite agreeable to one accustomed to work his own way to become, in a manner, dependent upon others'. Arrived in Africa he set to work with great zeal. He could not brook the idea of merely entering upon the labours of others, but cut out a large sphere of independent work, preparing himself for it by undertaking manual labour in building and other handicraft employment, in addition to teaching, which, he says, 'made me generally as much exhausted and unfit for study in the evenings as ever I had been when a cotton-spinner'. Whilst labouring amongst the Bechuanas, he dug canals, built houses, cultivated fields, reared cattle, and taught the natives to work as well as worship. One of his last known acts is thoroughly characteristic of the man. The

Birkenhead steam launch, which he took out with him to Africa, having proved a failure, he sent home orders for the construction of another vessel at an estimated cost of £2,000. This sum he proposed to defray out of the means which he had set aside for his children arising from the profits of his books of travels. 'The children must make it up themselves', was in effect his expression in sending home the order for the appropriation of the money.

Jonas Hanway was another of the many patient and persevering men who have made England what it is – content simply to do with energy the work they have been appointed to do, and go to their rest thankfully when it is done. He was born in 1712, at Portsmouth, where his father, a store-keeper in the dockyard, being killed by an accident, he was left an orphan at an early age. His mother removed with her children to London, where she had them put to school, and struggled hard to bring them up respectably. At seventeen Jonas was sent to Lisbon to be apprenticed to a merchant, where his close attention to business, his punctuality, and his strict honour and integrity gained for him the respect and esteem of all who knew him. Returning to London in 1743, he accepted the offer of a partnership in an English mercantile house at St Petersburg engaged in the Caspian trade, then in its infancy. Hanway went to Russia for the purpose of extending the business; and shortly after his arrival at the capital he set out for Persia, with a caravan of English bales of cloth making twenty carriage loads. At Astracan he sailed for Astrabad, on the south-eastern shore of the Caspian; but he had scarcely landed his bales, when an insurrection broke out, his goods were seized, and though he afterwards recovered the principal part of them, the fruits of his enterprise were in a great measure lost. A plot was set on foot to seize himself and his party; so he took to sea and, after encountering great perils, reached Ghilan in safety. His escape on this occasion gave him the first idea of the words which he afterwards adopted as the motto of his life – '*Never Despair*'. He afterwards resided in St Petersburg for five years, carrying on a prosperous business. But a relative having left him some property, and his own means being considerable, he left Russia, and arrived in his native country in 1750. His object in returning to England was, as he himself expressed it, 'to consult his own health [which was extremely delicate], and do as much good to himself and others as he was able'. The rest of his life was spent in deeds of active benevolence and usefulness to his fellow men. He lived in a quiet style, in order that he might employ a larger share of his income in works of benevolence. One of the first public improvements to which he devoted himself was that of the highways of the metropolis, in which he succeeded to a large extent. The rumour of a French invasion being prevalent in 1755, Mr Hanway turned his attention to the best mode of keeping up the supply of seamen. He summoned a meeting of merchants and shipowners at the Royal Exchange, and there proposed to them to form themselves into a society for fitting out landsmen volunteers and boys, to serve on board the king's ships. The proposal was received with enthusiasm: a society was formed, and officers were appointed, Mr Hanway directing its entire operations. The result was the establishment in 1756 of The Marine Society, an institution which has proved of much national advantage, and is to this day of great and substantial utility.

Mr Hanway devoted the other portions of his spare time to improving or establishing important public institutions in the metropolis. From an early period he took an active interest in the Foundling Hospital, which had been started by Thomas Coram many years before, but which, by encouraging parents to abandon their children to the charge of a charity, was threatening to do more harm than good. He determined to take steps to stem the evil, entering upon the work in the face of the fashionable philanthropy of the time; but by holding to his purpose he eventually succeeded in bringing the charity back to its proper objects; and time and experience have proved that he was right. The Magdalen Hospital was also established in a great measure through Mr Hanway's exertions. But his most laborious and persevering efforts were on behalf of the infant parish poor. The misery and neglect amidst which the children of the parish poor then grew up, and the mortality which prevailed amongst them, were frightful; but there was no fashionable movement on foot to abate the suffering, as in the case of the foundlings. So Jonas Hanway summoned his energies to the task. Alone and unassisted he first ascertained by personal inquiry the extent of the evil. He explored the dwellings of the poorest classes in London, and visited the poorhouse sick wards, by which he ascertained the management in detail of every workhouse in and near the metropolis. He next made a journey into France and through Holland, visiting the houses for the reception of the poor, and noting whatever he thought might be adopted at home with advantage. He was thus employed for five years; and on his return to England he published the results of his observations. The consequence was that many of the workhouses were reformed and improved. In 1761 he obtained an Act obliging every London parish to keep an annual register of all the infants received, discharged, and dead; and he took care that the Act should work, for he himself superintended its working with indefatigable watchfulness. He went about from workhouse to workhouse in the morning, and from one member of parliament to another in the afternoon, for day after day, and for year after year, enduring every rebuff, answering every objection, and accommodating himself to every humour. At length, after a persever-ance hardly to be equalled, and after nearly ten years' labour, he obtained another Act, at his sole expense (7 Geo. III c. 39), directing that all parish infants belonging to the parishes within the bills of mortality should not be nursed in the workhouses, but be sent to nurse a certain number of miles out of town until they were six years old, under the care of guardians to be elected triennially. The poor people called this 'the Act for keeping children alive'; and the regis-ters for the years which followed its passing, as compared with those which preceded it, showed that thousands of lives had been preserved through the judicious interference of this good and sensible man.

When he found his powers failing, he prepared for death with as much cheerfulness as he would have prepared himself for a journey into the country. He sent round and paid all his tradesmen, took leave of his friends, arranged his affairs, had his person neatly disposed of, and parted with life serenely and peacefully in his 74th year. The property which he left did not amount to two thousand pounds, and, as he had no relatives who wanted it, he divided it amongst sundry orphans and poor persons whom he had befriended during his lifetime. Such, in brief, was the beautiful life of Jonas Hanway – as honest, energetic, hard-working, and true-hearted a man as ever lived.

The life of Granville Sharp is another striking example of the same power of individual energy – a power which was afterwards transfused into the noble band of workers in the cause of Slavery Abolition, prominent among whom were Clarkson, Wilberforce, Buxton and

Brougham. But, giants though these men were in this cause, Granville Sharp was the first, and perhaps the greatest of them all, in point of perseverance, energy, and intrepidity. He began life as apprentice to a linen-draper on Tower-hill; but, leaving that business after his apprenticeship was out, he next entered as a clerk in the Ordnance Office; and it was while engaged in that humble occupation that he carried on in his spare hours the work of Negro Emancipation. He was always, even when an apprentice, ready to undertake any amount of volunteer labour where a useful purpose was to be served. Thus, while learning the linen-drapery business, a fellow apprentice who lodged in the same house, and was a Unitarian, led him into frequent discussions on religious subjects. The Unitarian youth insisted that Granville's Trinitarian misconception of certain passages of Scripture arose from his want of acquaintance with the Greek tongue; on which he immediately set to work in his evening hours, and shortly acquired an intimate knowledge of Greek. A similar controversy with another fellow-apprentice, a Jew, as to the interpretation of the prophecies, led him in like manner to undertake and overcome the difficulties of Hebrew.

But the circumstance which gave the bias and direction to the main labours of his life originated in his generosity and benevolence. His brother William, a surgeon in Mincing Lane, gave gratuitous service to the poor, and amongst the numerous applicants for relief at his surgery was a poor African named Jonathan Strong. It appeared that the negro had been brutally treated by his master, a Barbadoes lawyer then in London, and became lame, almost blind, and unable to work; on which his owner, regarding him as of no further value as a chattel, cruelly turned him adrift into the streets to starve. This poor man, a mass of disease, supported himself by begging for a time, until he found his way to William Sharp, who gave him some medicine, and shortly after got him admitted to St Bartholomew's hospital, where he was cured. On coming out of the hospital, the two brothers supported the negro in order to keep him off the streets, but they had not the least suspicion at the time that any one had claim upon his person. They even succeeded in obtaining a situation for Strong with an apothecary, in whose service he remained for two years; and it was while he was attending his mistress behind a hackney coach, that his former owner, the Barbadoes lawyer, recognized him, and determined to recover possession of the slave, again rendered valuable by the restoration of his health.

The lawyer employed two of the Lord Mayor's officers to apprehend Strong, and he was lodged in the Compter, until he could be shipped off to the West Indies. The negro, bethinking him in his captivity of the kind services which Granville Sharp had rendered him in his great distress some years before, despatched a letter to him requesting his help. Sharp had forgotten the name of Strong, but he sent a messenger to make inquiries, who returned saying that the keepers denied having any such person in their charge. His suspicions were roused, and he went forthwith to the prison, and insisted upon seeing Jonathan Strong. He was admitted, and recognized the poor negro, now in custody as a recaptured slave. Mr Sharp charged the master of the prison at his own peril not to deliver up Strong to any person whatever, until he had been carried before the Lord Mayor, to whom Sharp immediately went, and obtained a summons against those persons who had seized and imprisoned Strong without a warrant. The parties appeared before the Lord Mayor accordingly, and it appeared from the proceedings that Strong's former master had already sold him to a new one, who produced the bill of sale and claimed the negro as his property. As no charge of offence was made against Strong, and as the Lord Mayor was incompetent to deal with the legal question of Strong's liberty or otherwise, he discharged him, and the slave followed his benefactor out of court, no one daring to touch him. The man's owner immediately gave Sharp notice of an action to recover possession of his negro slave, of whom he declared he had been robbed.

The position of the reputed slave in England was undefined and doubtful. The judgements which had been given in the courts of law were fluctuating and various, resting on no settled principle. Although it was a popular belief that no slave could breathe in England, there were legal men of eminence who expressed a directly contrary opinion. The lawyers to whom Mr Sharp resorted for advice, in defending himself in the action raised against him in the case of Jonathan Strong, generally concurred in this view, and he was further told by Jonathan Strong's owner, that the eminent Lord Chief Justice Mansfield, and all the leading counsel, were decidedly of opinion that the slave, by coming into England, did not become free, but might legally be compelled to return again to the plantations. Such information would have caused despair in a mind less courageous and earnest than that of Granville Sharp; but it only served to stimulate his resolution to fight the battle of the negroes' freedom, at least in England.

Mr Sharp gave up every leisure moment that he could command during the next two years to the close study of the laws of England affecting personal liberty – wading through an immense mass of dry and repulsive literature, and making extracts of all the most important Acts of Parliament, decisions of the courts, and opinions of eminent lawyers as he went along. In this tedious and protracted inquiry he had no instructor, nor assistant, nor adviser. He could not find a single lawyer whose opinion was favourable to his undertaking. The results of his inquiries were, however, as gratifying to himself as they were surprising to the gentlemen of the law. 'God be thanked,' he wrote, 'there is nothing in any English law or statute – at least that I am able to find out – that can justify the enslaving of others.' He had planted his foot firm, and now he doubted nothing. He drew up the result of his studies in a summary form; it was a plain, clear, and manly statement, entitled, 'On the Injustice of Tolerating Slavery in England'; and numerous copies, made by himself, were circulated by him amongst the most eminent lawyers of the time. Strong's owner, finding the sort of man he had to deal with, invented various pretexts for deferring the suit against Sharp, and at length offered a compromise, which was rejected. Granville went on circulating his manuscript tract among the lawyers, until at length those employed against Jonathan Strong were deterred from proceeding further, and the result was, that the plaintiff was compelled to pay treble costs for not bringing forward his action. The tract was then printed in 1769.

In the meantime other cases occurred of the kidnapping of negroes in London, and their shipment to the West Indies for sale. Wherever Sharp could lay hold of any such case, he at once took proceedings to rescue the negro. Thus the wife of one Hylas, an African, was seized, and despatched to Barbadoes; on which Sharp, in the name of Hylas, instituted legal proceedings against the aggressor, obtained a verdict with damages, and Hylas's wife was brought back to England free.

The question of the personal liberty of the negro in England was therefore still undecided; but in the meantime Mr Sharp continued steadily in his benevolent course, and by his indefatigable exertions and promptitude of action many more were added to the list of the rescued. At length the important case of James Somerset occurred; a case which is said to have been selected, at the mutual desire of Lord Mansfield and Mr Sharp, in order to bring the great question involved to a clear legal issue. Somerset had been brought to England by his master, and left there. Afterwards his master sought to apprehend him and send him off to Jamaica for sale. Mr Sharp, as usual, at once took the negro's case in hand, and employed counsel to defend him. Lord Mansfield intimated that the case was of such general concern, that he should take the opinion of all the judges upon it.

The cause of personal liberty, now at stake, was fairly tried before Lord Mansfield, assisted by the three justices – and tried on the broad principle of the essential and constitutional right of every man in England to the liberty of his person, unless forfeited by the law. It is unnecessary here to enter into any account of this great trial; the arguments extended to a great length, the cause being carried over to another term – when it was adjourned and re-adjourned – but at length judgement was given by Lord Mansfield, in whose powerful mind so gradual a change had been worked by the arguments of counsel, based mainly on Granville Sharp's tract, that he now declared the court to be so clearly of one opinion, that there was no necessity for referring the case to the twelve judges. He then declared that the claim of slavery never can be supported; that the power claimed never was in use in England, nor acknowledged by the law; therefore the man James Somerset must be discharged. By securing this judgement Granville Sharp effectually abolished the slave trade until then carried on openly in the streets of Liverpool and London. But he also firmly established the glorious axiom, that as soon as any slave sets his foot on English ground, that moment he becomes free; and there can be no doubt that this great decision of Lord Mansfield was mainly owing to Mr Sharp's firm, resolute, and intrepid prosecution of the cause from the beginning to the end.

Mr Sharp also laboured, but ineffectually, to restore amity between England and her colonies in America; and when the fratricidal war of

163

the American Revolution was entered on, his sense of integrity was so scrupulous that, resolving not in any way to be concerned in so unnatural a business, he resigned his situation at the Ordnance Office. To the last he held to the great object of his life – the abolition of slavery. To carry on this work, and organize the efforts of the growing friends of the cause, the Society for the Abolition of Slavery was founded, and new men, inspired by Sharp's example and zeal, sprang forward to help him. His energy became theirs, and the self-sacrificing zeal in which he had so long laboured single-handed became at length transfused into the nation itself. His mantle fell upon Clarkson, upon Wilberforce, upon Brougham and upon Buxton, who laboured as he had done, with like energy and steadfastness of purpose, until at length slavery was abolished throughout the British dominions. But though the names last mentioned may be more frequently identified with the triumph of this great cause, the chief merit unquestionably belongs to Granville Sharp.

Before the death of Granville Sharp, Clarkson had already turned his attention to the question of negro slavery. He had even selected it for the subject of a college essay; and his mind became so possessed by it that he could not shake it off. The spot is pointed out near Wade's Mill, in Hertfordshire, where, alighting from his horse one day, he sat down disconsolate on the turf by the road side, and, after long thinking, determined to devote himself wholly to the work. He translated his essay from Latin into English, added fresh illustrations, and published it. Then fellow-labourers gathered around him. The Society for Abolishing the Slave Trade, unknown to him, had already been formed, and when he heard of it he joined it. He sacrificed all his prospects in life to prosecute this cause. Wilberforce was selected to lead in Parliament: but upon Clarkson chiefly devolved the labour of collecting and arranging the immense mass of evidence offered in support of the abolition. A remarkable instance of Clarkson's sleuth-hound sort of perseverance may be mentioned. The abettors of slavery, in the course of their defence of the system, maintained that only such negroes as were captured in battle were sold as slaves, and, if not so sold, then they were reserved for a still more frightful doom in their own country. Clarkson knew of the slave-hunts conducted by the slave-traders, but had no witnesses to prove it. Where was one to be found? Accidentally, a gentleman whom he met on one of his journeys informed him of a young sailor, in whose company he had been about a year before, who had been actually engaged in one of such slave-hunting expeditions. The gentleman did not know his name, and could but indefinitely describe his person. He did not know where he was, further than that he belonged to a ship of war in ordinary, but at what port he could not tell. With this mere glimmering of information, Clarkson determined to produce this man as a witness. He visited personally all the seaport towns where ships in ordinary lay; boarded and examined every ship without success, until he came to the very *last* port, and found the young man, his prize, in the very *last* ship that remained to be visited. The young man proved to be one of his most valuable and effective witnesses.

After years of protracted struggle, the slave trade was abolished. But still another great achievement remained to be accomplished – the abolition of slavery itself throughout the British dominions. And here again determined energy won the day. Of the leaders in the cause, none was more distinguished than Fowell Buxton, who took the position formerly occupied by Wilberforce in the House of Commons. Buxton was a dull, heavy boy, distinguished for his strong self-will, which first exhibited itself in violent, domineering, and headstrong obstinacy. His father died when he was a child; but fortunately he had a wise mother, who trained his will with great care, constraining him to obey, but encouraging the habit of deciding and acting for himself in matters which might safely be left to him. His mother believed that a strong will, directed upon worthy objects, was a valuable manly quality if properly guided, and she acted accordingly. When others about her commented on the boy's self-will, she would merely say, 'Never mind – he is self-willed now – you will see it will turn out well in the end.' Fowell learnt very little at school, and was regarded as a dunce and an idler. He got other boys to do his exercises for him, while he romped and scrambled about. He returned home at fifteen, a great, growing, awkward lad, fond only of boating, shooting, riding, and field sports – spending his time principally with the gamekeeper, a man possessed of a good heart – an intelligent observer of life and nature, though he could neither read nor write. Buxton had excellent raw material in him, but he wanted culture, training, and development. At this juncture of his life, when his habits were being formed for good or evil, he was happily thrown into the society of the Gurney family, distinguished for their fine social qualities not less than for their intellectual culture and public-spirited philanthropy. This intercourse with the Gurneys, he used afterwards to say, gave the colouring to his life. They encouraged his efforts at self-culture; and when he went to the University of Dublin and gained high honours there, the animating passion in his mind, he said, 'was to carry back to them the prizes which they prompted and enabled me to win'. He married one of the daughters of the family, and started in life, commencing as a clerk to his uncles Hanbury, the London brewers. His power of will, which made him so difficult to deal with as a boy, now formed the backbone of his character, and made him most indefatigable and energetic in whatever he undertook.

When only thirty-two, Buxton entered Parliament, and at once assumed that position of influence there of which every honest, earnest, well-informed man is secure who enters that assembly of the first gentlemen in the world. The principal question to which he devoted himself was complete emancipation of the slaves in the British colonies. He himself used to attribute the interest which he early felt in this question to the influence of Priscilla Gurney, one of the Earlham family – a woman of a fine intellect and warm heart, abounding in illustrious virtues. When on her death-bed, in 1821, she repeatedly sent for Buxton, and urged him 'to make the cause of the slaves the great object of his life'. Her last act was to attempt to reiterate the solemn charge, and she expired in the ineffectual effort. Buxton never forgot her counsel; he named one of his daughters after her; and on the day on which she was married from his house, on 1 August 1834 – the day of negro emancipation – after his Priscilla had been manumitted from her filial service, and left her father's home in the company of her husband, Buxton sat down and thus wrote to a friend: 'The bride is just gone; everything has passed off to admiration; and *there is not a slave in the British colonies!*'

Buxton was no genius – not a great intellectual leader nor discoverer, but mainly an earnest, straightforward, resolute, energetic man. Indeed, his whole character is most forcibly expressed in his own words, which every young man might well stamp upon his soul: 'The longer I live,' said he, 'the more I am certain that the great difference between men, between the feeble and the powerful, the great and the insignificant, is *energy – invincible determination* – a purpose once fixed, and then death or victory! That quality will do anything that can be done in this world; and no talents, no circumstances, no opportunities, will make a two-legged creature a Man without it.'

9. Men of Business

Hazlitt, in one of his clever essays, represents the man of business as a mean sort of person put in a go-cart, yoked to a trade or profession; alleging that all he has to do is, not to go out of the beaten track, but merely to let his affairs take their own course. 'The great requisite,' he says, 'for the prosperous management of ordinary business is the want of imagination, or of any idea but those of custom and interest on the narrowest scale.' But nothing could be more one-sided, and in effect untrue, than such a definition. Of course, there are narrow-minded men of business, as there are narrow-minded scientific men, literary men, and legislators; but there are also business men of large and comprehensive minds, capable of action on the very largest scale. As Burke said in his speech on the India Bill, he knew statesmen who were pedlars, and merchants who acted in the spirit of statesmen.

The greatest have not disdained to labour honestly and usefully for a living, though at the same time aiming after higher things. Thales, the first of the seven sages, Solon, the second founder of Athens, and Hyperates, the mathematician, were all traders. Plato, called the Divine by reason of the excellence of his wisdom, defrayed his travelling expenses in Egypt by the profits derived from the oil which he sold during his journey. Spinoza maintained himself by polishing glasses while he pursued his philosophical investigations. Linnaeus, the great botanist, prosecuted his studies while hammering leather and making shoes. Shakespeare was a successful manager of a theatre – perhaps priding himself more upon his practical qualities in that capacity than on his writing of plays and poetry. Pope was of opinion that Shakespeare's principal object in cultivating literature was to secure an honest independence. Indeed, he seems to have been altogether indifferent to literary reputation. It is not known that he superintended the publication of a single play, or even sanctioned the printing of one; and the chronology of his writings is still a mystery. It is certain, however, that he prospered in his business, and realized sufficient to enable him to retire upon a competency to his native town of Stratford-upon-Avon.

Chaucer was in early life a soldier, and afterwards an effective Commissioner of Customs, and Inspector of Woods and Crown Lands. Spenser was Secretary to the Lord Deputy of Ireland, was afterwards Sheriff of Cork, and is said to have been shrewd and attentive in matters of business. Milton, originally a schoolmaster, was elevated to the post of Secretary to the Council of State during the Commonwealth; and the extant Order-book of the Council, as well as many of Milton's letters which are preserved, give abundant evidence of his activity and usefulness in that office. Sir Isaac Newton proved himself an efficient Master of the Mint; the new coinage of 1694 having been carried on under his immediate personal superintendence. Cowper prided himself upon his business punctuality, though he confessed that he 'never knew a poet, except himself, who was punctual in anything'. But against this we may set the lives of Wordsworth and Scott – the former a distributor of stamps, the latter a clerk to the Court of Session – both of whom, though great poets, were eminently punctual and practical men of business. David Ricardo, amidst the occupations of his daily business as a London stock-jobber, in conducting which he acquired an ample fortune, was able to concentrate his mind upon his favourite subject – on which he was enabled to throw great light – the principles of political economy; for he united in himself the sagacious commercial man and the profound philosopher. Baily, the eminent astronomer, was another stockbroker; and Allen, the chemist, was a silk manufacturer.

The path of success in business is usually the path of common sense. Patient labour and application are as necessary here as in the acquisition of knowledge or the pursuit of science. The old Greeks said, 'to become an able man in any profession, three things are necessary – nature, study, and practice'. In business, practice, wisely and diligently improved, is the great secret of success. Some may make what are called 'lucky hits', but, like money earned by gambling, such 'hits' may only serve to lure one to ruin. Bacon was accustomed to say that it was in business as in ways – the nearest way was commonly the foulest, and that if a man would go the fairest way he must go somewhat about. The journey may occupy a longer time, but the pleasure of the labour involved by it, and the enjoyment of the results produced, will be more genuine and unalloyed. To have a daily appointed task of even common drudgery to do makes the rest of life feel all the sweeter.

The fable of the labours of Hercules is the type of all human doing and success. Every youth should be made to feel that his happiness and well-doing in life must necessarily rely mainly on himself and the exercise of his own energies, rather than upon the help and patronage of others. The late Lord Melbourne embodied a piece of useful advice in a letter which he wrote to Lord John Russell, in reply to an application for a provision for one of Moore the poet's sons: 'My dear John,' he said, 'I return you Moore's letter. I shall be ready to do what you like about it when we have the means. I think whatever is done should be done for Moore himself. This is more distinct, direct, and intelligible. Making a small provision for young men is hardly justifiable; and it is of all things the most prejudicial to themselves. They think what they have much larger than it really is; and they make no exertion. The young should never hear any language but this: "You have your own way to make, and it depends upon your own exertions whether you starve or not." Believe me, &c., MELBOURNE.'

Practical industry, wisely and vigorously applied, always produces its due effects. It carries a man onward, brings out his individual character, and stimulates the action of others. All may not rise equally, yet each, on the whole, very much according to his deserts. 'Though all cannot live on the piazza,' as the Tuscan proverb has it, 'every one may feel the sun.'

On the whole, it is not good that human nature should have the road of life made too easy. Better to be under the necessity of working hard and faring meanly, than to have everything done ready to hand and a pillow of down to repose upon. Indeed, to start in life with comparatively small means seems so necessary as a stimulus to work, that it may almost be set down as one of the conditions essential to success in life. Hence, an eminent judge, when asked what contributed most to success at the bar, replied, 'Some succeed by great talent, some by high connections, some by miracle, but the majority by commencing without a shilling.'

The necessity of labour may, indeed, be regarded as the main root and spring of all that we call progress in individuals, and civilization in nations; and it is doubtful whether any heavier curse could be imposed on man than the complete gratification of all his wishes without effort on his part, leaving nothing for his hopes, desires or struggles. The feeling that life is destitute of any motive or necessity for action must be of all others the most distressing and insupportable to a rational being. The Marquis de Spinola asking Sir Horace Vere what his brother died of, Sir Horace replied, 'He died, sir, of having nothing to do.' 'Alas!' said Spinola, 'that is enough to kill any general of us all.'

Those who fail in life are, however, very apt to assume a tone of injured innocence, and conclude too hastily that everybody excepting themselves has had a hand in their personal misfortunes. An eminent writer published a book in which he described his numerous failures in business, naïvely admitting, at the same time, that he was ignorant of the multiplication table; and he came to the conclusion that the real cause of his ill-success in life was the money-worshipping spirit of the age. Lamartine also did not hesitate to profess his contempt for arithmetic; but, had it been less, probably we should not have witnessed the unseemly spectacle of the admirers of that distinguished personage engaged in collecting subscriptions for his support in his old age.

Again, some consider themselves born to ill luck, and make up their minds that the world invariably goes against them without any fault on their own part. We have heard of a person of this sort, who went so far as to declare his belief that if he had been a hatter people would have been born without heads! There is, however, a Russian proverb which says that Misfortune is next door to Stupidity; and it will often be found that men who are constantly lamenting their luck are in some way or other reaping the consequences of their own neglect, mismanagement, improvidence, or want of application. Dr Johnson, who came up to London with a single guinea in his pocket, and who once accurately described himself in his signature to a letter addressed to a noble lord as *Impransus*, or Dinnerless, has honestly said, 'All the complaints which are made of the world are unjust; I never knew a man of merit neglected; it was generally by his own fault that he failed of success.'

Washington Irving, the American author, held like views. 'As for the talk,' said he, 'about modest merit being neglected, it is too often a cant, by which indolent and irresolute men seek to lay their want of success at the door of the public. Modest merit is, however, too apt to be inactive, or negligent, or uninstructed merit. Well matured and well disciplined talent is always sure of a market, provided it exerts itself;

but it must not cower at home and expect to be sought for. There is a good deal of cant, too, about the success of forward and impudent men, while men of retiring worth are passed over with neglect. But it usually happens that those forward men have that valuable quality of promptness and activity without which worth is a mere inoperative property. A barking dog is often more useful than a sleeping lion.'

Attention, application, accuracy, method, punctuality, and despatch are the principal qualities required for the efficient conduct of business of any sort. These, at first sight, may appear to be small matters; and yet they are of essential importance to human happiness, well-being, and usefulness. They are little things, it is true; but human life is made up of comparative trifles. It is the repetition of little acts which constitutes not only the sum of human character, but which determines the character of nations. And where men or nations have broken down, it will almost invariably be found that neglect of little things was the rock on which they split. Every human being has duties to be performed, and, therefore, has need of cultivating the capacity for doing them; whether the sphere of action be the management of a household, the conduct of a trade or profession, or the government of a nation.

The examples we have already given of great workers in various branches of industry, art, and science render it unnecessary further to enforce the importance of persevering application in any department of life. It is the result of every-day experience that steady attention to matters of detail lies at the root of human progress; and that diligence, above all, is the mother of good luck. Accuracy is also of much importance, and an invariable mark of good training in a man. Accuracy in observation, accuracy in speech, accuracy in the transaction of affairs. What is done in business must be done well; for it is better to accomplish perfectly a small amount of work than to half-do ten times as much. A wise man used to say, 'Stay a little, that we may make an end the sooner.'

Too little attention, however, is paid to this highly important quality of accuracy. As a man eminent in practical science lately observed to us, 'It is astonishing how few people I have met with in the course of my experience who can *define a fact* accurately.' Yet, in business affairs, it is the manner in which even small matters are transacted that often decides men for or against you. With virtue, capacity, and good conduct in other respects, the person who is habitually inaccurate cannot be trusted; his work has to be gone over again; and he thus causes an infinity of annoyance, vexation, and trouble.

It was one of the characteristic qualities of Charles James Fox, that he was thoroughly painstaking in all that he did. When appointed Secretary of State, being piqued at some observation as to his bad writing, he actually took a writing-master, and wrote copies like a schoolboy until he had sufficiently improved himself. Though a corpulent man, he was wonderfully active at picking up cut tennis balls, and when asked how he contrived to do so, he playfully replied, 'Because I am a very pains-taking man.' The same accuracy in trifling matters was displayed by him in things of greater importance; and he acquired his reputation, like the painter, by 'neglecting nothing'.

Method is essential, and enables a larger amount of work to be got through with satisfaction. 'Method,' said the Reverend Richard Cecil, 'is like packing things in a box; a good packer will get in half as much again as a bad one.' Cecil's despatch of business was extraordinary, his maxim being, 'The shortest way to do many things is to do only one thing at once'; and he never left a thing undone with a view of recurring to it at a period of more leisure. When business pressed, he rather chose to encroach on his hours of meals and rest than omit any part of his work. De Witt's maxim was like Cecil's: 'One thing at a time.' 'If,' said he, 'I have any necessary despatches to make, I think of nothing else till they are finished; if any domestic affairs require my attention, I give myself wholly up to them till they are set in order.'

Sir Walter Scott, writing to a youth who had obtained a situation and asked for his advice, gave him in reply this sound counsel: 'Beware of stumbling over a propensity which easily besets you from not having your time fully employed – I mean what the women call *dawdling*. Your motto must be, *Hoc age*. Do instantly whatever is to be done, and take the hours of recreation after business, never before it. If that which is first in hand is not instantly, steadily, and regularly despatched, other things accumulate behind, till affairs begin to press all at once, and no human brain can stand the confusion.'

Men of business are accustomed to quote the maxim that Time is money; but it is more; the proper improvement of it is self-culture, self-improvement, and growth of character. An hour wasted daily on trifles or in indolence would, if devoted to self-improvement, make an ignorant man wise in a few years, and employed in good works would make his life fruitful, and death a harvest of worthy deeds. Fifteen minutes a day devoted to self-improvement will be felt at the end of the year. Good thoughts and carefully gathered experience take up no room, and may be carried about as our companions everywhere, without cost or incumbrance. An economical use of time is the true mode of securing leisure: it enables us to get through business and carry it forward, instead of being driven by it. On the other hand, the miscalculation of time involves us in perpetual hurry, confusion, and difficulties; and life becomes a mere shuffle of expedients, usually followed by disaster. Nelson once said, 'I owe all my success in life to having been always a quarter of an hour before my time.'

Some take no thought of the value of money until they have come to an end of it, and many do the same with their time. The hours are allowed to flow by unemployed, and then, when life is fast waning, they bethink themselves of the duty of making a wiser use of it. But the habit of listlessness may already have become confirmed, and they are unable to break the bonds with which they have permitted themselves to become bound. Lost wealth may be replaced by industry, lost knowledge by study, lost health by temperance or medicine, but lost time is gone for ever.

In addition to the ordinary working qualities the business man of the highest class requires quick perception and firmness in the execution of his plans. Tact is also important; and though this is partly the gift of nature, it is yet capable of being cultivated and developed by observation and experience. Men of this quality are quick to see the right mode of action, and if they have decision of purpose, are prompt to carry out their undertakings to a successful issue. These qualities are especially valuable, and indeed indispensable in those who direct the action of other men on a large scale, as, for instance, in the case of the commander of an army in the field. It is not merely necessary that the general should be great as a warrior, but also as a man of business. He must possess great tact, much knowledge of character, and ability to organize the movements of a large mass of men, whom he has to feed, clothe, and furnish with whatever may be necessary in order that they may keep the field and win battles. In these respects Napoleon and Wellington were both first-rate men of business.

Though Napoleon had an immense love for details, he had also a vivid power of imagination, which enabled him to look along extended lines of action, and deal with those details on a large scale, with judgement and rapidity. He possessed such knowledge of character as enabled him to select, almost unerringly, the best agents for the execution of his designs. But he trusted as little as possible to agents in matters of great moment, on which important results depended.

Like Napoleon, the Duke of Wellington was a first-rate man of business; and it is not perhaps saying too much to aver that it was in no small degree because of his possession of a business faculty amounting to genius that the Duke never lost a battle. While a subaltern, he became dissatisfied with the slowness of his promotion, and having passed from the infantry to the cavalry twice, and back again, without advancement, he applied to Lord Camden, then Viceroy of Ireland, for employment in the Revenue or Treasury Board. Had he succeeded, no doubt he would have made a first-rate head of a department, as he would have made a first-rate merchant or manufacturer. But his application failed, and he remained with the army to become the greatest of British generals.

The Duke began his active military career under the Duke of York and General Walmoden, in Flanders and Holland, where he learnt, amidst misfortunes and defeats, how bad business arrangements and bad generalship serve to ruin the *morale* of an army. Ten years after entering the army we find him a colonel in India, reported by his superiors as an officer of indefatigable energy and application. He entered into the minutest details of the service, and sought to raise the discipline of his men to the highest standard. 'The regiment of Colonel Wellesley,' wrote General Harris in 1799, 'is a model regiment; on the score of soldierly bearing, discipline, instruction, and orderly behaviour it is above all praise.' Thus qualifying himself for posts of greater confidence, he was shortly after nominated governor of the capital of Mysore. In the war with the Mahrattas he was first called upon to try his hand at generalship; and at thirty-four he won the memorable battle of Assaye, with an army composed of 1,500 British and 5,000 sepoys, over 20,000 Mahratta infantry and 30,000 cavalry. But so brilliant a victory did not in the least disturb his equanimity, or affect the perfect honesty of his character.

The extraordinary qualities displayed by Lord Wellington can only be appreciated after a perusal of his despatches, which contain the unvarnished tale of the manifold ways and means by which he laid the foundations of his success. Never was man more tried by difficulty and opposition, arising not less from the imbecility, falsehood, and intrigues of the British Government of the day, than from the selfishness, cowardice, and vanity of the people he went to save. It may, indeed, be said of him, that he sustained the war in Spain by his individual firmness and self-reliance, which never failed him even in the midst of his great discouragements. He had not only to fight Napoleon's veterans, but also to hold in check the Spanish juntas and the Portuguese regency. He had the utmost difficulty in obtaining provisions and clothing for his troops; and it will scarcely be credited that while engaged with the enemy in the battle of Talavera, the Spaniards, who ran away, fell upon the baggage of the British army, and the ruffians actually plundered it!

These and other vexations the Duke bore with a sublime patience and self-control, and held on his course, in the face of ingratitude, treachery, and opposition, with indomitable firmness. He neglected nothing, and attended to every important detail of business himself. When he found that food for his troops was not to be obtained from England, and that he must rely upon his own resources for feeding them, he forthwith commenced business as a corn merchant on a large scale, in copartnery with the British Minister at Lisbon. Commissariat bills were created, with which grain was bought in the ports of the Mediterranean and in South America. When he had thus filled his magazines, the overplus was sold to the Portuguese, who were greatly in want of provisions. He left nothing whatever to chance, but provided for every contingency. He gave his attention to the minutest details of the service; and was accustomed to concentrate his whole energies, from time to time, on such apparently ignominious matters as soldiers' shoes, camp-kettles, biscuits and horse fodder. His magnificent business qualities were everywhere felt, and there can be no doubt that, by the care with which he provided for every contingency, and the personal attention which he gave to every detail, he laid the foundations of his great success. By such means he transformed an army of raw levies into the best soldiers in Europe, with whom he declared it to be possible to go anywhere and do anything.

We have already referred to his remarkable power of abstracting himself from the work, no matter how engrossing, immediately in hand, and concentrating his energies upon the details of some entirely different business. Thus Napier relates that it was while he was preparing to fight the battle of Salamanca that he had to expose to the Ministers at home the futility of relying upon a loan; it was on the heights of San Cristoval, on the field of battle itself, that he demonstrated the absurdity of attempting to establish a Portuguese bank; it was in the trenches of Burgos that he dissected Funchal's scheme of finance, and exposed the folly of attempting the sale of church property; and on each occasion he showed himself as well acquainted with these subjects as with the minutest detail in the mechanism of armies.

Another feature in his character, showing the upright man of business, was his thorough honesty. Whilst Soult ransacked and carried away with him from Spain numerous pictures of great value, Wellington did not appropriate to himself a single farthing's worth of property. Everywhere he paid his way, even when in the enemy's country. When he had crossed the French frontier, followed by 40,000 Spaniards, who sought to 'make fortunes' by pillage and plunder, he first rebuked their officers, and then, finding his efforts to restrain them unavailing, he sent them back into their own country. It is a remarkable fact, that, even in France, the peasantry fled from their own countrymen, and carried their valuables within the protection of the British lines! At the very same time Wellington was writing home to the British Ministry, 'We are overwhelmed with debts, and I can scarcely stir out of my house on account of public creditors waiting to demand payment of what is due to them.' Jules Maurel, in his estimate of the Duke's character, says, 'Nothing can be grander or more nobly original than this admission. This old soldier, after thirty years' service, this iron man and victorious general, established in an enemy's country at the head of an immense army, is afraid of his creditors! This is a kind of fear that has seldom troubled the minds of the conquerors and invaders; and I doubt if the annals of war could present anything comparable to this sublime simplicity.' But the Duke himself, had the matter been put to him, would most probably have disclaimed any intention of acting even grandly or nobly in the matter; merely regarding the punctual payment of his debts as the best and most honourable mode of conducting his business.

It must be admitted, that Trade tries character perhaps more severely than any other pursuit in life. It puts to the severest test honesty, self-denial, justice, and truthfulness; and men of business who pass through such trials unstained are perhaps worthy of as great honour as soldiers who prove their courage amidst the fires and perils of battle. And, to the credit of the multitudes of men engaged in the various departments of trade, we think it must be admitted that on the whole they pass through their trials nobly. If we reflect but for a moment on the vast amount of wealth daily entrusted even to subordinate persons, who themselves probably earn but a bare competency – the loose cash which is constantly passing through the hands of shopmen, agents, brokers, and clerks in banking houses – and note how comparatively few are the breaches of trust which occur amidst all this temptation, it will probably be admitted that this steady daily honesty of conduct is most honourable to human nature, if it do not even tempt us to be proud of it. The same trust and confidence reposed by men of business in each other, as implied by the system of Credit, which is mainly based upon the principle of honour, would be surprising if it were not so much a matter of ordinary practice in business transactions. Dr Chalmers has well said, that the implicit trust with which merchants are customed to confide in distant agents – separated from them perhaps by half the globe – often consigning vast wealth to persons, recommended only by their character, whom perhaps they have never seen – is probably the finest act of homage which men can render to one another.

Although common honesty is still happily in the ascendant amongst common people, and the general business community of England is still sound at heart, putting their honest character into their respective callings, there are, unhappily, as there have been in all times, but too many instances of flagrant dishonesty and fraud, exhibited by the unscrupulous, the over-speculative, and the intensely selfish in their haste to be rich. There are tradesmen who adulterate, contractors who 'scamp', manufacturers who give us shoddy instead of wool, 'dressing' instead of cotton, cast-iron tools instead of steel, needles without eyes, razors made only 'to sell', and swindled fabrics in many shapes. But these we must hold to be the exceptional cases, of low-minded and grasping men, who, though they may gain wealth which they probably cannot enjoy, will never gain an honest character, nor secure that without which wealth is nothing – a heart at peace. 'The rogue cozened not me, but his own conscience,' said Bishop Latimer of a cutler who made him pay twopence for a knife not worth a penny. Money earned by screwing, cheating, and over-reaching may for a time dazzle the eyes of the unthinking; but the bubbles blown by unscrupulous rogues, when full-blown, usually glitter only to burst.

It is possible that the scrupulously honest man may not grow rich so fast as the unscrupulous and dishonest one; but the success will be of a truer kind, earned without fraud or injustice. And even though a man should for a time be unsuccessful, still he must be honest: better lose all and save character. For character is itself a fortune; and if the high-principled man will but hold on his way courageously, success will surely come – nor will the highest reward of all be withheld from him.

10. Money: Its Use and Abuse

How a man uses money – makes it, saves it, and spends it – is perhaps one of the best tests of practical wisdom. Although money ought by no means to be regarded as a chief end of man's life, neither is it a trifling matter, to be held in philosophic contempt, representing as it does to so large an extent the means of physical comfort and social well-being. Indeed, some of the finest qualities of human nature are intimately related to the right use of money; such as generosity, honesty, justice, and self-sacrifice; as well as the practical virtues of economy and providence. On the other hand, there are their counterparts of avarice, fraud, injustice, and selfishness, as displayed by the inordinate lovers of gain; and the vices of thriftlessness, extravagance, and improvidence, on the part of those who misuse and abuse the means entrusted to them. 'So that,' as is wisely observed by Henry Taylor in his thoughtful *Notes from Life*, 'a right measure and manner in getting, saving, spending, giving, taking, lending, borrowing, and bequeathing would almost argue a perfect man.'

Comfort in worldly circumstances is a condition which every man is justified in striving to attain by all worthy means. It secures that physical satisfaction which is necessary for the culture of the better part of his nature; and enables him to provide for those of his own household, without which, says the Apostle, a man is 'worse than an infidel'. Nor ought the duty to be any the less indifferent to us, that the respect which our fellow-men entertain for us in no slight degree depends upon the manner in which we exercise the opportunities which present themselves for our honourable advancement in life. The very effort required to be made to succeed in life with this object is of itself an education; stimulating a man's sense of self-respect, bringing out his practical qualities, and disciplining him in the exercise of patience, perseverance, and such like virtues. The provident and careful man must necessarily be a thoughtful man, for he lives not merely in the present, but with provident forecast makes arrangements for the future. He must also be a temperate man, and exercise the virtue of self-denial, than which nothing is so much calculated to give strength to the character. John Sterling says truly that 'the worst education which teaches self-denial is better than the best which teaches everything else, and not that'. The Romans rightly employed the same word (*virtus*) to designate courage, which is in a physical sense what the other is in a moral; the highest virtue of all being victory over ourselves.

Hence the lesson of self-denial – the sacrificing of a present gratification for a future good – is one of the last that is learnt. Those classes which work the hardest might naturally be expected to value the most the money which they earn. Yet the readiness with which so many are accustomed to eat up and drink up their earnings as they go renders them to a great extent helpless and dependent upon the frugal. There are large numbers of persons among us who, though enjoying sufficient means of comfort and independence, are often found to be barely a day's march ahead of actual want when a time of pressure occurs; and hence a great cause of social helplessness and suffering. On one occasion a deputation waited on Lord John Russell, respecting the taxation levied on the working classes of the country, when the noble lord took the opportunity of remarking, 'You may rely upon it that the Government of this country durst not tax the working classes to anything like the extent to which they tax themselves in their expenditure upon intoxicating drinks alone!' Of all great public questions, there is perhaps none more important than this – no great work of reform calling more loudly for labourers. But it must be admitted that 'self-denial and self-help' would make a poor rallying cry for the hustings; and it is to be feared that the patriotism of this day has but little regard for such common things as individual economy and providence, although it is by the practice of such virtues only that the genuine independence of the industrial classes is to be secured. 'Prudence, frugality, and good management,' said Samuel Drew, the philosophical shoemaker, 'are excellent artists for mending bad times: they occupy but little room in any dwelling, but would furnish a more effectual remedy for the evils of life than any Reform Bill that ever passed the Houses of Parliament.' Socrates said, 'Let him that would move the world move first himself.'

Any class of men that lives from hand to mouth will ever be an inferior class. They will necessarily remain impotent and helpless, hanging on to the skirts of society, the sport of times and seasons. Having no respect for themselves, they will fail in securing the respect of others. In commercial crises such men must inevitably go to the wall. Wanting that husbanded power which a store of savings, no matter how small, invariably gives them, they will be at every man's mercy, and, if possessed of right feelings, they cannot but regard with fear and trembling the future possible fate of their wives and children. 'The world,' once said Mr Cobden to the working men of Huddersfield, 'has always been divided into two classes – those who have saved, and those who have spent – the thrifty and the extravagant. The building of all the houses, the mills, the bridges, and the ships, and the accomplishment of all other great works which have rendered man civilized and happy, has been done by the savers, the thrifty; and those who have wasted their resources have always been their slaves. It has been the law of nature and of Providence that this should be so; and I were an impostor if I promised any class that they would advance themselves if they were improvident, thoughtless, and idle.'

Equally sound was the advice given by Mr Bright to an assembly of working men at Rochdale, in 1847, when, after expressing his belief that, 'so far as honesty was concerned, it was to be found in pretty equal amount among all classes', he used the following words: 'There is only one way that is safe for any man, or any number of men, by which they can maintain their present position if it be a good one, or raise themselves above it if it be a bad one – that is, by the practice of the virtues of industry, frugality, temperance, and honesty. There is no royal road by which men can raise themselves from a position which they feel to be uncomfortable and unsatisfactory, as regards their mental or physical condition, except by the practice of those virtues by which they find numbers amongst them are continually advancing and bettering themselves.'

There is no reason why the condition of the average workman should not be a useful, honourable, respectable, and happy one. The whole body of the working classes might (with few exceptions) be as frugal, virtuous, well-informed, and well-conditioned as many individuals of the same class have already made themselves. What some men are, all without difficulty might be. Employ the same means, and the same results will follow. That there should be a class of men who live by their daily labour in every state is the ordinance of God, and doubtless is a wise and righteous one; but that this class should be otherwise than frugal, contented, intelligent, and happy is not the design of Providence, but springs solely from the weakness, self-indulgence, and perverseness of man himself. The healthy spirit of self-help created amongst working people would more than any other measure serve to raise them as a class, and this, not by pulling down others, but by levelling them up to a higher and still advancing standard of religion, intelligence, and virtue. 'All moral philosophy,' says Montaigne, 'is as applicable to a common and private life as to the most splendid. Every man carries the entire form of the human condition within him.'

When a man casts his glance forward, he will find that the three chief temporal contingencies for which he has to provide are want of employment, sickness, and death. The first two he may escape, but the last is inevitable. It is, however, the duty of the prudent man so to live, and so to arrange, that the pressure of suffering, in event of either contingency occurring, shall be mitigated to as great an extent as possible, not only to himself, but also to those who are dependent upon him for their comfort and subsistence. Viewed in this light the honest earning and the frugal use of money are of the greatest importance. Rightly earned, it is the representative of patient industry and untiring effort, of temptation resisted and hope rewarded; and, rightly used, it affords indications of prudence, forethought and self-denial – the true basis of manly character. Though money represents a crowd of objects without any real worth or utility, it also represents many things of great value; not only food, clothing, and household satisfaction, but personal self-respect and independence. Thus a store of savings is to the working man as a barricade against want; it secures him a footing, and enables him to wait, it may be in cheerfulness and hope, until better days come round. The very endeavour to gain a firmer position in the world has a certain dignity in it, and tends to make a man stronger and better. At all events, it gives him greater freedom of action, and enables him to husband his strength for future effort.

But the man who is always hovering on the verge of want is in a state not far removed from that of slavery. He is in no sense his own master, but is in constant peril of falling under the bondage of others, and accepting the terms which they dictate to him. He cannot help being, in a measure, servile, for he dares not look the world boldly in the face; and in adverse times he must look either to alms or the poor's rates. If work fails him altogether, he has not the means of moving to another field of employment; he is fixed to his parish like a limpet to its rock, and can neither migrate nor emigrate.

To secure independence, the practice of simple economy is all that is necessary. Economy requires neither superior courage nor eminent virtue; it is satisfied with ordinary energy, and the capacity of average minds. Economy, at bottom, is but the spirit of order applied in the administration of domestic affairs: it means management, regularity, prudence, and the avoidance of waste. The spirit of economy was expressed by our Divine Master in the words 'Gather up the fragments that remain, so that nothing may be lost.' His omnipotence did not disdain the small things of life; and even while revealing His infinite power to the multitude, He taught the pregnant lesson of carefulness of which all stand so much in need.

Economy also means the power of resisting present gratification for the purpose of securing a future good, and in this light it represents the ascendancy of reason over the animal instincts. It is altogether different from penuriousness: for it is economy that can always best afford to be generous. It does not make money an idol, but regards it as a useful agent. As Dean Swift observes, 'we must carry money in the head, not in the heart'. Economy may be styled the daughter of Prudence, the sister of Temperance, and the mother of Liberty. It is evidently conservative – conservative of character, of domestic happiness, and social well-being. It is, in short, the exhibition of self-help in one of its best forms.

Every man ought so to contrive as to live within his means. This practice is of the very essence of honesty. For if a man do not manage honestly to live within his own means, he must necessarily be living dishonestly upon the means of somebody else. Those who are careless about personal expenditure, and consider merely their own gratification, without regard for the comfort of others, generally find out the real uses of money when it is too late. Though by nature generous, these thriftless persons are often driven in the end to do very shabby things. They waste their money as they do their time; draw bills upon the future; anticipate their earnings; and are thus under the necessity of dragging after them a load of debts and obligations which seriously affect their action as free and independent men.

It was a maxim of Lord Bacon, that when it was necessary to economize, it was better to look after petty savings than to descend to petty gettings. The loose cash which many persons throw away uselessly, and worse, would often form a basis of fortune and independence for life. These wasters are their own worst enemies, though generally found amongst the ranks of those who rail at the injustice of 'the world'. But if a man will not be his own friend, how can he expect that others will? Orderly men of moderate means have always something left in their pockets to help others; whereas your prodigal and careless fellows who spend all never find an opportunity for helping anybody. It is poor economy, however, to be a scrub. Narrowmindedness in living and in dealing is generally short-sighted, and leads to failure.

The proverb says that 'an empty bag cannot stand upright'; neither can a man who is in debt. It is also difficult for a man who is in debt to be truthful; hence it is said that lying rides on debt's back. The debtor has to frame excuses to his creditor for postponing payment of the money he owes him; and probably also to contrive falsehoods. It is easy enough for a man who will exercise a healthy resolution to avoid incurring the first obligation; but the facility with which that has been incurred often becomes a temptation to a second; and very soon the unfortunate borrower becomes so entangled that no late exertion of industry can set him free. The first step in debt is like the first step in falsehood! almost involving the necessity of proceeding in the same course, debt following debt, as lie follows lie.

Dr Johnson held that early debt is ruin. His words on the subject are weighty, and worthy of being held in remembrance. 'Do not,' said he, 'accustom yourself to consider debt only as an inconvenience; you will find it a calamity. Poverty takes away so many means of doing good, and produces so much inability to resist evil, both natural and moral, but it is by all virtuous means to be avoided . . . Let it be your first care, then, not to be in any man's debt. Resolve not to be poor; whatever you have, spend less. Poverty is a great enemy to human happiness; it certainly destroys liberty, and it makes some virtues impracticable and others extremely difficult. Frugality is not only the basis of quiet, but of beneficence. No man can help others that wants help himself; we must have enough before we have to spare.'

It is the bounden duty of every man to look his affairs in the face, and to keep an account of his incomings and outgoings in money matters. The exercise of a little simple arithmetic in this way will be found of great value. Prudence requires that we shall pitch our scale of living a degree below our means, rather than up to them; but this can only be done by carrying out faithfully a plan of living by which both ends may be made to meet. John Locke strongly advised this course. 'Nothing,' said he, 'is likelier to keep a man within compass than having constantly before his eyes the state of his affairs in a regular course of account.' The Duke of Wellington kept an accurate detailed account of all the moneys received and expended by him. 'I make a point,' said he to Mr Gleig, 'of paying my own bills, and I advise every one to do the same; formerly I used to trust a confidential servant to pay them, but I was cured of that folly by receiving one morning, to my great surprise, duns of a year or two's standing. The fellow had speculated with my money, and left my debts unpaid.' Talking of debt, his remark was, 'It makes a slave of a man. I have often known what it was to be in want of money, but I never got into debt.' Washington was as particular as Wellington was, in matters of business detail; and it is a remarkable fact that he did not disdain to scrutinize the outgoings of his household – determined as he was to live honestly within his means – even while holding the high office of President of the American Union.

Admiral Jervis, Earl St Vincent, has told the story of his early struggles, and, amongst other things, of his determination to keep out of debt. 'My father had a very large family', said he, 'with limited means. He gave me twenty pounds at starting, and that was all he ever gave me. After I had been a considerable time at the station [at sea], I drew for twenty more, but the bill came back protested. I was mortified at this rebuke, and made a promise, which I have ever kept, that I would never draw another bill without a certainty of its being paid. I immediately changed my mode of living, quitted my mess, lived alone, and took up the ship's allowance, which I found quite sufficient; washed and mended my own clothes; made a pair of trousers out of the ticking of my bed; and having by these means saved as much money as would redeem my honour, I took up my bill, and from that time to this I have taken care to keep within my means.' Jervis for six years endured pinching privation, but preserved his integrity, studied his profession with success, and gradually and steadily rose by merit and bravery to the highest rank.

There is an ambition to bring up boys as gentlemen, or rather 'genteel' men; though the result frequently is only to make them gents. They acquire a taste for dress, style, luxuries, and amusements which can never form any solid foundation for manly or gentlemanly character; and the result is, that we have a vast number of gingerbread young gentry thrown upon the world, who remind one of the abandoned hulls sometimes picked up at sea, with only a monkey on board. There is a dreadful ambition abroad for being 'genteel'. We keep up appearances, too often at the expense of honesty; and, though we may not be rich, yet we must seem to be so. We must be 'respectable', though only in the meanest sense – in mere vulgar outward show. There is a constant struggle and pressure for front seats in the social amphitheatre; in the midst of which all noble self-denying resolve is trodden down, and many fine natures are inevitably crushed to death. What waste, what misery, what bankruptcy, come from all this ambition to dazzle others with the glare of the apparent worldly success we need not describe. The mischievous results show themselves in a thousand ways – in the rank frauds committed by men who dare to be dishonest, but do not dare to seem poor; and in the desperate dashes at fortune, in which the pity is not so much for those who fail as for the hundreds of innocent families who are so often involved in their ruin.

The famous Sir Charles Napier, in taking leave of his command in India, did a bold and honest thing in publishing his strong protest, embodied in his last General Order to the officers of the Indian army, against the 'fast' life led by so many young officers in that service, involving them in ignominious obligations. Sir Charles strongly urged, in that famous document – what had almost been lost sight of – that 'honesty is inseparable from the character of a thoroughbred gentleman'; and that 'to drink unpaid for champagne and unpaid for beer, and to ride unpaid for horses, is to be a cheat, and not a gentleman'. Men who lived beyond their means and were summoned, often by their own servants, before Courts of Requests for debts contracted in extravagant living, might be officers by virtue of their commissions, but they were not gentlemen. The habit of being constantly in debt, the Commander-in-Chief held, made men grow callous to the proper feelings of a gentleman. It was not enough that an officer should be able to fight: that any bulldog could do. But did he hold his word inviolate? – did he pay his debts? These were among the points of honour which, he insisted, illuminated the true gentleman's and soldier's career.

Hugh Miller has told how, by an act of youthful decision, he saved himself from one of the strong temptations so peculiar to a life of toil. When employed as a mason, it was usual for his fellow-workmen to have an occasional treat of drink, and one day two glasses of whisky fell to his share, which he swallowed. When he reached home, he found, on opening his favourite book, *Bacon's Essays* – that the letters danced before his eyes, and that he could no longer master the sense. 'The condition,' he says, 'into which I had brought myself was, I felt, one of degradation. I had sunk, by my own act, for the time, to a lower level of intelligence than that on which it was my privilege to be placed; and though the state could have been no very favourable one for forming a resolution, I in that hour determined that I should never again sacrifice my capacity of intellectual enjoyment to a drinking usage; and, with God's help, I was enabled to hold by the determination.' It is such decisions as this that often form the turning-points in a man's life, and furnish the foundation of his future character. And this rock, on which Hugh Miller might have been wrecked, if he had not at the right moment put forth his moral strength to strike away from it, is one that youth and manhood alike need to be constantly on their guard against. It is about one of the worst and most deadly, as well as extravagant, temptations which lie in the way of youth. Sir Walter Scott used to say that 'of all vices drinking is the most incompatible with greatness'. Not only so, but it is incompatible with economy, decency, health, and honest living. When a youth cannot restrain, he must abstain. Dr Johnson's case is the case of many. He said, referring to his own habits, 'Sir, I can abstain; but I can't be moderate.'

Many popular books have been written for the purpose of communicating to the public the grand secret of making money. But there is no secret whatever about it, as the proverbs of every nation abundantly testify. 'Take care of the pennies and the pounds will take care of themselves.' 'Diligence is the mother of good luck.' 'No pains, no gains.'

'No sweat, no sweet.' 'Work and thou shalt have.' 'The world is his who has patience and industry.' 'Better go to bed supperless than rise in debt.' Such are specimens of the proverbial philosophy, embodying the hoarded experience of many generations, as to the best means of thriving in the world. They were current in people's mouths long before books were invented; and, like other popular proverbs, they were the first codes of popular morals. Moreover, they have stood the test of time, and the experience of every day still bears witness to their accuracy, force, and soundness.

Simple industry and thrift will go far towards making any person of ordinary working faculty comparatively independent in his means. Even a working man may be so, provided he will carefully husband his resources, and watch the little outlets of useless expenditure. A penny is a very small matter, yet the comfort of thousands of families depends upon the proper spending and saving of pennies. If a man allows the little pennies, the results of his hard work, to slip out of his fingers – some to the beer-shop, some this way and some that – he will find that his life is little raised above one of mere animal drudgery. On the other hand, if he takes care of the pennies – putting some weekly into a benefit society or an insurance fund, others into a savings bank, and confiding the rest to his wife to be carefully laid out, with a view to the comfortable maintenance and education of his family – he will soon find that this attention to small matters will abundantly repay him, in increasing means, growing comfort at home, and a mind comparatively free from fears as to the future. And if a working man have high ambition and possess richness in spirit – a kind of wealth which far transcends all mere worldly possessions – he may not only help himself, but be a profitable helper of others in his path through life.

There is no discredit, but honour, in every right walk of industry, whether it be in tilling the ground, making tools, weaving fabrics, or selling the products behind a counter. A youth may handle a yard-stick, or measure a piece of ribbon; and there will be no discredit in doing so, unless he allows his mind to have no higher range than the stick and ribbon; to be as short as the one, and as narrow as the other. 'Let not those blush who *have*,' said Fuller, 'but those who *have not* a lawful calling.' And Bishop Hall said, 'Sweet is the destiny of all trades, whether of the brow or of the mind.' Men who have raised themselves from a humble calling need not be ashamed, but rather ought to be proud of the difficulties they have surmounted. An American President, when asked what was his coat-of-arms, remembering that he had been a hewer of wood in his youth, replied, 'A pair of shirt sleeves.' A French doctor once taunted Fléchier, Bishop of Nîmes, who had been a tallow-chandler in his youth, with the meanness of his origin, to which Fléchier replied, 'If you had been born in the same condition that I was, you would still have been but a maker of candles.'

Nothing is more common than energy in money-making, quite independent of any higher object than its accumulation. A man who devotes himself to this pursuit, body and soul, can scarcely fail to become rich. Very little brains will do; spend less than you earn; add guinea to guinea; scrape and save; and the pile of gold will gradually rise. Osterwald, the Parisian banker, began life a poor man. He was accustomed every evening to drink a pint of beer for supper at a tavern which he visited, during which he collected and pocketed all the corks that he could lay his hands on. In eight years he had collected as many corks as sold for eight louis d'ors. With that sum he laid the foundations of his fortune – gained mostly by stock-jobbing; leaving at his death some three millions of francs.

To provide for others and for our own comfort and independence in old age, is honourable, and greatly to be commended; but to hoard for mere wealth's sake is the characteristic of the narrow-souled and the miserly. It is against the growth of this habit of inordinate saving that the wise man needs most carefully to guard himself: else, what in youth was a simple economy may in old age grow into avarice, and what was a duty in the one case may become a vice in the other. It is the *love* of money – not money itself – which is 'the root of evil', a love which narrows and contracts the soul, and closes it against generous life and action. Hence, Sir Walter Scott makes one of his characters declare that 'the penny siller slew more souls than the naked sword slew bodies'. It is one of the defects of business too exclusively followed, that it insensibly tends to a mechanism of character. The business man gets into a rut, and often does not look beyond it. If he lives for himself only, he becomes apt to regard other human beings only in so far as they minister to his ends. Take a leaf from such men's ledger and you have their life.

Worldly success, measured by the accumulation of money, is no doubt a very dazzling thing; and all men are naturally more or less the admirers of worldly success. But though men of persevering, sharp, dexterous, and unscrupulous habits, ever on the watch to push opportunities, may and do 'get on' in the world, yet it is quite possible that they may not possess the slightest elevation of character, nor a particle of real goodness. He who recognizes no higher logic than that of the shilling, may become a very rich man, and yet remain all the while an exceedingly poor creature. For riches are no proof whatever of moral worth; and their glitter often serves only to draw attention to the worthlessness of their possessor, as the light of the glow-worm reveals the grub.

The power of money is on the whole overestimated. The greatest things which have been done for the world have not been accomplished by rich men, nor by subscription lists, but by men generally of small pecuniary means. Christianity was propagated over half the world by men of the poorest class; and the greatest thinkers, discoverers, inventors, and artists have been men of moderate wealth, many of them little raised above the condition of manual labourers in point of worldly circumstances. And it will always be so. Riches are oftener an impediment than a stimulus to action; and in many cases they are quite as much a misfortune as a blessing. The youth who inherits wealth is apt to have life made too easy for him, and he soon grows sated with it, because he has nothing left to desire. Having no special object to struggle for, he finds time hang heavy on his hands; he remains morally and spiritually asleep; and his position in society is often no higher than that of a polypus over which the tide floats.

Yet the rich man, inspired by a right spirit, will spurn idleness as unmanly; and if he bethink himself of the responsibilities which attain to the possession of wealth and property he will feel even a higher call to work than men of humbler lot. This, however, must be admitted to be by no means the practice of life. The golden mean of Agur's perfect prayer is, perhaps, the best lot of all, did we but know it; 'Give me neither poverty nor riches; feed me with food convenient for me.' Joseph Brotherton left a fine motto to be recorded upon his monument in the Peel Park at Manchester – the declaration in this case being strictly true: 'My richness consisted not in the greatness of my possessions, but in the smallness of my wants.' He rose from the humblest station, that of a factory boy, to an eminent position of usefulness, by the simple exercise of homely honesty, industry, punctuality, and self-denial. Down to the close of his life, when not attending Parliament, he did duty as minister in a small chapel in Manchester to which he was attached; and in all things he made it appear, to those who knew him in private life, that the glory he sought was *not* 'to be seen of men', or to excite their praise, but to earn the consciousness of discharging the every-day duties of life, down to the smallest and humblest of them, in an honest, upright, truthful, and loving spirit.

'Respectability', in its best sense, is good. The respectable man is one worthy of regard, literally worth turning to look at. But the respectability that consists in merely keeping up appearances is not worth looking at in any sense. Far better and more respectable is the good poor man than the bad rich one – better the humble silent man than the agreeable well-appointed rogue who keeps his gig. A well-balanced and well-stored mind, a life full of useful purpose, whatever the position occupied in it may be, is of far greater importance than average worldly respectability. The highest object of life we take to be to form a manly character, and to work out the best development possible, of body and spirit – of mind, conscience, heart, and soul. This is the end: all else ought to be regarded but as the means. Accordingly, that is not the most successful life in which a man gets the most pleasure, the most money, the most power or place, honour or fame; but that in which a man gets the most manhood, and performs the greatest amounts of useful work and of human duty. Money is power after its sort, it is true; but intelligence, public spirit, and moral virtue, are powers too, and far nobler ones.

The making of a fortune may no doubt enable some people to 'enter society', as it is called; but to be esteemed there, they must possess qualities of mind, manners, or heart, else they are merely rich people, nothing more. There are men 'in society' now, as rich as Croesus, who have no consideration extended towards them, and elicit no respect. For why? They are but as money-bags: their only power is in their till. The men of mark in society – the guides and rulers of opinion – the really successful and useful men – are not necessarily rich men; but men of sterling character, of disciplined experience, and of moral excellence. Even the poor man, though he possess but little of this world's goods, may, in the enjoyment of a cultivated nature, of opportunities used and not abused, of a life spent to the best of his means and ability, look down, without the slightest feeling of envy, upon the person of mere worldly success, the man of money-bags and acres.

11. Self-Culture: Facilities and Difficulties

'The best part of every man's education,' said Sir Walter Scott, 'is that which he gives to himself.' The late Sir Benjamin Brodie delighted to remember this saying, and he used to congratulate himself on the fact that professionally he was self-taught. But this is necessarily the case with all men who have acquired distinction in letters, science, or art. The education received at school or college is but a beginning, and is valuable mainly inasmuch as it trains the mind and habituates it to continuous application and study. That which is put into us by others is always far less ours than that which we acquire by our own diligent and persevering effort. Knowledge conquered by labour becomes a possession – a property entirely our own. A greater vividness and permanency of impression is secured; and facts thus acquired become registered in the mind in a way that mere imparted information can never effect. This kind of self-culture also calls forth power and cultivates strength. The solution of one problem helps the mastery of another; and thus knowledge is carried into faculty. Our own active effort is the essential thing; and no facilities, no books, no teachers, no amount of lessons learnt by rote will enable us to dispense with it.

The best teachers have been the readiest to recognize the importance of self-culture, and of stimulating the student to acquire knowledge by the active exercise of his own faculties. They have relied more upon *training* than upon *telling*, and sought to make their pupils themselves active parties to the work in which they were engaged; thus making teaching something far higher than the mere passive reception of the scraps and details of knowledge. This was the spirit in which the great Dr Arnold worked; he strove to teach his pupils to rely upon themselves, and develop their powers by their own active efforts, himself merely guiding, directing, stimulating, and encouraging them. 'I would far rather', he said, 'send a boy to Van Diemen's Land, where he must work for his bread, than send him to Oxford to live in luxury, without any desire in his mind to avail himself of his advantages.' 'If there be one thing on earth', he observed on another occasion, 'which is truly admirable, it is to see God's wisdom blessing an inferiority of natural powers, when they have been honestly, truly, and zealously cultivated.' Speaking of a pupil of this character, he said, 'I would stand to that man hat in hand.' Once at Laleham, when teaching a rather dull boy, Arnold spoke somewhat sharply to him, on which the pupil looked up in his face and said, 'Why do you speak angrily, sir? *Indeed*, I am doing the best I can.' Years afterwards, Arnold used to tell the story to his children, and added, 'I never felt so much in my life – that look and that speech I have never forgotten.'

From the numerous instances already cited of men of humble station who have risen to distinction in science and literature, it will be obvious that labour is by no means incompatible with the highest intellectual culture. Work in moderation is healthy, as well as agreeable to the human constitution. Work educates the body, as study educates the mind; and that is the best state of society in which there is some work for every man's leisure, and some leisure for every man's work. Even the leisure classes are in a measure compelled to work, sometimes as a relief from ennui, but in most cases to gratify an instinct which they cannot resist. Some go fox-hunting in the English counties, others grouse-shooting on the Scotch hills, while many others wander away every summer to climb mountains in Switzerland. Hence the boating, running, cricketing, and athletic sports of the public schools, in which our young men at the same time so healthfully cultivate their strength both of mind and body. It is said that the Duke of Wellington, when once looking on at the boys engaged in their sports in the playground at Eton, where he had spent many of his own younger days, made the remark, 'It was here that the battle of Waterloo was won!'

Daniel Malthus urged his son when at college to be most diligent in the cultivation of knowledge, but he also enjoined him to pursue manly sports as the best means of keeping up the full working power of his mind, as well as of enjoying the pleasures of intellect. 'Every kind of knowledge,' said he, 'every acquaintance with nature and art, will amuse and strengthen your mind, and I am perfectly pleased that cricket should do the same for your arms and legs; I love to see you excel in exercises of the body, and I think myself that the better half, and much the most agreeable part, of the pleasures of the mind is best enjoyed while one is upon one's legs.' But a still more important use of active employment is that referred to by the great divine, Jeremy Taylor. 'Avoid idleness,' he says, 'and fill up the spaces of thy time with severe and useful employment; for lust easily creeps in at those emptinesses where the soul is unemployed and the body is at ease; for no easy, healthful, idle person was ever chaste if he could be tempted; but of all employments bodily labour is the most useful, and of the greatest benefit for driving away the devil.'

Practical success in life depends more upon physical health than is generally imagined. Hodson, of Hodson's Horse, writing home to a friend in England, said, 'I believe, if I get on well in India, it will be owing, physically speaking, to a sound digestion.' The capacity for continuous working in any calling must necessarily depend in a great measure upon this; and hence the necessity for attending to health, even as a means of intellectual labour. It is perhaps to the neglect of physical exercise that we find amongst students so frequent a tendency towards discontent, unhappiness, inaction, and reverie – displaying itself in contempt for real life and disgust at the beaten tracks of men – a tendency which in England has been called Byronism, and in Germany Wertherism. Dr Channing noted the same growth in America, which led him to make the remark, that 'too many of our young men grow up in a school of despair'. The only remedy for this green-sickness in youth is physical exercise – action, work, and bodily occupation.

The use of early labour in self-imposed mechanical employments may be illustrated by the boyhood of Sir Isaac Newton. Though a comparatively dull scholar, he was very assiduous in the use of his saw, hammer, and hatchet – 'knocking and hammering in his lodging-room' – making models of windmills, carriages, and machines of all sorts; and as he grew older, he took delight in making little tables and cupboards for his friends. Smeaton, Watt and Stephenson were equally handy with tools when mere boys; and but for such kind of self-culture in their youth it is doubtful whether they would have accomplished so much in their manhood. Such was also the early training of the great inventors and mechanics described in the preceding pages, whose contrivance and intelligence were practically trained by the constant use of their hands in early life. Even where men belonging to the manual labour class have risen above it, and become more purely intellectual labourers, they have found the advantages of their early training in their later pursuits.

The training of young men in the use of tools would, at the same time that it educated them in 'common things', teach them the use of their hands and arms, familiarize them with healthy work, exercise their faculties upon things tangible and actual, give them some practical acquaintance with mechanics, impart to them the ability of being useful, and implant in them the habit of persevering physical effort. This is an advantage which the working classes, strictly so called, certainly possess over the leisure classes – that they are in early life under the necessity of applying themselves laboriously to some mechanical pursuit or other – thus acquiring manual dexterity and the use of their physical powers. The chief disadvantage attached to the calling of the laborious classes is, not that they are employed in physical work, but that they are too exclusively so employed, often to the neglect of their moral and intellectual faculties. While the youths of the leisure classes, having been taught to associate labour with servility, have shunned it, and been allowed to grow up practically ignorant, the poorer classes, confining themselves within the circle of their laborious callings, have been allowed to grow up in a large proportion of cases absolutely illiterate. It seems possible, however, to avoid both these evils by combining physical training or physical work with intellectual culture; and there are various signs abroad which seem to mark the gradual adoption of this healthier system of education.

Though Sir Walter Scott, when at Edinburgh College, went by the name of 'The Greek Blockhead', he was, notwithstanding his lameness, a remarkably healthy youth: he could spear a salmon with the best fisher on the Tweed, and ride a wild horse with any hunter in Yarrow. When devoting himself in after life to literary pursuits, Sir Walter never lost his taste for field sports; but while writing *Waverley* in the morning, he would in the afternoon course hares. Professor Wilson was a very fine athlete, as great at throwing the hammer as in his flights of eloquence and poetry; and Burns, when a youth, was remarkable chiefly for his leaping, putting, and wrestling. Some of our greatest divines were distinguished in their youth for their physical energies. Isaac Barrow, when at the Charterhouse School, was notorious for his pugilistic encounters, in which he got many a bloody nose; Andrew Fuller, when working as a farmer's lad at Soham, was chiefly famous for his skill in boxing; and Adam Clarke, when a boy, was only remarkable for the strength displayed by him in 'rolling large stones about' – the secret, possibly, of some of the power which he subsequently displayed in rolling forth large thoughts in his manhood.

While it is necessary, then, in the first place to secure this solid foundation of physical health, it must also be observed that the cultivation of the habit of mental application is quite indispensable for the education of the student. The maxim that 'Labour conquers all things' holds especially true in the case of the conquest of knowledge. The road into learning is alike free to all who will give the labour and the study requisite to gather it; nor are there any difficulties so great that the student of resolute purpose may not surmount and overcome them. It was one of the characteristic expressions of Chatterton, that God had sent His creatures into the world with arms long enough to reach anything if they chose to be at the trouble. In study, as in business, energy is the great thing. There must be the *fervet opus*: we must not only strike the iron while it is hot, but strike it till it is made hot. It is astonishing how much may be accomplished in self-culture by the energetic and the persevering, who are careful to avail themselves of opportunities, and use up the fragments of spare time which the idle permit to run to waste. Thus Ferguson learnt astronomy from the heavens, while wrapt in a sheep-skin on the highland hills; thus Stone learnt mathematics while working as a journeyman gardener; thus Drew studied the highest philosophy in the intervals of cobbling shoes; and thus Miller taught himself geology while working as a day labourer in a quarry.

Sir Joshua Reynolds, as we have already observed, was so earnest a believer in the force of industry that he held that all men might achieve excellence if they would but exercise the power of assiduous and patient working. He held that drudgery lay on the road to genius, and that there was no limit to the proficiency of an artist except the limit of his own painstaking. He would not believe in what is called inspiration, but only in study and labour. 'Excellence,' he said, 'is never granted to man but as the reward of labour.' 'If you have great talents, industry will improve them; if you have but moderate abilities, industry will supply their deficiency. Nothing is denied to well-directed labour; nothing is to be obtained without it.' Sir Fowell Buxton was an equal believer in the power of study; and he entertained the modest idea that he could do as well as other men if he devoted to the pursuit double the time and labour that they did. He placed his great confidence in ordinary means and extraordinary application.

One of Ignatius Loyola's maxims was, 'He who does well one work at a time, does more than all.' By spreading our efforts over too large a surface we inevitably weaken our force, hinder our progress, and acquire a habit of fitfulness and ineffective working. Lord St Leonards once communicated to Sir Fowell Buxton the mode in which he had conducted his studies, and thus explained the secret of his success. 'I resolved,' said he, 'when beginning to read law, to make everything I acquired perfectly my own, and never to go to a second thing until I had entirely accomplished the first. Many of my competitors read as much in a day as I read in a week; but at the end of twelve months, my knowledge was as fresh as the day it was acquired, whilst theirs had glided away from recollection.'

It is not the quantity of study that one gets through, or the amount of reading, that makes a wise man; but the appositeness of the study to the purpose for which it is pursued; the concentration of the mind for the time being on the subject under consideration; and the habitual discipline by which the whole system of mental application is regulated. Abernethy was even of opinion that there was a point of saturation in his own mind, and that if he took into it something more than it could hold, it only had the effect of pushing something else out. Speaking of the study of medicine, he said, 'If a man has a clear idea of what he desires to do, he will seldom fail in selecting the proper means of accomplishing it.'

Decision and promptitude are as requisite in self-culture as in business. The growth of these qualities may be encouraged by accustoming young people to rely upon their own resources, leaving them to enjoy as much freedom of action in early life as is practicable. Too much guidance and restraint hinder the formation of habits of self-help. They are like bladders tied under the arms of one who has not taught himself to swim. Want of confidence is perhaps a greater obstacle to improvement than is generally imagined. It has been said that half the failures in life arise from pulling in one's horse while he is leaping. Dr

Johnson was accustomed to attribute his success to confidence in his own powers. True modesty is quite compatible with a due estimate of one's own merits, and does not demand the abnegation of all merit. Though there are those who deceive themselves, by putting a false figure before their ciphers, the want of confidence, the want of faith in one's self, and consequently the want of promptitude in action, is a defect of character which is found to stand very much in the way of individual progress; and the reason why so little is done, is generally because so little is attempted.

There is usually no want of desire on the part of most persons to arrive at the results of self-culture, but there is a great aversion to pay the inevitable price for it, of hard work. Dr Johnson held that 'impatience of study was the mental disease of the present generation'; and the remark is still applicable. We may not believe that there is a royal road to learning, but we seem to believe very firmly in a 'popular' one. In education, we invent labour-saving processes, seek short cuts to science, learn French and Latin 'in twelve lessons', or 'without a master'. We resemble the lady of fashion, who engaged a master to teach her on condition that he did not plague her with verbs and participles. We get our smattering of science in the same way; we learn chemistry by listening to a short course of lectures enlivened by experiments, and when we have inhaled laughing gas, seen green water turned to red, and phosphorus burnt in oxygen, we have got our smattering, of which the most that can be said is, that though it may be better than nothing, it is yet good for nothing. Thus we often imagine we are being educated while we are only being amused.

Accustomed to acquire information under the guise of amusement, young people will soon reject that which is presented to them under the aspect of study and labour. Learning their knowledge and science in sport, they will be too apt to make sport of both; while the habit of intellectual dissipation, thus engendered, cannot fail, in course of time, to produce a thoroughly emasculating effect both upon their mind and character. 'Multifarious reading,' said Robertson of Brighton, 'weakens the mind like smoking, and is an excuse for its lying dormant. It is the idlest of all idlenesses, and leaves more of impotency than any other.'

The evil is a growing one, and operates in various ways. Its least mischief is shallowness; its greatest, the aversion to steady labour which it induces, and the low and feeble tone of mind which it encourages. If we would be really wise, we must diligently apply ourselves, and confront the same continuous application which our forefathers did; for labour is still, and ever will be, the inevitable price set upon everything which is valuable. We must be satisfied to work with a purpose, and wait the results with patience. All progress, of the best kind, is slow, but to him who works faithfully and zealously the reward will, doubtless, be vouchsafed in good time. The spirit of industry, embodied in a man's daily life, will gradually lead him to exercise his powers on objects outside himself, of greater dignity and more extended usefulness. And still we must labour on; for the work of self-culture is never finished. 'To be employed', said the poet Gray, 'is to be happy.' 'It is better to wear out than rust out,' said Bishop Cumberland. 'Have we not all eternity to rest in?' exclaimed Arnauld. 'Repos ailleurs' was the motto of Marnix de St Aldegonde, the energetic and ever-working friend of William the Silent.

It is possible that at this day we may even exaggerate the importance of literary culture. We are apt to imagine that, because we possess many libraries, institutes, and museums, we are making great progress. But such facilities may as often be a hindrance as a help to individual self-culture of the highest kind. The possession of a library, or the free use of it, no more constitutes learning, than the possession of wealth constitutes generosity. Though we undoubtedly possess great facilities, it is nevertheless true, as of old, that wisdom and understanding can only become the possession of individual men by travelling the old road of observation, attention, perseverance and industry. The possession of the mere materials of knowledge is something very different from wisdom and understanding, which are reached through a higher kind of discipline than that of reading – which is often but a mere passive reception of other men's thoughts; there being little or no active effort of mind in the transaction. Then how much of our reading is but the indulgence of a sort of intellectual dram-drinking, imparting a grateful excitement for the moment, without the slightest effect in improving and enriching the mind or building up the character. Thus many indulge themselves in the conceit that they are cultivating their minds, when they are only employed in the humbler occupation of killing time, of which perhaps the best that can be said is that it keeps them from doing worse things.

It is also to be borne in mind that the experience gathered from books, though often valuable, is but of the nature of *learning*: whereas the experience gained from actual life is of the nature of *wisdom*; and a small store of the latter is worth vastly more than any stock of the former. Lord Bolingbroke truly said that, 'Whatever study tends neither directly nor indirectly to make us better men and citizens is at best but a specious and ingenious sort of idleness and the knowledge we acquire by it only a creditable kind of ignorance – nothing more.'

Useful and instructive though good reading may be, it is yet only one mode of cultivating the mind; and is much less influential than practical experience and good example in the formation of character. There were wise, valiant, and true-hearted men bred in England long before the existence of a reading public. Magna Charta was secured by men who signed the deed with their marks. Though altogether unskilled in the art of deciphering the literary signs by which principles were denominated upon paper, they yet understood and appreciated, and boldly contended for, the things themselves. Thus the foundations of English liberty were laid by men who, though illiterate, were neverthe-less of the very highest stamp of character. And it must be admitted that the chief object of culture is, not merely to fill the mind with other men's thoughts, and to be the passive recipient of their impressions of things, but to enlarge our individual intelligence, and render us more useful and efficient workers in the sphere of life to which we may be called.

Self-discipline and self-control are the beginnings of practical wis-dom; and these must have their root in self-respect. Hope springs from it – hope, which is the companion of power, and the mother of success; for whoso hopes strongly has within him the gift of miracles. The humblest may say, 'To respect myself, to develop myself – this is my true duty in life. An integral and responsible part of the great system of society, I owe it to society and to its Author not to degrade or destroy either my body, mind or instincts. On the contrary, I am bound to the best of my power to give to those parts of my constitution the highest degree of perfection possible. I am not only to suppress the evil, but to evoke the good elements in my nature. And as I respect myself, so am

I equally bound to respect others, as they on their part are bound to respect me.' Hence mutual respect, justice and order, of which law becomes the written record and guarantee.

One way in which self-culture may be degraded is by regarding it too exclusively as a means of 'getting on'. Viewed in this light, it is unquestionable that education is one of the best investments of time and labour. In any line of life, intelligence will enable a man to adapt himself more readily to circumstances, suggest improved methods of working, and render him more apt, skilled and effective in all respects. He who works with his head as well as his hands will come to look at his business with a clearer eye; and he will become conscious of increasing power – perhaps the most cheering consciousness the human mind can cherish. The power of self-help will gradually grow: and in proportion to a man's self-respect, will he be armed against the temptation of low indulgences. Society and its action will be regarded with quite a new interest, his sympathies will widen and enlarge, and he will thus be attracted to work for others as well as for himself.

Self-culture may not, however, end in eminence, as in the numerous instances above cited. The great majority of men, in all times, however enlightened, must necessarily be engaged in the ordinary avocations of industry; and no degree of culture which can be conferred upon the community at large will ever enable them – even were it desirable, which it is not – to get rid of the daily work of society, which must be done. But this, we think, may also be accomplished. We can elevate the condition of labour by allying it to noble thoughts, which confer a grace upon the lowliest as well as the highest rank. For no matter how poor or humble a man may be, the great thinker of this and other days may come in and sit down with him, and be his companion for the time, though his dwelling be the meanest hut. It is thus that the habit of well-directed reading may become a source of the greatest pleasure and self-improvement, and exercise a gentle coercion, with the most beneficial results, over the whole tenor of a man's character and conduct. And even though self-culture may not bring wealth, it will at all events give one the companionship of elevated thoughts. A nobleman once contemptuously asked of a sage, 'What have you got by all your philosophy?' 'At least I have got society in myself,' was the wise man's reply.

But many are apt to feel despondent, and become discouraged in the work of self-culture, because they do not 'get on' in the world so fast as they think they deserve to do. Having planted their acorn, they expect to see it grow into an oak at once. They have perhaps looked upon knowledge in the light of a marketable commodity, and are consequently mortified because it does not sell as they expected it would do. Mr Tremenheere, in one of his 'Education Reports' (for 1840–41), states that a schoolmaster in Norfolk, finding his school rapidly falling off, made inquiry into the cause, and ascertained that the reason given by the majority of the parents for withdrawing their children was, that they had expected 'education was to make them better off than they were before', but that having found it had 'done them no good', they had taken their children from school, and would give themselves no further trouble about education!

The same low idea of self-culture is but too prevalent in other classes, and is encouraged by the false views of life which are always more or less current in society. But to regard self-culture either as a means of getting past others in the world or of intellectual dissipation and amusement, rather than as a power to elevate the character and expand the spiritual nature, is to place it on a very low level. To use the words of Bacon, 'Knowledge is not a shop for profit or sale, but a rich storehouse for the glory of the Creator and the relief of man's estate.' It is doubtless most honourable for a man of labour to elevate himself, and to better his condition in society, but this is not to be done at the sacrifice of himself. To make the mind the mere drudge of the body is putting it to a very servile use; and to go about whining and bemoaning our pitiful lot because we fail in achieving that success in life which, after all, depends rather upon habits of industry and attention to business details than upon knowledge, is the mark of a small, and often of a sour mind. Such a temper cannot better be reproved than in the words of Robert Southey, who thus wrote to a friend who sought his counsel: 'I would give you advice if it could be of use; but there is no curing those who choose to be diseased. A good man and a wise man may at times be angry with the world, at times grieved for it; but be sure no man was ever discontented with the world if he did his duty in it. If a man of education, who has health, eyes, hands and leisure, wants an object, it is only because God

Almighty has bestowed all those blessings upon a man who does not deserve them.'

Another way in which education may be prostituted is by employing it as a mere means of intellectual dissipation and amusement. Many are the ministers to this taste in our time. There is almost a mania for frivolity and excitement, which exhibits itself in many forms in our popular literature. To meet the public taste, our books and periodicals must now be highly spiced, amusing and comic, not disdaining slang, and illustrative of breaches of all laws, human and divine. Douglas Jerrold once observed of this tendency, 'I am convinced the world will get tired (at least, I hope so) of this eternal guffaw about all things. After all, life has something serious in it. It cannot be all a comic history of humanity. Some men would, I believe, write a Comic Sermon on the Mount. Think of a Comic History of England, the drollery of Alfred, the fun of Sir Thomas More, the farce of his daughter begging the dead head and clasping it in her coffin on her bosom. Surely the world will be sick of this blasphemy.'

As a rest from toil and a relaxation from graver pursuits, the perusal of a well-written story, by a writer of genius, is a high intellectual pleasure; and it is a description of literature to which all classes of readers, old and young, are attracted as by a powerful instinct; nor would we have any of them debarred from its enjoyment in a reasonable degree. But to make it the exclusive literary diet as some do – to devour the garbage with which the shelves of circulating libraries are filled – and to occupy the greater portion of the leisure hours in studying the preposterous pictures of human life which so many of them present, is worse than waste of time: it is positively pernicious. The habitual novel-reader indulges in fictitious feelings so much, that there is great risk of sound and healthy feeling becoming perverted or benumbed.

Amusement in moderation is wholesome, and to be commended; but amusement in excess vitiates the whole nature, and is a thing to be carefully guarded against. The maxim is often quoted of 'All work and no play makes Jack a dull boy'; but all play and no work makes him something greatly worse. Nothing can be more hurtful to a youth than to have his soul sodden with pleasure. The best qualities of his mind are impaired; common enjoyments become tasteless; his appetite for the higher kind of pleasures is vitiated; and when he comes to face the work and the duties of life, the result is usually aversion and disgust. 'Fast' men waste and exhaust the powers of life, and dry up the sources of true happiness. Having forestalled their spring, they can produce no healthy growth of either character or intellect. A child without simplicity, a maiden without innocence, a boy without truthfulness, are not more piteous sights than the man who has wasted and thrown away his youth in self-indulgence. Mirabeau said of himself, 'My early years have already in a great measure disinherited the succeeding ones, and dissipated a great part of my vital powers.' As the wrong done to another today returns upon ourselves tomorrow, so the sins of our youth rise up in our age to scourge us. When Lord Bacon says that 'strength to nature in youth passeth over many excesses which are owing a man until he is old', he exposes a physical as well as a moral fact which cannot be too well weighed in the conduct of life. The worst of youthful indiscretions is, not that they destroy health, so much as that they sully manhood. The dissipated youth becomes a tainted man; and often he cannot be pure, even if he would. If cure there be, it is only to be found in inoculating the mind with a fervent spirit of duty, and in energetic application to useful work.

Robert Nicoll wrote to a friend, after reading *Recollections of Coleridge*, 'What a mighty intellect was lost in that man for want of a little energy – a little determination!' Nicoll himself was a true and brave spirit, who died young, but not before he had encountered and overcome great difficulties in life. At his outset, while carrying on a small business as a bookseller, he found himself weighed down with a debt of only twenty pounds, which he said he felt 'weighing like a millstone round his neck', and that, 'if he had it paid he never would borrow again from mortal man'. Writing to his mother at the time he said, 'Fear not for me, dear mother, for I feel myself daily growing firmer and more hopeful in spirit. The more I think and reflect – and thinking, not reading, is now my occupation – I feel that, whether I be growing richer or not, I am growing a wiser man, which is far better. Pain, poverty, and all the other wild beasts of life which so affrighten others, I am so bold as to think I could look in the face without shrinking, without losing respect for myself, faith in man's high destinies, or trust in God. There is a point which it costs much mental toil and struggle to gain, but which, when once gained, a man can look down from, as a traveller from a lofty mountain, on storms raging below, while he is walking in sunshine. That I have yet gained this point in life I will not say, but I feel myself daily nearer to it.'

It is not ease, but effort – not facility, but difficulty, that makes men. There is, perhaps, no station in life in which difficulties have not to be encountered and overcome before any decided measure of success can be achieved. Those difficulties are, however, our best instructors, as our mistakes often form our best experience. Charles James Fox was accustomed to say that he hoped more from a man who failed, and yet went on in spite of his failure, than from the buoyant career of the successful. 'It is all very well,' said he, 'to tell me that a young man has distinguished himself by a brilliant first speech. He may go on, or he may be satisfied with his first triumph; but show me a young man who has *not* succeeded at first, and nevertheless has gone on, and I will back that young man to do better than most of those who have succeeded at the first trial.'

We learn wisdom from failure much more than from success. We often discover what *will* do, by finding out what will not do; and probably he who never made a mistake never made a discovery. It was the failure in the attempt to make a sucking-pump act, when the working bucket was more than thirty-three feet above the surface of the water to be raised, that led observant men to study the law of atmospheric pressure, and opened a new field of research to the genius of Galileo, Torrecelli, and Boyle. John Hunter used to remark that the art of surgery would not advance until professional men had the courage to publish their failures as well as their successes. Watt the engineer said, of all things most wanted in mechanical engineering was a history of failures: 'We want', he said, 'a book of blots.' When Sir Humphry Davy was once shown a dexterously manipulated experiment, he said: 'I thank God I was not made a dexterous manipulator, for the most important of my discoveries have been suggested to me by failures.' Another distinguished investigator in physical science has left it on record that, whenever in the course of his researches he encountered an apparently insuperable obstacle, he generally found himself on the brink of some discovery. The very greatest things – great thoughts, discoveries, inventions – have usually been nurtured in hardship, often pondered over in sorrow, and at length established with difficulty.

Beethoven said of Rossini, that he had in him the stuff to have made a good musician if he had only, when a boy, been well flogged; but that he had been spoilt by the facility with which he produced. Men who feel their strength within them need not fear to encounter adverse opinions; they have far greater reason to fear undue praise and too friendly criticism. When Mendelssohn was about to enter the orchestra at Birmingham, on the first performance of his 'Elijah', he said laughingly to one of his friends and critics, 'Stick your claws into me! Don't tell me what you like, but what you don't like!'

It has been said, and truly, that it is the defeat that tries the general more than the victory. Washington lost more battles than he gained; but he succeeded in the end. The Romans, in their most victorious campaigns, almost invariably began with defeats. Moreau used to be compared by his companions to a drum, which nobody hears of except it be beaten. Wellington's military genius was perfected by encounter with difficulties of apparently the most overwhelming character, but which only served to nerve his resolution, and bring out more prominently his great qualities as a man and a general. So the skilful mariner obtains his best experience amidst storms and tempest, which train him to self-reliance, courage, and the highest discipline; and we probably owe to rough seas and wintry nights the best training of our race of British seamen, who are, certainly, not surpassed by any in the world.

'Sweet indeed are the uses of adversity.' They reveal to us our powers, and call forth our energies. If there be real worth in the character, like sweet herbs, it will give forth its finest fragrance when pressed. 'Crosses,' says the old proverb, 'are the ladders that lead to heaven.' 'What is even poverty itself,' asks Richter, 'that a man should murmur under it? It is but as the pain of piercing a maiden's ear, and you hang precious jewels in the wound.' In the experience of life it is found that the wholesome discipline of adversity in strong natures usually carries with it a self-preserving influence. Many are found capable of bravely bearing up under privations, and cheerfully encountering obstructions, who are afterwards found unable to withstand the more dangerous influences of prosperity. It is only a weak man whom the wind deprives of his cloak: a man of average strength is more in danger of losing it when assailed by the means of a too genial sun. Thus it often needs a higher discipline and a stronger character to bear up under good fortune than under adverse. Some generous natures kindle and warm with prosperity, but there are many on whom wealth has no such influence. Base hearts it only hardens, making those who were mean and servile, mean and proud. But while prosperity is apt to harden the heart to pride, adversity in a man of resolution will serve to ripen it into fortitude. To use the words of Burke, 'Difficulty is a severe instructor, set over us by the supreme ordinance of a parental Guardian and Instructor, who knows us better than we know ourselves, as He loves us better too. He that wrestles with us strengthens our nerves, and sharpens our skill: our antagonist is thus our helper.' Without the necessity of encountering difficulty, life might be easier, but men would be worthless. For trials, wisely improved, train the character, and teach self-help; thus hardship itself may often prove the wholesomest discipline for us, though we recognize it not. When the gallant young Hodson, unjustly removed from his Indian command, felt himself sore pressed down by unmerited calumny and reproach, he yet preserved the courage to say to a friend, 'I strive to look the worst boldly in the face, as I would an enemy in the field, and to do my appointed work resolutely and to the best of my ability, satisfied that there is a reason for all; and that even irksome duties well done bring their own reward, and that, if not, still they *are* duties.'

The battle of life is, in most cases, fought uphill; and to win it without a struggle were perhaps to win it without honour. If there were no difficulties there would be no success; if there were nothing to struggle for, there would be nothing to be achieved. Difficulties may intimidate the weak, but they act only as a wholesome stimulus to men of resolution and valour. All experience of life indeed serves to prove that the impediments thrown in the way of human advancement may for the most part be overcome by steady good conduct, honest zeal, activity, perseverance, and above all by a determined resolution to surmount difficulties, and stand up manfully against misfortune.

The school of Difficulty is the best school of moral discipline, for nations as for individuals. Indeed, the history of difficulty would be but a history of all the great and good things that have yet been accomplished by men. It is hard to say how much northern nations owe to their encounter with a comparatively rude and changeable climate and an originally sterile soil, which is one of the necessities of their condition –

involving a perennial struggle with difficulties such as the natives of sunnier climes know nothing of. And thus it may be, that, though our finest products are exotic, the skill and industry which have been necessary to rear them have issued in the production of a native growth of men not surpassed on the globe.

Wherever there is difficulty, the individual man must come out for better, for worse. Encounter with it will train his strength, and discipline his skill; heartening him for future effort, as the racer, by being trained to run against the hill, at length courses with facility. The road to success may be steep to climb, and it puts to the proof the energies of him who would reach the summit. But by experience a man soon learns that obstacles are to be overcome by grappling with them – that the nettle feels as soft as silk when it is boldly grasped – and that the most effective help towards realizing the object proposed is the moral conviction that we can and will accomplish it. Thus difficulties often fall away of themselves before the determination to overcome them.

Much will be done if we do but try. Nobody knows what he can do till he has tried; and few try their best till they have been forced to do it. '*If* I could do such and such a thing,' sighs the desponding youth. But nothing will be done if he only wishes. The desire must ripen into purpose and effort; and one energetic attempt is worth a thousand aspirations. It is these thorny 'ifs' – the mutterings of impotence and despair – which so often hedge round the field of possibility, and prevent anything being done or even attempted. 'A difficulty', said Lord Lyndhurst, 'is a thing to be overcome'; grapple with it at once; facility will come with practice, and strength and fortitude with repeated effort. Thus the mind and character may be trained to an almost perfect discipline, and enabled to act with a grace, spirit, and liberty almost incomprehensible to those who have not passed through a similar experience.

Everything that we learn is the mastery of a difficulty; and the mastery of one helps to the mastery of others. Things which may at first sight appear comparatively valueless in education – such as the study of dead languages, and the relations of lines and surfaces which we call mathematics – are really of the greatest practical value, not so much because of the information which they yield, as because of the development which they compel. The mastery of these studies evokes effort, and cultivates powers of application, which otherwise might have lain dormant. Thus one thing leads to another, and so the work goes on through life – encounter with difficulty ending only when life and culture end. But indulging in the feeling of discouragement never helped any one over a difficulty, and never will. D'Alembert's advice to the student who complained about his want of success in mastering the first elements of mathematics was the right one: 'Go on, sir, and faith and strength will come to you.'

The danseuse who turns a pirouette, the violinist who plays a sonata, have acquired their dexterity by patient repetition and after many failures. Carissimi, when praised for the ease and grace of his melodies, exclaimed, 'Ah! you little know with what difficulty this ease has been acquired.' Sir Joshua Reynolds, when once asked how long it had taken him to paint a certain picture, replied, 'All my life.' Henry Clay, the American orator, when giving advice to young men, thus described to them the secret of his success in the cultivation of his art: 'I owe my success in life', said he, 'chiefly to one circumstance – that at the age of twenty-seven I commenced, and continued for years, the process of daily reading and speaking upon the contents of some historical or scientific book. These off-hand efforts were made, sometimes in a corn-field, at others in the forest, and not infrequently in some distant barn, with the horse and the ox for my auditors. It is to this early practice of the art of all arts that I am indebted for the primary and leading impulses that stimulated me onward and have shaped and moulded my whole subsequent destiny.'

Curran, the Irish orator, when a youth, had a strong defect in his articulation, and at school he was known as 'stuttering Jack Curran'. While he was engaged in the study of the law, and still struggling to overcome his defect, he was stung into eloquence by the sarcasms of a member of a debating club, who characterized him as 'Orator Mum'; for, like Cowper, when he stood up to speak on a similar occasion, Curran had not been able to utter a word. The taunt stung him and he replied in a triumphant speech. This accidental discovery in himself of the gift of eloquence encouraged him to proceed in his studies with renewed energy. He corrected his enunciation by reading aloud, em-phatically and distinctly, the best passages in literature, for several hours every day, studying his features before a mirror, and adopting a method of gesticulation suited to his rather awkward and ungraceful figure. He also proposed cases to himself, which he argued with as much care as if he had been addressing a jury. Curran began business with the qualification which Lord Eldon stated to be the first requisite for distinction, that is, 'to be not worth a shilling'. While working his way laboriously at the bar, still oppressed by the diffidence which had overcome him in his debating club, he was on one occasion provoked by the Judge (Robinson) into making a very severe retort. In the case under discussion, Curran observed 'that he had never met the law as laid down by his lordship in any book in his library'. 'That may be, sir,' said the judge, in a contemptuous tone, 'but I suspect that *your* library is very small.' His lordship was notoriously a furious political partisan, the author of several anonymous pamphlets characterized by unusual violence and dogmatism. Curran, roused by the allusion to his straitened circumstances, replied thus: 'It is very true, my lord, that I am poor, and the circumstance has certainly curtailed my library; my books are not numerous, but they are select, and I hope they have been perused with proper dispositions. I have prepared myself for this high profession by the study of a few good works, rather than by the composition of a great many bad ones. I am not ashamed of my poverty; but I should be ashamed of my wealth, could I have stooped to acquire it by servility and corruption. If I rise not to rank, I shall at least be honest; and should I ever cease to be so, many an example shows me that an ill-gained elevation, by making me the more conspicuous, would only make me the more universally and the more notoriously contemptible.'

The extremest poverty has been no obstacle in the way of men devoted to the duty of self-culture. Professor Alexander Murray, the linguist, learnt to write by scribbling his letters on an old woolcard with the end of a burnt heather stem. The only book which his father, who was a poor shepherd, possessed was a penny Shorter Catechism; but that, being thought too valuable for common use, was carefully preserved in a cupboard for the Sunday catechizings. Professor Moor, when a young man, being too poor to purchase Newton's *Principia*, borrowed the book, and copied the whole of it with his own hand. Many poor students, while labouring daily for their living, have only been able to snatch an atom of knowledge here and there at intervals, as birds do their food in winter time when the fields are covered with snow. They have struggled on, and faith and hope have come to them. A well-known author and publisher, William Chambers, of Edinburgh, speaking before an assemblage of young men in that city, thus briefly described to them his humble beginnings, for their encouragement: 'I stand before you,' he said, 'a self-educated man. My education was that which is supplied at the humble parish schools of Scotland; and it was only when I went to Edinburgh a poor boy, that I devoted my evenings, after the labours of the day, to the cultivation of that intellect which the Almighty has given me. From seven or eight in the morning till nine or ten at night was I at my business as a bookseller's apprentice, and it was only during hours after these, stolen from sleep, that I could devote myself to study. I did not read novels: my attention was devoted to physical science, and other useful matters. I also taught myself French. I look back to those times with great pleasure, and am almost sorry I have not to go through the same experience again; for I reaped more pleasure when I had not a sixpence in my pocket, studying in a garret in Edinburgh, than I now find when sitting amidst all the elegances and comforts of a parlour.'

William Cobbett's account of how he learnt English Grammar is full of interest and instruction for all students labouring under difficulties. 'I learned grammar', said he, 'when I was a private soldier on the pay of sixpence a day. The edge of my berth, or that of my guard-bed, was my sea to study in; my knapsack was my book-case; a bit of board lying on my lap was my writing-table; and the task did not demand anything like a year of my life. I had no money to purchase candle or oil; in winter time it was rarely that I could get any evening light but that of the fire, and only my turn even of that. And if I, under such circumstances, and without parent or friend to advise or encourage me, accomplished this undertaking, what excuse can there be for any youth, however poor, however pressed with business, or however circumstanced as to room or other conveniences?'

Sir Samuel Romilly was not less indefatigable as a self-cultivator. The son of a jeweller, descended from a French refugee, he received little education in his early years, but overcame all his disadvantages by unwearied application, and by efforts constantly directed towards the same end. 'I determined,' he says, in his autobiography, 'when I was between fifteen and sixteen years of age, to apply myself seriously to learning Latin, of which I, at that time, knew little more than some of the most familiar rules of grammar. In the course of three or four years, during which I thus applied myself, I had read almost every prose writer of the age of pure Latinity, except those who have treated merely of technical subjects, such as Varro, Columella, and Celsus. I had gone three times through the whole of Livy, Sallust and Tacitus. I had studied the most celebrated orations of Cicero, and translated a great deal of Homer. Terence, Virgil, Horace, Ovid and Juvenal I had read over and over again.' He also studied geography, natural history, and natural philosophy, and obtained a considerable acquaintance with general knowledge. At sixteen he was articled to a clerk in Chancery; worked hard; was admitted to the bar; and his industry and perseverance ensured success. He became Solicitor-General under the Fox administration in 1806, and steadily worked his way to the highest celebrity in his profession. Yet he was always haunted by a painful and almost oppressive sense of his own disqualifications, and never ceased labouring to remedy them.

Sir Walter Scott was accustomed to cite the case of his young friend John Leyden as one of the most remarkable illustrations of the power of perseverance which he had ever known. The son of a shepherd in one of the wildest valleys of Roxburghshire, he was almost entirely self-educated. Like many Scotch shepherds' sons – like Hogg, who taught himself to write by copying the letters of a printed book as he lay watching his flock on the hillside – like Cairns, who, from tending sheep on the Lammermoors, raised himself by dint of application and industry to the professor's chair which he now so worthily holds – like Murray, Ferguson and many more – Leyden was early inspired by a thirst for knowledge. When a poor barefooted boy, he walked six or eight miles across the moors daily to learn reading at the little village schoolhouse of Kirkton; and this was all the education he received, the rest he acquired for himself. He found his way to Edinburgh to attend the college there, setting the extremest penury at defiance. He was first discovered as a frequenter of a small bookseller's shop kept by Archibald Constable, afterwards so well known as a publisher. He would pass hour after hour perched on a ladder in mid-air, with some great folio in his hand, forgetful of the scanty meal of bread and water which

214

awaited him at his miserable lodging. Access to books and lectures comprised all within the bounds of his wishes.

Thus he toiled and battled at the gates of science until his unconquerable perseverance carried everything before it. Before he had attained his nineteenth year he had astonished all the professors in Edinburgh by his profound knowledge of Greek and Latin, and the general mass of information he had acquired. Having turned his views to India, he sought employment in the civil service, but failed. He was, however, informed that a surgeon's assistant's commission was open to him. But he was no surgeon, and knew no more of the profession than a child. He could, however, learn. Then he was told that he must be ready to pass in six months! Nothing daunted, he set to work, to acquire in six months what usually required three years. At the end of six months, he took his degree with honour. Scott and a few friends helped to fit him out; and he sailed for India, after publishing his beautiful poem, 'The Scenes of Infancy'. In India he promised to become one of the greatest of Oriental scholars, but was unhappily cut off by fever, caught by exposure, and died at an early age.

There are many other illustrious names which might be cited to prove the truth of the common saying that 'it is never too late to learn'. Even at advanced years men can do much, if they will determine on making a beginning. Sir Henry Spelman did not begin the study of science until he was between fifty and sixty years of age. Franklin was fifty before he fully entered upon the study of natural philosophy. Dryden and Scott were not known as authors until each was in his fortieth year. Boccaccio was thirty-five when he commenced his literary career, and Alfieri was forty-six when he began the study of Greek. Dr Arnold learnt German at an advanced age, for the purpose of reading Niebuhr in the original; and in like manner James Watt, when about forty, while working at his trade of an instrument maker in Glasgow, learnt French, German and Italian, to enable himself to peruse the valuable works on mechanical philosophy which existed in those languages. Thomas Scott was fifty-six before he began to learn Hebrew. Robert Hall was once found lying upon the floor, racked by pain, learning Italian in his old age, to enable him to judge of the parallel drawn by Macaulay between Milton and Dante. Handel was forty-eight before he published any of his great works. Indeed, hundreds of instances might be given of men who struck out an entirely new path, and successfully entered on new studies, at a comparatively advanced time of life. None but the frivolous or the indolent will say, 'I am too old to learn.'

Ulysses Grant, the Commander-in-Chief of the United States, was called 'Useless Grant' by his mother – he was so dull and unhandy when a boy; and Stonewall Jackson, Lee's greatest lieutenant, was, in his youth, chiefly noted for his slowness. While a pupil at West Point Military Academy he was, however, equally remarkable for his indefatigable application and perseverance. When a task was set him, he never left it until he had mastered it; nor did he ever feign to possess knowledge which he had not entirely acquired.

John Howard, the philanthropist, was another illustrious dunce, learning next to nothing during the seven years that he was at school. Stephenson, as a youth, was distinguished chiefly for his skill at putting and wrestling, and attention to his work. The brilliant Sir Humphry Davy was no cleverer than other boys: his teacher, Dr Cardew, once said of him, 'While he was with me I could not discern the faculties by which he was so much distinguished.' Indeed, Davy himself in later life considered it fortunate that he had been left to 'enjoy so much idleness' at school. Watt was a dull scholar, notwithstanding the stories told about his precosity; but he was, what was better, patient and perseverant, and it was by such qualities, and by his carefully cultivated inventiveness, that he was enabled to perfect his steam-engine.

What Dr Arnold said of boys is equally true of men – that the difference between one boy and another consists not so much in talent as in energy. Given perseverance and energy soon becomes habitual. Provided the dunce has persistency and application he will inevitably head the cleverer fellow without those qualities. Slow but sure wins the race. It is perseverance that explains how the position of boys at school is so often reversed in real life; and it is curious to note how some who were then so clever have since become so commonplace; whilst others, dull boys, of whom nothing was expected, slow in their faculties but sure in their pace, have assumed the position of leaders of men.

The tortoise in the right road will beat a racer in the wrong. It matters not though a youth be slow, if he be but diligent. Quickness of parts may even prove a defect, inasmuch as the boy who learns readily will often forget as readily; and also because he finds no need of cultivating that quality of application and perseverance which the slower youth is compelled to exercise, and which proves so valuable an element in the formation of every character. Davy said, 'What I am I have made myself': and the same holds true universally.

12. Example: Models

Example is one of the most potent of instructors, though it teaches without a tongue. It is the practical school of mankind, working by action, which is always more than words. Precept may point to us the way, but it is silent continuous example, conveyed to us by habits, and living with us in fact, that carries us along. Good advice has its weight: but without the accompaniment of a good example it is of comparatively small influence; and it will be found that the common saying of 'Do as I say, not as I do', is usually reversed in the actual experience of life.

All persons are more or less apt to learn through the eye rather than the ear; and, whatever is seen in fact, makes a far deeper impression than anything that is merely read or heard. This is especially the case in early youth, when the eye is the chief inlet of knowledge. Whatever children see they unconsciously imitate. They insensibly come to resemble those who are about them – as insects take the colour of the leaves they feed on. Hence the vast importance of domestic training. For whatever may be the efficiency of schools, the examples set in our Homes must always be of vastly greater influence in forming the characters of our future men and women. The Home is the crystal of society – the nucleus of national character; and from that source, be it pure or tainted, issue the habits, principles and maxims which govern public as well as private life. The nation comes from the nursery. Public opinion itself is for the most part the outgrowth of the home; and the best philanthropy comes from the fireside. 'To love the little platoon we belong to in society,' says Burke, 'is the gem of all public affections.' From this little central spot the human sympathies may extend in an ever widening circle, until the world is embraced; for, though true philanthropy, like charity, begins at home, assuredly it does not end there.

Example in conduct, therefore, even in apparently trivial matters, is of no light moment, inasmuch as it is constantly becoming interwoven with the lives of others, and contributing to form their natures for better or for worse. The characters of parents are thus constantly repeated in their children; and the acts of affection, discipline, industry, and self-control, which they daily exemplify, live and act when all else which may have been learned through the ear has long been forgotten. Hence a wise man was accustomed to speak of his children as his 'future state'. Even the mute action and unconscious look of a parent may give a stamp to the character which is never effaced; and who can tell how much evil act has been stayed by the thought of some good parents, whose memory their children may not sully by the commission of an unworthy deed, or the indulgence of an impure thought? The veriest trifles thus become of importance in influencing the characters of men. 'A kiss from my mother', said West, 'made me a painter.' It is on the direction of such seeming trifles when children that the future happiness and success of men mainly depend. Fowell Buxton, when occupying an eminent and influential station in life, wrote to his mother, 'I constantly feel, especially in action and exertion for others, the effects of principles early implanted by you in my mind.'

Lord Langdale, looking back upon the admirable example set him by his mother, declared, 'If the whole world were put into one scale, and my mother into the other, the world would kick the beam.' Mrs Schimmel Penninck, in her old age, was accustomed to call to mind the personal influence exercised by her mother upon the society amidst which she moved. When she entered a room it had the effect of immediately raising the tone of the conversation, and as if purifying the moral atmosphere – all seeming to breathe more freely, and stand more erectly. 'In her presence', says the daughter, 'I became for the time transformed into another person.' So much does the moral health depend upon the moral atmosphere that is breathed, and so great is the influence daily exercised by parents over their children by living a life before their eyes, that perhaps the best system of parental instruction might be summed up in these two words, 'Improve thyself.'

There is something solemn and awful in the thought that there is not an act done or a word uttered by a human being but carries with it a train of consequences, the end of which we may never trace. Not one but, to a certain extent, gives a colour to our life, and insensibly influences the lives of those about us. The good deed or word will live, even though we may not see it fructify, but so will the bad; and no person is so insignificant as to be sure that his example will not do good on the one hand, or evil on the other. The spirits of men do not die: they still live and walk abroad among us. It was a fine and a true thought uttered by Mr Disraeli in the House of Commons on the death of Richard Cobden, that 'he was one of those men who, though not present, were still members of that House, who were independent of dissolutions, of the caprices of constituencies, and even of the course of time'.

There is, indeed, an essence of immortality in the life of man, even in this world. No individual in the universe stands alone; he is a component part of a system of mutual dependencies; and by his several acts he either increases or diminishes the sum of human good now and for ever. As the present is rooted in the past, and the lives and examples of our forefathers still to a great extent influence us, so are we by our daily acts contributing to form the condition and character of the future. Man is a fruit formed and ripened by the culture of all the foregoing centuries; and the living generation continues the magnetic current of action and example destined to bind the remotest past with the most distant future. No man's acts die utterly; and though his body may resolve into dust and air, his good or his bad deeds will still be bringing forth fruit after their kind, and influencing future generations for all time to come. It is in this momentous and solemn fact that the great peril and responsibility of human existence lies.

Thus, every act we do or word we utter, as well as every act we witness or word we hear, carries with it an influence which extends over, and gives a colour, not only to the whole of our future life, but makes itself felt upon the whole frame of society. We may not, and indeed cannot, possibly trace the influence working itself into action in its various ramifications amongst our children, our friends, our associates; yet there it is assuredly, working on for ever. And herein lies the great significance of setting forth a good example – a silent teaching which even the poorest and least significant person can practise in his daily life. There is no one so humble but that he owes to others this simple but priceless instruction. Even the meanest condition may thus be made useful; for the light set in a low place shines as faithfully as that set upon a hill. Everywhere, and under almost all circumstances, however externally adverse – in moorland shielings, in cottage hamlets, in the close alleys of great towns – the true man may grow. He who tills a space of earth scarce bigger than is needed for his grave, may work as faithfully, and to as good purpose, as the heir to thousands. The commonest workshop may thus be a school of industry, science, and good morals, on the one hand; or of idleness, folly and depravity, on the other. It all depends on the individual men, and the use they make of the opportunities for good which offer themselves.

A life well spent, a character uprightly sustained, is no slight legacy to leave to one's children, and to the world; for it is the most eloquent lesson of virtue and the severest reproof of vice, while it continues an enduring source of the best kind of riches. Well for those who can say, as Pope did, in rejoinder to the sarcasm of Lord Hervey, 'I think it enough that my parents, such as they were, never cost me a blush, and that their son, such as he is, never cost them a tear.'

It is not enough to *tell* others what they are to do, but to exhibit the actual example of doing. What Mrs Chisholm described to Mrs Stowe as the secret of her success, applies to all life. 'I found,' she said, 'that if we want anything *done*, we must go to work and *do*: it is of no use merely to talk – none whatever.' It is poor eloquence that only shows how a person can talk. Had Mrs Chisholm rested satisfied with lecturing, her project, she was persuaded, would never have got beyond the region of talk; but when people saw what she was doing and had actually accomplished, they fell in with her views and came forward to help her. Hence the most beneficent worker is not he who says the most eloquent things, or even who thinks the most loftily, but he who does the most eloquent acts.

True-hearted persons, even in the humblest station in life, who are energetic doers, may thus give an impulse to good works out of all proportion, apparently, to their actual station in society. Thomas Wright might have talked about the reclamation of criminals, and John Pounds about the necessity for Ragged Schools, and yet done nothing; instead of which they simply set to work without any other idea in their minds than that of doing, not talking.

The education of character is very much a question of models; we mould ourselves so unconsciously after the characters, manners, habits, and opinions of those who are about us. Good rules may do much, but good models far more; for in the latter we have instruction in action – wisdom at work. Good admonition and bad example only build with one hand and pull down with the other. Hence the vast importance of exercising great care in the selection of companions, especially in youth. There is a magnetic affinity in young persons which insensibly tends to assimilate them to each other's likeness. Mr Edgeworth was so strongly convinced that from sympathy they involuntarily imitated or caught the tone of the company they frequented, for he held it to be of the most essential importance that they should be taught to select the very best models. 'No company, or good company,' was his motto. Lord Collingwood, writing to a young friend, said, 'Hold it as a maxim that you had better be alone than in mean company. Let your companions be such as yourself, or superior; for the worth of a man will always be ruled by that of his company.' It was a remark of the famous Dr Sydenham that everybody some time or other would be the better or the worse for having but spoken to a good or a bad man. As Sir Peter Lely made it a rule never to look at a bad picture if he could help it, believing that whenever he did so, his pencil caught a taint from it, so, whoever chooses to gaze often upon a debased specimen of humanity and to frequent his society, cannot help gradually assimilating himself to that sort of model.

It is therefore advisable for young men to seek the fellowship of the good, and always to aim at a higher standard than themselves. Francis Horner, speaking of the advantages to himself of direct personal intercourse with high-minded, intelligent men, said, 'I cannot hesitate to decide that I have derived more intellectual improvement from them than from all the books I have turned over.' Lord Shelburne (afterwards Marquis of Lansdowne), when a young man, paid a visit to the venerable Malesherbes, and was so much impressed by it that he said: 'I have travelled much, but I have never been so influenced by personal contact with any man; and if I ever accomplish any good in the course of my life, I am certain that the recollection of M. de Malesherbes will animate my soul.' So Fowell Buxton was always ready to acknowledge the powerful influence exercised upon the formation of his character in early life by the example of the Gurney family: 'It has given a colour to my life,' he used to say. Speaking of his success at the Dublin University, he confessed, 'I can ascribe it to nothing but my Earlham visits.' It was from the Gurneys he 'caught the infection' of self-improvement.

Contact with the good never fails to impart good, and we carry away with us some of the blessing, as travellers' garments retain the odour of the flowers and shrubs through which they have passed. Those who knew the late John Sterling intimately have spoken of the beneficial influence which he exercised on all with whom he came into personal contact. Many owed to him their first awakening to a higher being; from him they learnt what they were, and what they ought to be. Mr Trench says of him: 'It was impossible to come in contact with his noble nature without feeling one's self in some measure *ennobled* and *lifted up*, as I ever felt when I left him, into a higher region of objects and aims than that in which one is tempted habitually to dwell.' It is thus that the noble character always acts; we become insensibly elevated by him; and cannot help feeling as he does and acquiring the habit of looking at things in the same light. Such is the magical action and reaction of minds upon each other.

The example of the brave is an inspiration to the timid, their presence thrilling through every fibre. Hence the miracles of valour so often performed by ordinary men under the leadership of the heroic. The very recollection of the deeds of the valiant stirs men's blood like the sound of a trumpet. Ziska bequeathed his skin to be used as a drum to inspire the valour of the Bohemians. When Scanderbeg, prince of Epirus, was dead, the Turks wished to possess his bones, that each might wear a piece next to his heart, hoping thus to secure some portion of the courage he had displayed while living, and which they had so often experienced in battle. When the gallant Douglas, bearing the heart of Bruce to the Holy Land, saw one of his knights surrounded and sorely pressed by the Saracens, he took from his neck the silver case containing the hero's bequest, and throwing it amidst the thickest press of his foes, cried, 'Pass first in fight, as thou wert wont to do, and Douglas will follow thee, or die'; and so saying, he rushed forward to the place where it fell, and was there slain.

The chief use of biography consists in the noble models of character in which it abounds. Our great forefathers still live among us in the records of their lives, as well as in the acts they have done, which live also: still sit by us at table, and hold us by the hand; furnishing examples for our benefit, which we may still study, admire and imitate. Indeed, whoever has left behind him the record of a noble life, has bequeathed to posterity an enduring source of good, for it serves as a model for others to form themselves by in all time to come; still breathing fresh life into men, helping them to reproduce his life anew, and to illustrate his character in other forms. Hence a book containing the life of a true man is full of precious seed. It is a still living voice; it is an intellect. To use Milton's words, 'It is the precious life-blood of a master spirit, embalmed and treasured up on purpose to a life beyond life.' Such a book never ceases to exercise an elevating and ennobling influence.

Again, no young man can rise from the perusal of such lives as those of Buxton and Arnold, without feeling his mind and heart made better, and his best resolves invigorated. Such biographies increase a man's self-reliance by demonstrating what men can be, and what they can do; fortifying his hopes and elevating his aims in life. Sometimes a young man discovers himself in a biography, as Correggio felt within him the risings of genius on contemplating the works of Michael Angelo: 'And I, too, am a painter,' he exclaimed. Sir Samuel Romilly, in his autobiography, confessed himself to have been powerfully influenced by the life of the great and noble-minded French Chancellor Daguesseau: 'The works of Thomas', says he, 'had fallen into my hands, and I had read with admiration his *Eloge of Daguesseau*; and the career of honour which he represented that illustrious magistrate to have run, excited to a great degree my ardour and ambition, and opened to my imagination new paths of glory.'

Franklin was accustomed to attribute his usefulness and eminence to his having early read Cotton Mather's *Essays to do Good* – a book which grew out of Mather's own life. And see how good example draws other men after it, and propagates itself through future generations in all lands. For Samuel Drew avers that he framed his own life, and especially his business habits, after the model left on record by Benjamin Franklin. Thus it is impossible to say where a good example may not reach, or where it will end, if indeed it have an end. Hence the advantage, in literature as in life, of keeping the best society, reading the best books, and wisely admiring and imitating the best things we find in them. 'In literature,' said Lord Dudley, 'I am fond of confining myself to the best company, which consists chiefly on my old acquaintance, with whom I am desirous of becoming more intimate; and I suspect that nine times out of ten it is more profitable, if not more agreeable, to read an old book over again than to read a new one for the first time.'

Sometimes a book containing a noble exemplar of life, taken up at random, merely with the object of reading it as a pastime, has been known to call forth energies whose existence had not before been suspected. Alfieri was first drawn with passion to literature by reading *Plutarch's Lives*. Loyola, when a soldier serving at the siege of Pampeluna, and laid up by a dangerous wound in his leg, asked for a book to divert his thoughts: the *Lives of the Saints* was brought to him, and its perusal so inflamed his mind, that he determined thenceforth to devote himself to the founding of a religious order. Luther, in like manner, was inspired to undertake the great labours of his life by a perusal of the *Life and Writings of John Huss*. Dr Wolff was stimulated to enter upon his missionary career by reading the *Life of Francis Xavier*; and the book fired his youthful bosom with a passion the most sincere and ardent to devote himself to the enterprise of his life. William Carey, also, got the first idea of entering upon his sublime labours as a missionary from a perusal of the Voyages of Captain Cook.

Francis Horner was accustomed to note in his diary and letters the books by which he was most improved and influenced. Amongst these were Condorcet's *Eloge of Haller*, Sir Joshua Reynolds' *Discourses*, the writings of Bacon, and *Burnet's Account of Sir Matthew Hale*. The perusal of the last-mentioned book – the portrait of a prodigy of labour – Horner says, filled him with enthusiasm. Of Condorcet's *Eloge of Haller*, he said: 'I never rise from the account of such men without a sort of thrilling palpitation about me, which I know not whether I should call admiration, ambition, or despair.' And speaking of the *Discourses* of Sir Joshua Reynolds, he said: 'Next to the writings of Bacon, there is no book which has more powerfully impelled me to self-culture. He is one of the first men of genius who has condescended to inform the world of the steps by which greatness is attained. The confidence with which he asserts the omnipotence of human labour has the effect of familiarizing his reader with the idea that genius is an acquisition rather than a gift; whilst with all there is blended so naturally and eloquently the most elevated and passionate admiration of excellence, that upon the whole there is no book of a more *inflammatory* effect.' It is remarkable that

Reynolds himself attributed his first passionate impulse towards the study of art to reading Richardson's account of a great painter; and Haydon was in like manner afterwards inflamed to follow the same pursuit by reading of the career of Reynolds. Thus the brave and aspiring life of one man lights a flame in the midst of others of like faculties and impulse; and where there is equally vigorous effort, like distinction and success will almost surely follow. Thus the chain of example is carried down through time in an endless succession of links – admiration exciting imitation, and perpetuating the true aristocracy of genius.

In another sphere of action, Dr Arnold was a noble and a cheerful worker, throwing himself into the great business of his life, the training and teaching of young men, with his whole heart and soul. It is stated in his admirable biography, that 'the most remarkable thing in the Laleham circle was the wonderful healthiness of tone which prevailed there. It was a place where a new-comer at once felt that a great and earnest work was going forward. Every pupil was made to feel that there was a work for him to do; that his happiness, as well as his duty, lay in doing that work well. Hence an indescribable zest was communicated to a young man's feeling about life; a strange joy came over him on discerning that he had the means of being useful, and thus of being happy; and a deep respect and ardent attachment sprang up towards him who had taught him thus to value life and his own self, and his work and mission in the world. All this was founded on the breadth and comprehensiveness of Arnold's character, as well as its striking truth and reality; on the unfeigned regard he had for work of all kinds, and the sense he had of its value, both for the complex aggregate of society and the growth and protection of the individual. In all this there was no excitement; no predilection for one class of work above another; no enthusiasm for any one-sided object: but a humble, profound, and most religious consciousness that work is the appointed calling of man on earth; the end for which his various faculties were given; the element in which his nature is ordained to develop itself, and in which his progressive advance towards heaven is to lie.' Among the many valuable men trained for public life and usefulness by Arnold, was the gallant Hodson, of Hodson's Horse, who, writing home from India, many years after, thus spoke of his revered master: 'The influence he produced has been most lasting and striking in its effects. It is felt even in India; I cannot say more than *that*.'

The useful influence which a right-hearted man of energy and industry may exercise amongst his neighbours and dependants, and accomplish for his country, cannot, perhaps, be better illustrated than by the career of Sir John Sinclair; characterized by the Abbé Gregoire as 'the most indefatigable man in Europe'. He was originally a country laird, born to a considerable estate situated near John o' Groat's House, almost beyond the beat of civilization, in a bare, wild country fronting the stormy North Sea. His father dying while he was a youth of sixteen, the management of the family property thus early devolved upon him; and at eighteen he began a course of vigorous improvement in the county of Caithness, which eventually spread all over Scotland. The country was without roads or bridges; and drovers driving their cattle south had to swim the rivers along with their beasts. The chief track leading into Caithness lay along a high shelf on a mountain side, the road being some hundred feet of clear perpendicular height above the sea which dashed below. Sir John, though a mere youth, determined to make a new road over the hill of Ben Cheilt, the old let-alone proprietors, however, regarding his scheme with incredulity and derision. But he himself laid out the road, assembled some twelve hundred workmen early one summer's morning, set them simultaneously to work, superintending their labours, and stimulating them by his presence and example; and before night, what had been a dangerous sheep track, six miles in length, hardly passable for led horses, was made practicable for wheel-carriages as if by the power of magic. It was an admirable example of energy and well-directed labour, which could not fail to have a most salutary influence upon the surrounding population. He then proceeded to make more roads, to erect mills, to build bridges, and to enclose and cultivate the waste lands. He introduced improved methods of culture, and regular rotation of crops, distributing small premiums to encourage industry; and he thus soon quickened the whole frame of society within reach of his influence, and infused an entirely new spirit into the cultivators of the soil. From being one of the most inaccessible districts of the North – the very *ultima Thule* of civilization –

Caithness became a pattern county for its roads, its agriculture, and its fisheries.

The circle of his benevolent operation gradually widened. Observing the serious deterioration which had taken place in the quality of British wool – one of the staple commodities of the country – he forthwith, though but a private and little-known country gentleman, devoted himself to its improvement. By his personal exertions he established the British Wool Society for the purpose, and himself led the way to practical improvement by importing 800 sheep from all countries, at his own expense. The result was the introduction into Scotland of the celebrated Cheviot breed.

Returned by Caithness to Parliament, in which he remained for thirty years, rarely missing a division, his position gave him further opportunities of usefulness, which he did not neglect to employ. Mr Pitt, observing his persevering energy in all useful public projects, sent for him to Downing Street, and voluntarily proposed his assistance in any object he might have in view. Another man might have thought of himself and his own promotion; but Sir John characteristically replied, that he desired no favour for himself, but intimated that the reward most gratifying to his feelings would be Mr Pitt's assistance in the establishment of a National Board of Agriculture. Arthur Young laid a bet with the baronet that his scheme would never be established, adding, 'Your Board of Agriculture will be in the moon!' But vigorously setting to work, he roused public attention to the subject, enlisted a majority of Parliament on his side, and eventually established the Board, of which he was appointed President. The result of its action need not be described, but the stimulus which it gave to agriculture and stock-raising was shortly felt throughout the whole United Kingdom, and tens of thousands of acres were redeemed from barrenness by its operation.

Sir John threw his personal energy into every work in which he engaged, rousing the inert, stimulating the idle, encouraging the hopeful, and working with all. But the great monument of his indefatigable industry, a work that would have appalled other men, but only served to rouse and sustain his energy, was his *Statistical Account of Scotland*, in twenty-one volumes, one of the most valuable practical works ever published in any age or country. Amid a host of other pursuits it occupied him nearly eight years of hard labour, during which he received, and attended to, upwards of 20,000 letters on the subject. It was a thoroughly patriotic undertaking, from which he derived no personal advantage whatever, beyond the honour of having completed it. The publication of the book led to great public improvements; it was followed by the immediate abolition of several oppressive feudal rights, to which it called attention: the salaries of schoolmasters and clergymen in many parishes were increased; and an increased stimulus was given to agriculture throughout Scotland. Sir John then publicly offered to undertake the much greater labour of collecting and publishing a similar Statistical Account of England; but unhappily the then Archbishop of Canterbury refused to sanction it, lest it should interfere with the tithes of the clergy, and the idea was abandoned.

A remarkable illustration of his energetic promptitude was the manner in which he once provided, on a great emergency, for the relief of the manufacturing districts. In 1793 the stagnation produced by the war led to an unusual number of bankruptcies, and many of the first houses in Manchester and Glasgow were tottering, not so much from want of property, but because the usual sources of trade and credit were for the time closed up. A period of intense distress amongst the labouring classes seemed imminent, when Sir John urged, in Parliament, that Exchequer notes to the amount of five millions should be issued immediately as a loan to such merchants as could give security. This suggestion was adopted, and his offer to carry out his plan, in conjunction with certain members named by him, was also accepted. The vote was passed late at night, and early next morning Sir John, anticipating the delays of officialism and red tape, proceeded to bankers in the city, and borrowed of them, on his own personal security, the sum of £70,000, which he despatched the same evening to those merchants who were in the most urgent need of assistance. Pitt meeting Sir John in the House, expressed his great regret that the pressing wants of Manchester and Glasgow could not be supplied so soon as was desirable, adding, 'The money cannot be raised for some days.' 'It is already gone! it left London by tonight's mail!' was Sir John's triumphant reply; and in afterwards relating the anecdote he added, with a smile of pleasure, 'Pitt was as much startled as if I had stabbed him.' To the last this great, good man worked on usefully and cheerfully, setting a great example for his family and for his country. In so laboriously seeking others' good, it might be said that he found his own — not wealth, for his generosity seriously impaired his private fortune, but happiness, and self-satisfaction, and the peace that passes knowledge.

13. Character: The True Gentleman

The crown and glory of life is Character. It is the noblest possession of a man, constituting a rank in itself, and an estate in the general goodwill; dignifying every station, and exalting every position in society. It exercises a greater power than wealth, and secures all the honour without the jealousies of fame. It carries with it an influence which always tells; for it is the results of proved honour, rectitude and consistency – qualities which, perhaps more than any other, command the general confidence and respect of mankind.

Character is human nature in its best form. It is moral order embodied in the individual. Men of character are not only the conscience of society, but in every well-governed State they are its best motive power; for it is moral qualities in the main which rule the world. Even in war, Napoleon said the moral is to the physical as ten to one. The strength, the industry, and the civilization of nations – all depend upon individual character; and the very foundations of civil security rest upon it. Laws and institutions are but its outgrowth. In the just balance of nature, individuals, nations, and races will obtain just so much as they deserve, and no more. And as effect finds its cause, so surely does quality of character amongst a people produce its befitting results.

Though a man have comparatively little culture, slender abilities, and but small wealth, yet, if his character be of sterling worth, he will always command an influence, whether it be in the workshop, the counting-house, the mart, or the senate. Canning wisely wrote in 1801, 'My road must be through Character to power; I will try no other course; and I am sanguine enough to believe that this course, though not perhaps the quickest, is the surest.' You may admire men of intellect; but something more is necessary before you will trust them. Hence Lord John Russell once observed in a sentence full of truth, 'It is the nature of party in England to ask the assistance of men of genius, but to follow the guidance of men of character.' This was strikingly illustrated in the career of Francis Horner – a man of whom Sydney

Smith said that the Ten Commandments were stamped upon his countenance. 'The valuable and peculiar light,' says Lord Cockburn, 'in which his history is calculated to inspire every right-minded youth, is this. He died at the age of thirty-eight; possessed of greater public influence than any other private man; and admired, beloved, trusted, and deplored by all, except the heartless or the base. No greater homage was ever paid in Parliament to any deceased member. Now let every young man ask – how was this attained? By rank? He was the son of an Edinburgh merchant. By wealth? Neither he, nor any of his relations, ever had a superfluous sixpence. By office? He held but one, and only for a few years, of no influence, and with very little pay. By talents? His were not splendid, and he had no genius. Cautious and slow, his only ambition was to be right. By eloquence? He spoke in calm, good taste, without any of the oratory that either terrifies or seduces. By any fascination of manner? His was only correct and agreeable. By what, then, was it? Merely by sense, industry, good principles, and a good heart – qualities which no well-constituted mind need ever despair of attaining. It was the force of his character that raised him; and this character not impressed upon him by nature, but formed, out of no peculiarly fine elements, by himself. There were many in the House of Commons of far greater ability and eloquence. But no one surpassed him in the combination of an adequate portion of these with moral worth. Horner was born to show what moderate powers, unaided by anything whatever except culture and goodness, may achieve, even when these powers are displayed amidst the competition and jealousy of public life.'

Franklin, also, attributed his success as a public man, not to his talents or his powers of speaking – for these were but moderate – but to his known integrity of character. Hence it was, he says, 'that I had so much weight with my fellow-citizens. I was but a bad speaker, never eloquent, subject to much hesitation in my choice of words, hardly correct in language, and yet I generally carried my point.' Character creates confidence in men of high station as well as in humble life. It was said of the first Emperor Alexander of Russia, that his personal character was equivalent to a constitution. During the wars of the Fronde, Montaigne was the only man amongst the French gentry who kept his castle gates unbarred; and it was said of him, that his personal character was a better protection for him than a regiment of horse would have been.

That character is power, is true in a much higher sense than that knowledge is power. Mind without heart, intelligence without conduct, cleverness without goodness, are powers in their way, but they may be powers only for mischief. We may be instructed or amused by them; but it is sometimes as difficult to admire them as it would be to admire the dexterity of a pick-pocket or the horsemanship of a highwayman.

Truthfulness, integrity and goodness – qualities that hang not on any man's breath – form the essence of manly character, or, as one of our old writers has it, 'that inbred loyalty unto Virtue which can serve her without a livery'. He who possesses these qualities, united with strength of purpose, carries with him a power which is irresistible. He is strong to do good, strong to resist evil, and strong to bear up under difficulty and misfortune. When Stephen of Colonna fell into the hands of his base assailants, and they asked him in derision, 'Where is now your fortress?' 'Here', was his bold reply, placing his hand upon his heart. It is in misfortune that the character of the upright man shines forth with the greatest lustre; and when all else fails, he takes stand upon his integrity and his courage.

The rules of conduct followed by Lord Erskine – a man of sterling independence of principle and scrupulous adherence to truth – are worthy of being engraven on every young man's heart. 'It was a first command and counsel of my earliest youth,' he said, 'always to do what my conscience told me to be a duty, and to leave the consequence to God. I shall carry with me the memory, and I trust the practice, of this parental lesson to the grave. I have hitherto followed it, and I have no reason to complain that my obedience to it has been a temporal sacrifice. I have found it, on the contrary, the road to prosperity and wealth, and I shall point out the same path to my children for their pursuit.'

Every man is bound to aim at the possession of a good character as one of the highest objects of life. The very effort to secure it by worthy means will furnish him with a motive for exertion; and his idea of manhood, in proportion as it is elevated, will steady and animate his motive. It is well to have a high standard of life, even though we may not be able altogether to realize it. 'The youth,' says Mr Disraeli, 'who does not look up will look down; and the spirit that does not soar is destined perhaps to grovel.'

There are many counterfeits of character, but the genuine article is difficult to be mistaken. Some, knowing its money value, would assume its disguise for the purpose of imposing upon the unwary. Colonel Charteris said to a man distinguished for his honesty, 'I would give a thousand pounds for your good name.' 'Why?' 'Because I could make ten thousand by it,' was the knave's reply.

Integrity in word and deed is the backbone of character; and loyal adherence to veracity its most prominent characteristic. One of the finest testimonies to the character of Sir Robert Peel was that borne by the Duke of Wellington in the House of Lords, a few days after the great statesman's death. 'Your lordships,' he said, 'must all feel the high and honourable character of the late Sir Robert Peel. I was long connected with him in public life. We were both in the councils of our Sovereign together, and I had long the honour to enjoy his private friendship. In all the course of my acquaintance with him I never knew a man in whose truth and justice I had greater confidence, or in whom I saw a more invariable desire to promote the public service. In the whole course of my communication with him, I never knew an instance in which he did not show the strongest attachment to truth; and I never saw in the whole course of my life the smallest reason for suspecting that he stated anything which he did not firmly believe to be the fact.'

There is a truthfulness in action as well as in words, which is essential to uprightness of character. A man must really be what he seems or purposes to be. When an American gentleman wrote to Granville Sharp, that from respect for his great virtues he had named one of his sons after him, Sharp replied: 'I must request you to teach him a favourite maxim of the family whose name you have given him – *Always endeavour to be really what you would wish to appear*. This maxim, as my father informed me, was carefully and humbly practised by *his* father, whose sincerity, as a plain and honest man, thereby became the principal feature of his character, both in public and private life.' Every man who respects himself, and values the respect of others, will carry out the maxim in act – doing honestly what he proposes to do – putting the highest character into his work, scamping nothing, but priding himself upon his integrity and conscientiousness. Once Cromwell said to

Bernard – a clever but somewhat unscrupulous lawyer – 'I understand that you have lately been vastly wary in your conduct; do not be too confident of this; subtlety may deceive you, integrity never will.' Men whose acts are at direct variance with their words command no respect, and what they say has but little weight; even truths, when uttered by them, seem to come blasted from their lips.

The true character acts rightly, whether in secret or in the sight of men. That boy was well trained who, when asked why he did not pocket some pears, for nobody was there to see, replied, 'Yes, there was: I was there to see myself; and I don't intend ever to see myself do a dishonest thing.' This is a simple but not inappropriate illustration of principle, or conscience, dominating in the character, and exercising a noble protectorate over it; not merely a passive influence, but an active power regulating the life. Such a principle goes on moulding the character hourly and daily, growing with a force that operates every movement. Without this dominating influence, character has no protection, but is constantly liable to fall away before temptation; and every such temptation succumbed to, every act of meanness or dishonesty, however slight, causes self-degradation. It matters not whether the act be successful or not, discovered or concealed; the culprit is no longer the same, but another person; and he is pursued by a secret uneasiness, by self-reproach, or the workings of what we call conscience, which is the inevitable doom of the guilty.

And here it may be observed how greatly the character may be strengthened and supported by the cultivation of good habits. Man, it has been said, is a bundle of habits; and habit is second nature. Metastasio entertained so strong an opinion as to the power of repetition in act and thought, that he said, 'All is habit in mankind, even virtue itself.' Butler, in his *Analogy*, impresses the importance of careful self-discipline and firm resistance to temptation, as tending to make virtue habitual, so that at length it may become more easy to be good than to give way to sin. 'As habits belonging to the body', he said, 'are produced by external acts, so habits of the mind are produced by the execution of inward practical purposes, i.e. carrying them into act, or acting upon them – the principles of obedience, veracity, justice and charity.'

It is indeed scarcely possible to over-estimate the importance of training the young to virtuous habits. In them they are the easiest formed, and when formed they last for life; like letters cut on the bark of a tree, they grow and widen with age. 'Train up a child in the way he should go, and when he is old he will not depart from it.' The beginning holds within it the end; the first start on the road of life determines the direction and the destination of the journey; *ce n'est que le premier pas qui coûte*. 'Remember,' said Lord Collingwood to a young man whom he loved, 'before you are five-and-twenty you must establish a character that will serve you all your life.' As habit strengthens with age, and character becomes formed, any turning into a new path becomes more and more difficult. Hence, it is often harder to unlearn than to learn; and for this reason the Grecian flute-player was justified who charged double fees to those pupils who had been taught by an inferior master. To uproot an old habit is sometimes a more painful thing, and vastly more difficult, than to wrench out a tooth. Hence, as Mr Lynch observes, 'The wisest habit of all is the habit of care in the formation of good habits.'

Even happiness itself may become habitual. There is a habit of looking at the bright side of things, and also of looking at the dark side. Dr Johnson has said that the habit of looking at the best side of a thing is worth more to a man than a thousand pounds a year. And we possess the power, to a great extent, of so exercising the will as to direct the thoughts upon objects calculated to yield happiness and improvement rather than their opposites. In this way the habit of happy thought may be made to spring up like any other habit. And to bring up men or women with a genial nature of this sort, a good temper, and a happy frame of mind, is perhaps of even more importance, in many cases, than to perfect them in much knowledge and many accomplishments.

As daylight can be seen through very small holes, so little things will illustrate a person's character. Indeed, character consists in little acts, well and honourably performed; daily life being the quarry from which we build it up, and rough-hew the habits which form it. One of the most marked tests of character is the manner in which we conduct ourselves towards others. A graceful behaviour towards superiors, inferiors, and equals is a constant source of pleasure. It pleases others because it indicates respect for their personality; but it gives tenfold more pleasure to ourselves. Every man may to a large extent be a self-educator in good behaviour, as in everything else; he can be civil and kind, if he will, though he have not a penny in his purse. Gentleness in society is like the silent influence of light, which gives colour to all nature; it is far more powerful than loudness or force, and far more fruitful. It pushes its way quietly and persistently, like the tiniest daffodil in spring, which raises the clod and thrusts it aside by the simple persistency of growing.

Morals and manners, which give colour to life, are of much greater importance than laws, which are but their manifestations. The law touches us here and there, but manners are about us everywhere, pervading society like the air we breathe. Good manners, as we call them, are neither more nor less than good behaviour; consisting of courtesy and kindness; benevolence being the preponderating element in all kinds of mutually beneficial and pleasant intercourse amongst human beings. 'Civility', said Lady Montague, 'costs nothing and buys everything.' The cheapest of all things is kindness, its exercise requiring the least possible trouble and self-sacrifice. 'Win hearts,' said Burleigh to Queen Elizabeth, 'and you have all men's hearts and purses.' If we would only let nature act kindly, free from affectation and artifice, the results on social good humour and happiness would be incalculable. The little courtesies which form the small change of life may separately appear of little intrinsic value, but they acquire their importance from repetition, and accumulation.

The cultivation of manner – though in excess it is foppish and foolish – is highly necessary in a person who has occasion to negotiate with others in matters of business. Affability and good breeding may even be regarded as essential to the success of a man in any eminent station and enlarged sphere of life; for the want of it has not infrequently been found in a great measure to neutralize the results of much industry, integrity, and honesty of character. There are, no doubt, a few strong, tolerant minds which can bear with defects and angularities of manner, and look only to the more genuine qualities; but the world at large is not so forbearant, and cannot help forming its judgements and likings mainly according to outward conduct.

Another mode of displaying true politeness is consideration for the opinions of others. It has been said of dogmatism that it is only puppyism come to its full growth; and certainly the worst form this quality can assume is that of opinionativeness and arrogance. Let men agree to differ, and when they do differ, bear and forbear. Principles and opinions may be maintained with perfect suavity, without coming to blows or uttering hard words; and there are circumstances in which words are blows, and inflict wounds far less easy to heal.

The inbred politeness which springs from right-heartedness and kindly feelings is of no exclusive rank or station. The mechanic who works at the bench may possess it, as well as the clergyman or the peer. It is by no means a necessary condition of labour that it should, in any respect, be either rough or coarse. The politeness and refinement which distinguish all classes of the people in many continental countries show that those qualities might become ours too – as doubtless they will become with increased culture and more general social intercourse – without sacrificing any of our more genuine qualities as men. From the highest to the lowest, the richest to the poorest, to no rank or condition in life has nature denied her highest boon – the great heart. There never yet existed a gentleman but was lord of the great heart. And this may exhibit itself under the hodden grey of the peasant as well as under the laced coat of the noble. Robert Burns was once taken to task by a young Edinburgh blood, with whom he was walking, for recognizing an honest farmer in the open street. 'Why you fantastic gomeral,' exclaimed Burns, 'it was not the great-coat, the scone bonnet, and the saunders-boot hose that I spoke to, but *the man* that was in them; and the man, sir, for true worth, would weigh down you and me, and ten more such, any day.'

William and Charles Grant were the sons of a farmer in Inverness-shire, whom a sudden flood stripped of everything, even to the very soil which he tilled. The farmer and his sons, with the world before them where to choose, made their way southward in search of employment until they arrived in the neighbourhood of Bury, in Lancashire. From the crown of the hill near Walmersley they surveyed the wide extent of country which lay before them, the river Irwell making its circuitous course through the valley. They were utter strangers in the neighbour-hood, and knew not which way to turn. To decide their course they put up a stick and agreed to pursue the direction in which it fell. Thus their decision was made, and they journeyed on accordingly until they reached the village of Ramsbotham, not far distant. They found employment in a print-works, in which William served his apprentice-

238

ship; and they commended themselves to their employers by their diligence, sobriety, and strict integrity. They plodded on, rising from one station to another, until at length the two men themselves became employers, and after many long years of industry, enterprise and benevolence, they became rich, honoured, and respected by all who knew them. Their cotton-mills and print-works gave employment to a large population. Their well-directed diligence made the valley teem with activity, joy, health and opulence. Out of their abundant wealth they gave liberally to all worthy objects, erecting churches, founding schools, and in all ways promoting the well-being of the class of working-men from which they had sprung. They afterwards erected, on the top of the hill above Walmersley, a lofty tower in commemoration of the early event in their history which had determined the place of their settlement. The brothers Grant became widely celebrated for their benevolence and their various goodness, and it is said that Mr Dickens had them in his mind's eye when delineating the character of the brothers Cheeryble.

The True Gentleman is one whose nature has been fashioned after the highest models. It is a grand old name, that of Gentleman, and has been recognized as a rank and power in all stages of society. 'The Gentleman is always the Gentleman,' said the old French General to his regiment of Scottish gentry at Roussillon, 'and invariably proves himself such in need and in danger.' To possess this character is a dignity of itself, commanding the instinctive homage of every generous mind, and those who will not bow to titular rank will yet do homage to the gentleman. His qualities depend not upon fashion or manners, but upon moral worth – not on personal possessions, but on personal qualities. The Psalmist briefly describes him as one 'that walketh uprightly, and worketh righteously, and speaketh the truth in his heart'.

The gentleman is eminently distinguished for his self-respect. He values his character – not so much of it only as can be seen of others, but as he sees it himself; having regard for the approval of his inward monitor. And, as he respects himself, so, by the same law, does he respect others. Humanity is sacred in his eyes: and thence proceed politeness and forbearance, kindness and charity. It is related of Lord Edward Fitzgerald that, while travelling in Canada, in company with the Indians, he was shocked by the sight of a poor squaw trudging along laden with her husband's trappings, while the chief himself walked on unencumbered. Lord Edward at once relieved the squaw of her pack by placing it upon his own shoulders – a beautiful instance of what the French call *politesse de coeur* – the inbred politeness of the true gentleman.

The true gentleman has a keen sense of honour, scrupulously avoiding mean actions. His standard of probity in word and action is high. He does not shuffle or prevaricate, dodge or skulk; but is honest, upright, and straightforward. His law is rectitude – action in right lines. When he says *yes*, it is a law; and he dares to say the valiant *no* at the fitting season. The gentleman will not be bribed; only the low-minded and unprincipled will sell themselves to those who are interested in buying them. It was to Wellington's great honour, that though uniformly successful in India, and with the power of earning in such modes as this enormous wealth, he did not add a farthing to his fortune, and returned to England a comparatively poor man.

Sir Charles Napier exhibited the same noble self-denial in the course of his Indian career. He rejected all the costly gifts which barbaric princes were ready to lay at his feet, and said with truth, 'Certainly I could have got £30,000, since my coming to Scinde, but my hands do not want washing yet. Our dear father's sword, which I wore in both battles (Meeanee and Hyderabad), is unstained.'

Riches and rank have no necessary connection with genuine gentlemanly qualities. The poor man may be a true gentleman – in spirit and in daily life. He may be honest, truthful, upright, polite, temperate, courageous, self-respecting and self-helping – that is, be a true gentleman. The poor man with a rich spirit is in all ways superior to the rich man with a poor spirit. To borrow St Paul's words, the former is as 'having nothing, yet possessing all things', while the other, though possessing all things, has nothing. The former hopes everything, and fears nothing; the latter hopes nothing, and fears everything. Only the poor in spirit are really poor.

Mr Turnbull, in his work on *Austria*, relates an anecdote of the Emperor Francis, in illustration of the manner in which the Government of that country had been indebted, for its hold upon the people, to the personal qualities of its princes. 'At the time when the cholera was raging at Vienna, the emperor, with an aide-de-camp, was strolling about the streets of the city and suburbs, when a corpse was dragged past on a litter unaccompanied by a single mourner. The unusual circumstance attracted his attention, and he learnt, on inquiry, that the deceased was a poor person who had died of cholera, and that the relatives had not ventured on what was then considered the very dangerous office of attending the body to the grave. "Then", said Francis, "we will supply their place, for none of my poor people should go to the grave without that last mark of respect"; and he followed the body to the distant place of interment, and, bareheaded, stood to see every rite and observance respectfully performed.'

Above all, the gentleman is truthful. He feels that truth is the 'summit of being', and the soul of rectitude in human affairs. Lord Chesterfield declared that Truth made the success of a gentleman. The Duke of Wellington, writing to Kellerman, on the subject of prisoners on parole, when opposed to that general in the Peninsula, told him that if there was one thing on which an English officer prided himself more than another, excepting his courage, it was his truthfulness. 'When English officers,' said he, 'have given their parole of honour not to escape, be sure they will not break it. Believe me – trust to their word; the word of an English officer is a surer guarantee than the vigilance of sentinels.'

True courage and gentleness go hand in hand. The brave man is generous and forbearant, never unforgiving and cruel. It was finely said of Sir John Franklin by his friend Parry, that 'he was a man who never turned his back upon a danger, yet of that tenderness that he would not brush away a mosquito'. A fine trait of character – truly gentle, and worthy of the spirit of Bayard – was displayed by a French officer in the cavalry combat of El Bodon, in Spain. He had raised his sword to strike Sir Felton Harvey, but perceiving his antagonist had only one arm, he instantly stopped, brought down his sword before Sir Felton in the usual salute and rode past. To this may be added a noble and gentle deed of Ney during the same Peninsular War. Charles Napier was taken prisoner at Corunna, desperately wounded; and his friends did not know whether he was alive or dead. A special messenger was sent out from England with a frigate to ascertain his fate. Baron Clouet received the flag, and informed Ney of the arrival. 'Let the prisoner see his friends,' said Ney, 'and tell them he is well, and well treated.' Clouet lingered, and Ney asked, smiling, 'what more he wanted'? 'He has an old mother, a widow, and blind.' 'Has he? then let him go himself, and tell her he is alive.' As the exchange of prisoners between the countries was not then allowed, Ney knew that he risked the displeasure of the emperor by setting the young officer at liberty; but Napoleon approved the generous act.

Notwithstanding the wail which we occasionally hear for the chivalry that is gone, our own age has witnessed deeds of bravery and gentleness – of heroic self-denial and manly tenderness – which are unsurpassed in history. The events of the last few years have shown that our countrymen are as yet an undegenerate race. On the bleak plateau of Sebastopol, in the dripping perilous trenches of that twelve-month's leaguer, men of all classes proved themselves worthy of the noble inheritance of character which their forefathers have bequeathed to them. But it was in the hour of the great trial in India that the qualities of our countrymen shone forth the brightest. The march of Neill on Cawnpore, of Havelock on Lucknow – officers and men alike urged on by the hope of rescuing the women and children – are events which the whole history of chivalry cannot equal. Outram's conduct to Havelock, in resigning to him, though his inferior officer, the honour of leading the attack on Lucknow, was a trait worthy of Sydney, and alone justifies the title which has been awarded to him of 'the Bayard of India'. The death of Henry Lawrence – that brave and gentle spirit – his last words before dying, 'Let there be no fuss about me; let me be buried *with the men*' – the anxious solicitude of Sir Colin Campbell to rescue the beleaguered of Lucknow, and to conduct his long train of women and children by night from thence to Cawnpore, which he reached amidst the all but overpowering assault of the enemy – the care with which he led them across the perilous bridge, never ceasing his charge over them until he had seen the precious convoy safe on the road to Allahabad, and then burst upon the Gwalior contingent like a thunderclap; – such things make us feel proud of our countrymen, and inspire the conviction that the best and purest glow of chivalry is not dead, but vigorously lives among us yet.

Even the common soldiers proved themselves gentlemen under their trials. At Agra, where so many poor fellows had been scorched and wounded in their encounter with the enemy, they were brought into the fort, and tenderly nursed by the ladies; and the rough, gallant fellows proved gentle as any children. And when all was over – when the mortally wounded had died, and the sick and maimed who survived were able to demonstrate their gratitude – they invited their nurses and the chief people of Agra to an entertainment in the beautiful gardens of the Taj, where, amidst flowers and music, the rough veterans, all scarred and mutilated as they were, stood up to thank their gentle countrywomen who had clothed and fed them, and ministered to their wants during their time of sore distress. In the hospitals at Scutari, too, many wounded and sick blessed the kind English ladies who nursed them; and nothing can be finer than the thought of the poor sufferers, unable to rest through pain, blessing the shadow of Florence Nightingale as it fell upon their pillow in the night watches.

There are many tests by which a gentleman may be known; but there is one that never fails – How does he *exercise power* over those subordinate to him? How does he conduct himself towards women and children? How does the officer treat his men, the employer his servants, the master his pupils, and man in every station those who are weaker than himself? The discretion, forbearance, and kindliness with which power in such cases is used may indeed be regarded as the crucial test of gentlemanly character. When La Motte was one day passing through a crowd, he accidentally trod upon the foot of a young fellow, who forthwith struck him on the face: 'Ah, sir,' said La Motte, 'you will surely be sorry for what you have done, when you know that *I am blind.*' He who bullies those who are not in a position to resist may be a snob, but cannot be a gentleman. He who tyrannizes over the weak and helpless may be a coward, but no true man. The tyrant, it has been said, is but a slave turned inside out. Strength, and the consciousness of strength, in a right-hearted man imparts a nobleness to his character; but he will be most careful how he uses it; for

> *It is excellent*
> *To have giant's strength; but it is tyrannous*
> *To use it like a giant.*

Gentleness is indeed the best test of gentlemanliness. A consideration for the feelings of others, for his inferiors and dependants as well as his equals, and respect for their self-respect, will pervade the true gentleman's whole conduct. He will rather himself suffer a small injury, than by an uncharitable construction of another's behaviour incur

243

the risk of committing a great wrong. He will be forbearant of the weaknesses, the failings, and the errors of those whose advantages in life have not been equal to his own. He will be merciful even to his beast. He will not boast of his wealth, or his strength, or his gifts. He will not be puffed up by success, or unduly depressed by failure. He will not obtrude his views on others, but speak his mind freely when occasion calls for it. He will not confer favours with a patronizing air. Sir Walter Scott once said of Lord Lothian, 'He is a man from whom one may receive a favour, and that's saying a great deal in these days.'

Lord Chatham has said that the gentleman is characterized by his sacrifice of self and preference of others to himself in the little daily occurrences of life. In illustration of this ruling spirit of considerateness in a noble character, we may cite the anecdote of the gallant Sir Ralph Abercromby, of whom it is related, that when mortally wounded in the battle of Aboukir, he was carried in a litter on board the *Foudroyant*; and, to ease his pain, a soldier's blanket was placed under his head, from which he experienced considerable relief. He asked what it was. 'It's only a soldier's blanket,' was the reply. '*Whose* blanket is it?' said he, half lifting himself up. 'Only one of the men's.' 'I wish to know the name of the man whose blanket this is.' 'It is Duncan Roy's, of the 42nd, Sir Ralph.' 'Then see that Duncan Roy gets his blanket this very night.' The incident is as good in its way as that of the dying Sydney handing his cup of water to the private soldier on the field of Zutphen.

Index

Abercromby, Sir Ralph, anecdote of, 244

Accuracy, 172

Acts and consequences, 219–20

Addison, 26, 96

Adrian VI, 27

Adversity, uses of, 208–9

Akenside, poet, 25

Angelo, Michael, 88, 113, 224

Application and perseverance, 76 et seq.

Arkwright, Sir R., 42–5

Arne, Dr, musician, 136

Arnold, Dr, on self-education, 194; a cheerful worker, 226–7

Attention, habit of, 41, 172

Austria, Emperor of, anecdote of, 240–41

Bach, John Sebastian, 135

Bacon, Lord, 23, 33, 112, 169; his notes, 97; on economy, 185; on knowledge, 204

Banks, T., sculptor, 115–16

Barrow, Isaac, 197

Beethoven, 135, 208, 219

Bell, Sir Charles, 102

Bewick, wood-engraver, 92

Biography, its uses, 23, 223–6

Bird, artist, 113, 114

Blackstone, Sir William, 27

Böttgher, J. F., the potter, 63; his early life, 68; his boyish trick in alchemy, 68; his troubles, 68–71; makes red porcelain, 70; makes white porcelain, 73; his death, 72

Books, inspiration from, 223–6

Borrowing, danger of, 184–5

Boulton and Watt, 45

Bright, John, on frugality, 182

Brindley, engineer, 24

Britton, John, his early life, difficulties surmounted, 83–4

Brotherton, Joseph, M.P., 30, 191

Brougham, Lord, 34

Brown, John, geologist, 110

Brown, Sir S., 89

Brunel, Sir I., a thoughtful observer, 90

Buffon, Comte de, as student 80–82

Burney, Dr, 96

Burritt, Elihu, 96

Business men, 168–9

Business qualities of great men, 173–9

Buxton, Sir T. Fowell, philanthropist, 165–7; will, 150, 199; on mother's influence, 219; on good company, 222

Caesarism, fallacy of, 21

Callcott, Sir A., 114

Callot, Jacques, artist, 117–18

Campbell, Lord, 26

Canning, on character, 231

Carey, William, missionary, 24, 155

245

247

Method, 173
Meyerbeer, musician, 135
Mill, John Stuart, 20
Miller, Hugh, geologist, his origin, 32; on work as a teacher, 39–40, 109, 149; on drink, 188
Milton, John, 27; a man of business, 169
Misfortune and stupidity, 171
Models of character, 221–3
Money, its use and abuse, 180–81; making and saving, 188–9
Moreau, General, greatest in defeat, 208
Mother's influence, 219
Motte, La, anecdote of, 243
Mulready, artist, 116
Murat, Marshal, 29
Murchison, Sir Roderick, 110
Murray, Professor Alexander, 212
Musicians, industry of, 135–6

Napier, Sir Charles, 146; on debt, 187; on rectitude, 240
Napoleon, and Jacquard, 58; his character, and on will, 151; as a business man, attentive to details, 175
Negroes and Granville Sharp, 161
Nelson, Admiral, 26; his punctuality, 174
Newton, Sir I., sayings of, 76; loss of papers, 78; fall of apple, 89; aids to discovery, 92; his labour, 96; as a man of business, 169
Ney, Marshal, 29; generous conduct, 24
Nicoll, Robert, poet, 216
Northcote, painter, 113
Note-making, 97

Observation, intelligent, 89, 94, 107
Opie, painter, 24, 91, 113
Owen, Richard, naturalist, 27, 98

Palissy, the potter, 63–8
Paré, Ambrose, surgeon, 98–100
Parental example, 218
Patient labour, its results, 21, 76, 77, 80, 211
Paton, Noel, artist, 132
Peel family, the, 46–7
Peel, Sir Robert, statesman, his truthfulness, 234
Peerages founded by tradesmen, 139; by lawyers, 143
Perrier, François, artist, 117
'Perseus', casting of, 119–20
Perseverance, its value and results, 63–8, 77–82, 95, 147, 172, 213–5; commands success, 216
Petty, Sir William, and the Lansdowne peerage, 141
Physical health and education, 196
Pleasure, pursuit of, 203
Politeness, 237
Pope, Alexander, 27, 221
Porcelain, invention of, 70
Potters, illustrious, 63
Pottery manufacture, 75, 123–5
Pounds, John, and Ragged Schools, 221
Poussin, Nicolas, artist, 88, 121–2
Priestley, Dr, 93
Promptitude, importance of, 173–4, 199, 229
Pugin, architect, 129–30
Punctuality, importance of, 82, 173–4
Purpose, force of, 149

Ramus, Pierre, 28

249

MORE ABOUT PENGUINS, PELICANS
AND PUFFINS

For further information about books available from Penguins please write to Dept EP, Penguin Books Ltd, Harmondsworth, Middlesex UB7 0DA.

In the U.S.A.: For a complete list of books available from Penguins in the United States write to Dept DG, Penguin Books, 299 Murray Hill Parkway, East Rutherford, New Jersey 07073.

In Canada: For a complete list of books available from Penguins in Canada write to Penguin Books Canada Ltd, 2801 John Street, Markham, Ontario L3R 1B4.

In Australia: For a complete list of books available from Penguins in Australia write to the Marketing Department, Penguin Books Australia Ltd, P.O. Box 257, Ringwood, Victoria 3134.

In New Zealand: For a complete list of books available from Penguins in New Zealand write to the Marketing Department, Penguin Books (N.Z.) Ltd, Private Bag, Takapuna, Auckland 9.

In India: For a complete list of books available from Penguins in India write to Penguin Overseas Ltd, 706 Eros Apartments, 56 Nehru Place, New Delhi 110019.

A CHOICE OF PENGUINS

☐ *The Complete Penguin Stereo Record and Cassette Guide*
Greenfield, Layton and March £7.95

A new edition, now including information on compact discs. 'One of the few indispensables on the record collector's bookshelf' – *Gramophone*

☐ *Selected Letters of Malcolm Lowry*
Edited by Harvey Breit and Margerie Bonner Lowry £5.95

'Lowry emerges from these letters not only as an extremely interesting man, but also a lovable one' – Philip Toynbee

☐ *The First Day on the Somme*
Martin Middlebrook £3.95

1 July 1916 was the blackest day of slaughter in the history of the British Army. 'The soldiers receive the best service a historian can provide: their story told in their own words' – *Guardian*

☐ *A Better Class of Person* **John Osborne** £2.50

The playwright's autobiography, 1929–56. 'Splendidly enjoyable' – John Mortimer. 'One of the best, richest and most bitterly truthful autobiographies that I have ever read' – Melvyn Bragg

☐ *The Winning Streak* **Goldsmith and Clutterbuck** £2.95

Marks & Spencer, Saatchi & Saatchi, United Biscuits, GEC . . . The UK's top companies reveal their formulas for success, in an important and stimulating book that no British manager can afford to ignore.

☐ *The First World War* **A. J. P. Taylor** £4.95

'He manages in some 200 illustrated pages to say almost everything that is important . . . A special text . . . a remarkable collection of photographs' – *Observer*

A CHOICE OF PENGUINS

☐ *Man and the Natural World* **Keith Thomas** £4.95

Changing attitudes in England, 1500–1800. 'An encyclopedic study of man's relationship to animals and plants . . . a book to read again and again' – Paul Theroux, *Sunday Times* Books of the Year

☐ *Jean Rhys: Letters 1931–66*
Edited by Francis Wyndham and Diana Melly £4.95

'Eloquent and invaluable . . . her life emerges, and with it a portrait of an unexpectedly indomitable figure' – Marina Warner in the *Sunday Times*

☐ *The French Revolution* **Christopher Hibbert** £4.95

'One of the best accounts of the Revolution that I know . . . Mr Hibbert is outstanding' – J. H. Plumb in the *Sunday Telegraph*

☐ *Isak Dinesen* **Judith Thurman** £4.95

The acclaimed life of Karen Blixen, 'beautiful bride, disappointed wife, radiant lover, bereft and widowed woman, writer, sibyl, Scheherazade, child of Lucifer, Baroness; always a unique human being . . . an assiduously researched and finely narrated biography' – *Books & Bookmen*

☐ *The Amateur Naturalist*
Gerald Durrell with Lee Durrell £4.95

'Delight . . . on every page . . . packed with authoritative writing, learning without pomposity . . . it represents a real bargain' – *The Times Educational Supplement*. 'What treats are in store for the average British household' – *Daily Express*

☐ *When the Wind Blows* **Raymond Briggs** £2.95

'A visual parable against nuclear war: all the more chilling for being in the form of a strip cartoon' – *Sunday Times*. 'The most eloquent anti-Bomb statement you are likely to read' – *Daily Mail*

A CHOICE OF
PELICANS AND PEREGRINES

☐ *The Knight, the Lady and the Priest*
Georges Duby £6.95

The acclaimed study of the making of modern marriage in medieval France. 'He has traced this story – sometimes amusing, often horrifying, always startling – in a series of brilliant vignettes' – *Observer*

☐ *The Limits of Soviet Power* **Jonathan Steele** £3.95

The Kremlin's foreign policy – Brezhnev to Chernenko, is discussed in this informed, informative 'wholly invaluable and extraordinarily timely study' – *Guardian*

☐ *Understanding Organizations* **Charles B. Handy** £4.95

Third Edition. Designed as a practical source-book for managers, this Pelican looks at the concepts, key issues and current fashions in tackling organizational problems.

☐ *The Pelican Freud Library: Volume 12* £5.95

Containing the major essays: *Civilization, Society and Religion, Group Psychology* and *Civilization and Its Discontents*, plus other works.

☐ *Windows on the Mind* **Erich Harth** £4.95

Is there a physical explanation for the various phenomena that we call 'mind'? Professor Harth takes in age-old philosophers as well as the latest neuroscientific theories in his masterly study of memory, perception, free will, selfhood, sensation and other richly controversial fields.

☐ *The Pelican History of the World*
J. M. Roberts £5.95

'A stupendous achievement . . . This is the unrivalled World History for our day' – A. J. P. Taylor